STUFF ABOUT BIRDS

Clive Denby

Tim Saunders Publications

TS
Tim Saunders Publications

Copyright © 2025 Clive Denby

All rights reserved

No part of this book may be reproduced, or stored in a retrieval system, or transmitted in any form or by any means, electronic, mechanical, photocopying, recording, or otherwise, without express written permission of the publisher.

All cartoons by Heather-Anne Everett

CONTENTS

Title Page
Copyright
An explanation and thanks · 1
Acknowledgements... · 3
Some notes on the text · 7
Introduction... · 9
1. Whatever turns you on... · 15
2. I name this bird... · 29
3. La Plume De Ma Tante · 44
4. Up, Up and Away... · 50
5. See Me, See Me Not... · 59
6. Pack up your troubles... · 67
7. A Bird in the Hand... · 76
8. Table for two... · 86
9. Home Sweet Home... · 103
10. Sunny Side Up... · 113
11. Who goes there...? · 121

12. E = mc²	127
13. Do not disturb...	139
14. Why am I here?	145
15. Is it, or isn't it?	159
16. A look on the down side...	165
17. Running the gauntlet	176
18. And may I introduce...	196
19. Going, going, gone...	202
20. The Dodo - a Tribute...	211
21. High Flyers...	215
22. Come and join my gang...	242
23. Never Again...	255
24. Warden's Eye View (1)...	269
25. Warden's Eye View (2)...	304
26. With This Ring...	334
27. Getting Cold Feet - May be, May be Not...	371
28. All at Sea...	382
29. 'Twas a Cold Dark Night...	388
30. Automatic Pilot...?	396
This is all for you my child...	404
Appendix (i)	422
Appendix (ii)	471
Appendix (iii)	474
Also available	479

AN EXPLANATION AND THANKS

Clive Denby died in 2022 after an eventful and fulfilled life that some of us, at times, were privileged to share. He left behind a complete document that has become this book. He had been working on it for some time and but for the Covid epidemic, with consequential disruption to normal life, it might well have been published in 2020.

It has fallen to some of his friends to see the book published and we believe it is a fitting memorial to the man we knew and loved. We hope that it is acceptable to Clive's family. Publication has been financed by the residue of Clive's estate and some financial contributions from friends.

Among Clive's friends, Clare Sulston took on the burden of administering Clive's estate and I was proofreading while Clive was alive and have helped to progress the publication.

We owe a particular debt of thanks to our publisher, Tim Saunders, who took on the book although it was outside his normal scope and has always been enthusiastic, helpful and tolerant of my slowness in carrying out my work on the book.

I hope you enjoy 'Stuff about birds' and find the information that Clive put together as fascinating as we do.

> John Cockaday and Clive's friends, September 2025

ACKNOWLEDGEMENTS...

It is here that an author normally reels off a list of people who supported them throughout the entire project and put up with temper tantrums, interminable periods of sulking, near-defeatism and bad spelling. There is the long-suffering partner who stood by through thick and thin and the children who were largely neglected as the writer buried himself away in a cupboard under the stairs. Well... not quite.

At the very first I give enormous thanks to Heather Everett who has graced this work with fine cartoons. I believe she has successfully captured the essence of what was required in each case.

I acknowledge my dear partner Zandile with whom I shared a wonderful eleven years in Swaziland. We still keep in touch and when I told her I was starting out on a new book she asked unhesitatingly, "Am I going to be in it?" I promised that she would almost certainly pop up here and there where she would add to the narrative. I never once threw a temper tantrum whilst writing the book and only rarely did I slip into a deep sulk, mostly brought on by the rather unreliable internet link that prevails in my local area. My spelling is fine but my computer seems not to think so and I have had some frustration as it thinks I am an American and wants to tell me that *colour* is spelt *color* along with a host of other irritating examples.

One of my neighbouring residents, June, who is neither a birder nor a scientist in any way whatsoever asked if she could read bits and pieces as I completed them. She has since uttered such kindly words saying that although she knew little of the subject she felt she had learnt something and liked 'the way I put things'. Her comments have been most appreciated. Several of my birdy and scientific friends have read odd chapters and urged me to get the thing finished so they too, who know who they are, receive my genuine gratitude.

But my deepest thanks go way back in time. In 1971, I went to the Shetland Islands to act as senior warden for the Royal Society for the Protection of Birds (RSPB) on the island of Fetlar where a pair of Snowy Owls was breeding. There I met the rest of the team. Digby Cyrus, Rob Munro, Dave Hulme and I were all to live in a small bothy for five months, each of us from very different backgrounds. I left school at sixteen having not even sat examinations, and completed a boat-building apprenticeship. My three Snowy Owl colleagues were all graduates and there was I without an O-level to my name. Between them, over the season they convinced me I should 'go back to school' and get some qualifications. I did just that one year after the

Snowy job finished by enrolling as a full-time student in a technical college for three years to do O- and A-levels. Another four years at university (I messed up one year) got me my degree in Bio-geography. And so it is I often think of those three fine chaps who set me on the right path. I really don't think I would have done it without their pushing me and much later would have been too late.

I wish also to thank all those pea-brained narrow-minded relatives who collectively ganged up on me and wrote a 'family letter' to my parents asking if they were going to allow me (aged 22) to give up work and become a drug-crazed and long-haired hippie student. My parents were one hundred per cent supportive of my intentions and told them where to get off. I thank those relatives because they gave me that extra determination to succeed.

Another time I was obliged to work in a team was in the summer of 1977 when I worked on the RSPB Ouse Washes bird reserve as an assistant. Working under the warden Cliff Carson, I experienced one of the most wonderful chapters of my life, a real 'salad days' summer working with good people and learning all the time. So, it is huge thanks to Cliff, Dave, Les, Mark and Joy who all brought out the best in me.

Three expeditions to the NW Himalaya of India catching and ringing migrant birds was my third team experience and I still maintain contact with those people. We had two Himalayan reunions over the last two years and it is Simon Delany, Clare Sulston, Anne White, John Norton and Dr Charlie Williams who I shower with gratitude for entering my life.

All three of these team experiences made me who I am and each is covered in separate chapters towards the end of the book.

So, this book you hold is not just sciency but also anecdotal and will not just inform but, hopefully, entertain. And finally it is you my dear reader I thank in advance for not putting this book back on the shelf.

Clive Denby
Hampshire
January 2022

SOME NOTES ON THE TEXT

All measurements are metric. For those not so familiar with the metric system, one kilometre (km) is 1,000 metres (m), which is close to five-eighths of a mile. One foot approximates to 30 centimetres (cm). One metre is very close to 39 inches, not so far removed from one yard which is 36 inches. One ounce is 28 grammes. One kilogramme is 1,000 grammes. One thousand kilogrammes is one metric tonne. There are about 2.2 pounds to a kilogramme.

Regarding names of birds, where a definitive single species is being discussed, it is capitalised. Examples are Herring Gull, Little Stint, Short-eared Owl and Black-throated Diver. Where there exists more than one species of a bird being discussed, the names are all lower case. Examples are gulls, stints, owls and divers, all of which have more than one species. Some sentences may be mixed thus: Bullfinches, Goldfinches and various buntings.

There may be rare but justifiable instances of limited repetition of certain facts between chapters but this is kept to a minimum. The glossary explains selected words, mostly scientific or geographical terms used throughout the text, although in some cases these are also partly explained within the text if not self-explanatory. Scientific names are seldom used except in chapters two and three where they are essential to the content of those chapters.

English spellings are used throughout despite my computer often telling me to do otherwise - such as *centre* rather than *center*.

Throughout the book I have intentionally, when giving examples, drawn from the global pool of bird species. Since my childhood days when you were a pretty cool dude to go across to France for a birdwatching trip, birders today are highly cosmopolitan animals who whizz off quite readily to African game parks, rainforests, arctic wilderness and just about anywhere else. I have also tried to draw upon some of the lesser-known groups of birds and to demonstrate the sheer diversity of the world's avifauna. For instance, I was amazed to learn there are more than three hundred species of hummingbirds. I sincerely hope you too may have a few surprises.

INTRODUCTION...

Having retired from teaching/lecturing in Africa for twenty-seven years, I returned to the UK in 2012. I knew it was going to be difficult – the last twenty-three of those years had been continuous during which I had not stepped out of that wonderful continent.

I had not even kept up very much with world events, for instance, I was blissfully unaware of the 2008 economic crisis until after having returned to the UK several years later. After a very short while I ached to return, to be back in those huge open vistas so characteristic of Africa and yearning to be biking irresponsibly helmetless down the mind-blowing East African Rift Valley. My mind wandered also to the sheer joy and sanctuary of the classrooms or biology labs that had been my niche in nine schools of seven African countries. I yearned to be in my daily workplace with its spirited students arising collectively from between fifty and seventy countries.

I even taught a lad from Iceland whose dad was a geothermal-power advisor. Three of us laid friendly bets on where some of next year's students would come from – I lost mine on Philippines but Martin won his on Madagascar. Some were 'rich kids' (they couldn't help that) and many were on scholarships, particularly nationals of that country.

Without exception all of my postings were highly edifying and I learnt so, oh so much, in places where skin colour, ethnicity, politics, wealth or lack thereof and religion or lack thereof were not even considered. For twenty-seven years I was part of an ethnic minority and never once did I experience any bad feelings from either African nationals or indeed any other nationals from any of five other continents.

From the age of eight I was into birds. My mum was a domestic on a rather posh estate and sometimes I would go with her and immerse myself in a large gallery full of mahogany cabinets displaying stuffed birds from various bits of the world. Armed with the Observer's Book of Birds and a small ex-army canvas shoulder bag with lunch and orange juice, I would spend weekends and evenings walking along narrow lanes of Hawthorn and Sycamore to Hanningfield Reservoir in Essex. That was my stamping ground for many a year and, at the age of twelve, I got a rural paper round that took me across the causeway of the reservoir every morning for the next four years. The occasional camping weekend with my good mate Stewart, who lived next door and was also, to a lesser extent, into birds and other nature stuff, saw my bird list growing.

At the age of thirteen, I became the proud possessor of Petersen's Field Guide to the Birds of Britain and Europe. 'And Europe'... wow I couldn't wait – I was a 'real' ornithologist now. I even made it a mission to learn the Latin names of all the British birds and I got some of my more tolerant school mates to test me periodically.

At the age of sixteen, I hitchhiked with Stewart and with our parents' blessings down to Istanbul, I having just left school. It was Stewart's summer holidays as he had another year of school to come back to. With part of my paper round money I bought a decent pair of binoculars (Swift Audubon 8.5 x 44) and a middle of the range camera for scenic shots and a record of our 'adventure'. And it was an adventure too – I was nurtured on and influenced by Famous Five books (all twenty-two of them) and loved the way Enid Blyton managed to dispense with the parents in chapter one leaving the children to their adventures and ginger beer (she never once mentioned 'lashings' by the way – entirely apocryphal). I loved my parents of course and even more so for here was I literally on the road for seven wonderful bird-packed weeks. Hoopoes, Bee-Eaters, Black winged Stilts, and Subalpine Warblers were added to my non-existent 'list' along with many, many others.

On my return home I embarked on a four-year boat-building apprenticeship in Leigh-on-Sea, Essex building fourteen foot clinker fishing dinghies (skiffs). Although my parents moved house a couple of times (including our fourteen months living on a double decker bus in a field) I still kept in touch with Stewy. In 1969, we had a three-week trip down to the Camargue, southern France. We camped and moved around at our leisure but spent a whole week in a village where the local people treated us like heroes, including lending us a rowing boat for a day and inviting us into their village hall to see Mick Jagger playing Ned Kelly in a black and white film. I very much enjoyed exercising and expanding my limited schoolboy French.

In 1971, I secured my first job with the RSPB working for five months on the breeding of Snowy Owls on Fetlar, Shetland. This also included various surveys of other birds such as Arctic Terns and various auks (Puffins, Guillemots). I was senior warden and in charge of three fresh graduates. I can still see the Puffins flying into their burrows with beakfuls of fish for their young. I sat on a grassy headland festooned with Sea Pink flowers looking down at this wonderful spectacle.

The following September I embarked on a one-year course of O-levels in a technical college in Colchester. For the next two years I did three A-levels in biology, geography and geology. I now had my ticket to university and went to Southampton to read bio-geography (it was actually geography with a few modules of ecology such as soils and vegetation distribution). Those were the good old days when full-time students got grants and not loans, forcing them to live the first few years of their working lives in crippling debt. I entered university at age twenty-five and was determined that I was giving myself a second chance in life and was going to maximise my time at university. Clubs, theatre visits (Southampton University had the Nuffield Theatre on its campus), girls, expeditions, rigorous debates and of course the acquisition of knowledge all made my life most satisfactory. I really had promised myself to mount some form of birdy expedition while at uni' and a few months later that chance came to me. A detailed narrative of four resulting ornithological expeditions to the NW Himalaya is given in a separate chapter towards the end of the book.

For a few years after graduating I did a number of short term jobs, most of which were connected with wildlife and conservation and one which saw me identifying animal bone from Bronze-age middens (domestic rubbish tips) in Orkney to assess what our ancestors had for lunch. Seabirds featured quite a lot. Other jobs, such as washing up in a hospital, a bakery round, delivering ice to various events, picking fruit, renumbering library books at my former university and the traditional student GPO Christmas Post all kept me alive and I suppose all helped make me a 'well rounded' and satisfied human being.

At age thirty-six, I abandoned a PhD after just two months in favour of a one-year PGCE (Post Graduate Certificate in Education) at Bangor University, North Wales and metamorphosed into a teacher. I decided from the outset I was bound for foreign parts together of course with loads of new birds.

My first post was in Ethiopia and thereafter in six other African countries, all in international schools teaching biology and geography (and even some lower school secondary chemistry). At the end of my two years in Kenya I was employed by the Kenyan Wildlife Service for six weeks to make counts of flamingo colonies at four of the Rift Valley lakes including Lake Naivasha and Lake Baringo. Having never held a pensionable post, funds were now tight so I had to make any money as legally as I could by going out and giving talks and publishing the occasional article.

1. WHATEVER TURNS YOU ON...

"Come and join my gang".

In the '50s and '60s when I was at school, most children had a hobby or even more than one. My own included Meccano, Bayko (a sort of precursor to Lego but specifically for building houses), collecting bank notes from around the world and of course... birds. All of these faded away in my mid-teens, except birds.

Bird-watching and fishing seemed to be the two most popular schoolboy hobbies. I never had the patience for the latter and also fish don't sing. I say schoolboy hobbies as I was never aware of any girls in those early days showing any interest in either of these past-times. That is changing slowly. I suspect that many of today's birders started from a young age while others have slipped into the subject as an adult or perhaps on retirement influenced by the many wildlife programmes on TV, local societies, magazines and an overall national/global awareness of environmental issues, birds being an obvious and accessible focus.

I became aware in the late '60s of travel companies specializing in purely birding tours, Ornitholidays and Sunbird Travel being examples. I went on an Ornitholidays two-week trip to Austria when I was nineteen and thus almost doubled the number of those bird species I had seen previously.

So, what's the attraction? I mention below merely my own thoughts and I am sure some of these will apply more to some people than others. Firstly, birds are generally most attractive in form, many having fine colourful plumages. This is perhaps why we prefer Robins on our Christmas cards rather than dowdy Corncrakes or Water Rails. The birds of paradise found predominantly in New Guinea (which interestingly are closely related to the crow family), the hummingbirds of the Americas and their African equivalent, the sunbirds are well-known for their splendid and sometimes iridescent feathering. Turacos, kingfishers, bee-eaters, rollers and pheasants also spring to mind.

Many birds are sexually dimorphic, meaning

that the males are brighter and more gaudily coloured than the females. The males need to attract females while the drabber females need some protective camouflage as they spend a lot of time sitting on nests incubating their eggs or protecting their young. This is not to say male birds do not assist with incubating – many certainly do.

Sexual dimorphism is extremely prevalent in members of the duck family of which we have over twenty-five species in Britain. Other species are sexually the same in their plumage such as most waders, gulls, owls and pigeons or there may be just the slightest, often imperceptible differences between the sexes.

The male Green Woodpecker is much the same as the female but he has that extra dash of crimson in the middle of each of his black moustachial stripes. The Pied Kingfisher, common in parts of Africa have sexes similar but the males have two black incomplete chest-bands as opposed to just the one of the females. Sexual dimorphism has a notable exception in the phalaropes wherein males are duller versions of the females and are also responsible for most of the incubation of the eggs.

Some male birds will resemble the females except just prior to the breeding season. The wydahs are a group of seed eating birds of the African plains related to sparrows. The Paradise

Wydah spends much energy in growing a ridiculously long tail (nearly three times its body length). This it will use to display to the females but after the breeding season the extended tail feathers are moulted out. It does this as carting this cumbersome structure around makes it easier for him to be caught by a predator plus it takes valuable energy to maintain it. This is an example of compromise or a 'trade-off' in nature. The tail had its use but then that was it… it had to go.

The male Ruff, a wader we can see in a few places in Britain, adopts well… a ruff around its neck, resembling the decorative and totally non-functional ruffs that Elizabethan dandies and even monarchs wore round their necks (look at any picture of Henry VIII). The colour of the birds' ruffs can be almost anything - orange, tawny, yellow, black, white and even variegated and the males group together in small clusters called leks and leap about in a small arena flaunting themselves to prospective females. After the breeding season the ruff disappears through moulting and the sexes look similar save for the fact that the male is much larger than the female.

Differences between the sexes need not be just related to plumage. Many female birds of prey are considerably larger than their male counterparts. This is particularly noticeable in European Sparrowhawks and Goshawks. The male Mute Swan and the male Shelduck have prominent knobs at the base of their bills.

Secondly, birds sing... well not all of them but certainly the males of many species, notably among the smaller bird families we call Passerines (perching birds). My favourite is the Song Thrush but Sedge and Reed Warblers can rattle off a good tune and of course we all know about Nightingales. But how many of us have actually heard them? Nightingales don't just sing at night. They sing at any time of day but we notice them more at night when other birds are, more sensibly, getting some kip.

A lot of research has been done on bird song, notably Chaffinches and it seems that bird songs are learnt from the parents. Regional dialects have also been noticed just like we can recognise the accent of a Yorkshireman or maybe a Liverpudlian. It was once popular in Britain to keep a canary in a cage in the boudoir so it could sing to us.

On a number of occasions I raised the question, "Why do birds sing?"

Surprisingly a few people, largely religious zealots who feel that everything is here on Earth to serve our species, say birds sing to make us happy. Now I know none of my readers will go for that one... I hope! If that were true then birds have been holding a dress-rehearsal for 180 million years, patiently waiting for us humans to evolve and appreciate their efforts.

Male birds sing to attract mates, to warn off other males and to defend a territory and all that is in it including his female, his nest, eggs and young and of course his family's food supply.

Bird calls are different to songs and may be uttered by both sexes and serve a different function. These are more for communication to young birds and incubating mates maybe warning them of a prowling pussy cat or an overhead hawk. Contact calls are helpful within groups of migrating birds to help keep the flocks safely together. Here's a good one. We all know the "tu whit, tu whoo" call of the Tawny Owl and not the Barn Owl as once portrayed in an episode of Midsomer Murders… (me, pedantic?). It has been discovered that the bird calling "tu whit" is not the same as that calling "tu whoo" – that is provided by the other of the pair as a reply to the first contact call. The two calls follow on without a discernible interval so it sounds like it's coming from the same bird. Other bird species have a similar call set-up.

Thirdly, birds are very 'see-able' and being generally active can be observed easily and even better with a decent pair of binoculars. Some birders derive pleasure from the challenge of seeing secretive species such as crakes, rails and quails. I gave up on looking for francolins in Africa. They form a quite uniformly dull, very elusive, ground-hugging family and most species are difficult to sort out from one another.

Most bird species which spend their time in the undergrowth will have rather dull plumage. I have only once seen a quail, and that was just before eating it when wined and dined by a high up military man when in India who had heard of our migration research in Ladakh, NW Himalaya.

A wide range of species can be attracted to well stocked bird tables. Depending on the locality and nearby habitat and time of year, you may attract Blue and Great Tits, Greenfinches and other finches, Nuthatches, Great Spotted Woodpeckers, Starlings (the bully-boys of bird tables), Magpies, Jays, Fieldfares, Redwings and Blackbirds. You may even get some real surprises. Some people can boast Hawfinches, a bird I have never seen during my seventy years on this planet, sixty-two as a birder. Perhaps you have your own 'bogey birds'?

In secondary school when opting for a woodwork project I made a luxury two-storey bird table – it really was a fine piece of real estate. My woodwork teacher was somewhat disappointed as it had not a single carpentry joint on which to judge its merit but he let me go through with it (he probably liked birds). I attended to it religiously, especially in winter when birds really do need some help.

My fourth point is that you can see birds everywhere. Thus you can add to your bird sightings seeing new stuff the further you venture out of your own backyard. I can think of no habitat (apart from high mountain tops and down in the ocean depths) where birds do not dwell. The odd special trip away for a weekend or even better a holiday can do wonders for the avid birder. Imagine my sheer delight when I went up to Shetland to work on the breeding Snowy Owls (see chapter 25). There I saw for the first time Razorbills, Guillemots, Black Guillemots, Little Auks, Puffins, Storm and Leach's Petrels, Fulmars, Kittiwakes, Great and Arctic Skuas and oh yes... Snowy Owls. It was not just seeing the birds themselves but the unbelievably large colonies. There were thousands of pairs of Manx Shearwaters nesting underground although we seldom saw them. But you could certainly hear their strange and spooky caterwauling at nights when walking near their burrows. Light brushes past your face were made by incoming Storm Petrels returning to their own underground chambers. So, Shetland was something else and that was still in Britain. What of Africa?

On being offered my first teaching job in Ethiopia, I went out and bought the relevant field guide (Birds of East Africa) and treated myself to a new pair of Swift Audubon 8.5 x 44 binoculars, an optic I had come to prefer (I am currently on my fourth pair). On arrival at Ethiopian customs they were confiscated and I was informed they were illegal. I never got them back. There was a very nasty war raging with Eritrea and various items were banned, but strangely not cameras!

My headmaster lent me a pair of 6 x 30 binoculars, which had separate lens focusing but still I was very grateful. My first birding session in Ethiopia produced over a hundred species in one day. Subsequent trips gave me so much more in the way of new sightings and a great deal of my Ethiopian birding was well out of the way down in the Rift Valley, mostly around the huge Lake Langano. As I later worked my way round teaching in seven African countries I was getting to grips with the birds of eastern and southern Africa, plus another dozen or so African countries I visited during my holidays, which generally totalled sixteen weeks per year!

The fifth reason I am suggesting for our deep affinity to birds is that they are so diverse in form, coming packaged in all manner of shapes, colour schemes and sizes and many bear distinctive features such as crests, wagging tails, different shaped beaks to suit their different feeding functions, bald patches of skin, wattles, moustaches, wide splaying feet and so much more. Variety, seemingly infinite is the key word here. Regarding size differences, I made a calculation recently. The Bee Hummingbird of Latin America has a weight of just 2.6 grammes. The weight of a male Ostrich may be 136 kilogrammes. Simple maths tells us that it can take 52,000 hummingbirds to equal a single Ostrich. How's that for a pub quiz question? And let us bear in mind here that as recently as the fifteenth century there were enormous birds up to twelve feet tall and weighing up to 230kg called moas living in New Zealand, which were having a good time until humans came along and pushed them to extinction.

Number six... we are getting there... birds are generally not dangerous, not even large birds of prey so that maybe another reason we venture readily into their territories. Having said that there are exceptions. I once ended up leaping onto a complete stranger's 4x4 Pajero in Kenya (outside a game park) when I saw a displeased male Ostrich running towards me without so much as a smile on his beak. I was very lucky as I could not have outrun it. A couple of well-placed kicks from an unhappy Ostrich would be like being kicked by a horse and think of the damage they could do if you were down on the ground.

The Cassowary of Indonesia (another ratite) can also inflict nasty wounds on the unwary as they each proceed through thick rainforest. These birds are known to kill a few humans almost annually.

Eric Hosking, the world famous bird photographer, who passed away in 1991, had an eye hooked out by a Tawny Owl he was photographing. Obviously, it left him half-blinded... not an impediment a bird photographer can easily cope with being deprived of stereoscopic vision. He did however cope and went on to write an autobiography called An Eye for a Bird. It makes a good read, published in 1970.

In Shetland one of us wardens was attacked by a Snowy Owl (see Chapter 25) and we were more than once 'attacked' by Great black-backed Gulls as we wandered through a breeding colony. They made no physical contact but came uncomfortably close as the enormous audible waft of their long powerful wings passed close by our heads. Some gulls would pick up bits of offal and drop them down onto us. Arctic Terns actually sat on our heads and pecked our scalps as we tried to do counts so we devised some make-shift mortar-board type headpieces to protect us.

Finally, birds undertake lengthy migrations, say between Europe and sub-Saharan Africa, and then do the return journey later in the year. This alone is enough reason to take up an interest in birds. The British Trust for Ornithology was set up with this very much in mind. A number of Bird Observatories was set up around the British coast in the '50s and '60s to trap birds temporarily while they were ringed with numbered rings and then released after various biometric data had been taken (see Chapter 8). The re-trapping of birds ringed at other world sites has given us so much information of migration routes, migration timings, life, longevity, pre-migration weight gains and more). I mentioned in the Introduction our work in the NW Himalaya, which involved the ringing of many birds (see chapter 27).

Finally finally, I will add that birding can be a very inexpensive hobby. Most people's birding takes place in nearby locations with perhaps the occasional special trips and holidays to see new stuff. Having said that, it is worthwhile to have a decent pair of binoculars ('bins' as us 'real' birders call them). Don't skimp on binoculars and try out several types before buying. Birders are often very particular about their bins and I can confirm this. More 'serious' birders will sport telescopes with tripods, which are especially useful for watching birds out at sea. One other basic tool is a decent field guide to the birds of your region. These today cover most of the world and more general books on birds are indeed numerous. Averaging around £1 each you can pick up all manner of wildlife books in charity shops, some of which are in pristine condition and bear original price tags of £20 or more. I have even picked up a couple of bird field-guides, one covering the birds of the West Indies even though I shall probably not now get to that part of the world. That book was written by Caribbean bird expert James Bond... yes I mean the real and original James Bond. Ian Fleming, living in Jamaica, had a copy of Bond's field guide and used the name for his now globally famous and much-loved character. If you like islands then I recommend the dozen or so books of birdman RM Lockley who, incidentally, set up Britain's first bird observatory on Skokholm off the Welsh coast (see Reading List).

If you want to venture into the art of bird photography (I didn't) then the bill starts to go up and can be astronomical if you want the serious equipment needed for professional standards of wildlife photography, which have improved dramatically in recent decades. Just see the David Attenborough TV series and you appreciate just how much skill has been drawn upon but not without super-duper cameras and associated bells and whistles that are available today.

If you are one of these hyper devoted characters who are willing to take days off work and charter planes to see a couple of vagrant birds then you clearly have money to burn. These 'twitchers' can cause a great deal of distress to an exhausted bird, which has been wind-driven off course and has luckily hit land so it can now feed. But it can't if it is being hounded by thoughtless fanatics who will see that bird at all costs. Horrendous tales abound of demented twitchers going to any measures, legal or otherwise, to tick off a new bird or a bird for that particular year. To me, obsessively and competitively maintaining lists of birds is little more than stamp-collecting. I must stress however that not all twitchers behave in this way and many have contributed much to our knowledge of bird distributions and abundance over time.

2. I NAME THIS BIRD...

First some basics. Why do we classify things? If you looked at ten sites on Google to find out how many animal and plant species exist on

Earth today, you would probably get ten widely varying figures. These range from 1.5 million to up to eighty million but these higher figures must relate to assumptions and not those animals, which have been observed, described and named. Let's play safe and go for a figure which possibly satisfies that for confirmed species, around two million. Quite simply, even that is far too many to get a handle on unless we can break them down into smaller groupings, each successively trending down to a particular species. Whether it be animals, plants, fungi or bacteria we use the same system of classification which comprises seven groupings. These range from the largest grouping, the Kingdom through Phylum, Class, Order, Family, Genus and Species. [If you want to remember them, think of the mnemonic 'king peter came over for general smith'].

I will deal with sub-species shortly. Let's say you want to classify the African Lion. That clearly belongs to the animal kingdom. Then it comes under the phylum of chordata, animals with well-developed or semblances of backbones (what we would generally term Vertebrates). Next, our lion fits into the class of mammals (the same group as us of course). We move down to order, in this case carnivores followed by family... no guesses here, the cat family (Felidae). Finally, we arrive at Genus, Panthera followed by species leo. The domestic cat bears the Latin name Felis domesticus, which is why many cats are called Felix. The genus of some crows is Corvus and is used for five of the eight British types of crow. We then further delineate these down to species – Corvus corax (Raven), Corvus frugilegus (Rook) and Corvus monedula (Jackdaw). Three of the British crows each have their own different genera such as the Magpie (Pica) and the Jay (Garrulus). All living organisms bear a Latin name (generally known as its scientific name, which is made up of these last two groupings, genus and species, so an African Lion becomes Panthera leo, with genus always capitalized and species in lower case. Also, scientific names are traditionally italicized and underlined (although I have not done so throughout this book) an example being *Loxidonta Africana,* the African Elephant.

Us humans share the first three animal classification groups with African Lions and indeed all other mammals but our order is primates while our family is hominids (Hominidae). We end up as the genus Homo and species sapiens thus our Latin name is Homo sapiens ('wise ape', although one may wonder why at times as we are the only species, which seems hell-bent on destroying the world's habitats along with their collective enormous biodiversity). There have been times when other Homo genera existed such as Homo habilis (handy man), Homo erectus (upright or bipedal man) and the Australopithecines, which included the famous 'Lucy'. We, Homo sapiens, entered the stage around 0.5 – 0.3 million years ago.

A European Robin then comes out as kingdom, animals: phylum, chordata; class, Aves (birds); order, Passeriformes (perching birds); family Turdidae, thrushes then finely tuned to genus Erithacus and species rubecula, so Erithacus rubecula is the Latin name.

If I were describing a European Robin to an American, I would have to make it clear I was not talking about an American Robin, which is of the same family but of the genus Turdus (true thrushes) and species migratorius. Such possible confusions would be rampant among the 10,900 species of birds known to exist today. So, Latin names pinpoint a single species, allowing international communication among, in this case, ornithologists.

Were I to give a talk about warblers, I would first have to establish whether I was referring to Old World Warblers (those living in Europe, Asia and Africa) or to the New World Warblers of the Americas. Both groups are of totally different families and they are not really that closely related. The same can be said of Old and New World Flycatchers and several other groups.

And it is important to appreciate that new birds are discovered almost every year – ten new species were discovered in early 2020 on three islands in Indonesia and these were not just subspecies but full-blown species. When you take trouble to really stare at a good atlas, you will see that there are so many places, remote forests, swamplands, the slopes of specific volcanoes, hidden valleys, inaccessible sea-stacks, small specks of islands all waiting to be scientifically studied. Many birds might be familiar to local communities but unless they are observed by ornithologists who can identify them as new species and then go on to report them, they will continue to await discovery. There is surely plenty of new stuff out there.

There is a wonderful book titled A Complete Checklist of the Birds of the World (Second edition) by Howard and Moore, 1991. It is a reference work and not the kind of book one reads from cover to cover. It has no pictures and is basically a six hundred page list of birds, ordered in the latest classification so a huge percentage of the book comprises Latin nomenclature. Hardly a book then to settle down by the fireside for the evening. I love this book and occasionally I leaf through its pages, ever learning more. There is so much stuff that most, including myself of course, have never heard of. Let me quote one of the authors' favourites, the Guttulated Forest-gleaner (stand on a chair and say it out loud). Or imagine dashing into your local bar screaming, "Hey guys, there's a Black-capped Sibia on my allotment." I said above, 'latest' classification. This is because taxonomy (the science of classification) is constantly being adjusted, tweaked here and there or even having some surprisingly large alterations, especially now we have DNA analytical methods at our disposal. Similarities of DNA between species indicate closeness of relationship, so taxonomists will continue to upset the proverbial applecart. Good for them, I say. Taxonomists classify. Taxidermists stuff and mount animals for display. Taxon simply means scientific group.

I promised to deal with sub-species. Most birds have sub-specific variants, these differences generally being quite subtle. As populations of a given species may occur over a broad geographical region, then there will inevitably be variations as these become separated. An example is the St Kilda Wren. This bird differs just slightly, but discernibly, from our mainland Wren. Our common Pied Wagtail is a sub-species of the White Wagtail more common on the European continent. They are not separate species but there are some subtle plumage differences. Look at the page showing heads of Yellow Wagtails in Peterson's Field Guide to the Birds of Britain and Europe. You will see the Yellow (the most common in Britain), the Spanish, the Blue-headed, the Ashy-headed, the Grey-headed and the Black-headed. All are gradations of the same species,

Yellow Wagtails. We call the main bird the nominate species, generally the one which was first discovered and named, in this case the Blue-headed Wagtail, which sometimes visits Britain. Technically, these birds can interbreed but generally don't as they are found in different parts of Europe. So, where we have sub-species we add on a third part of the Latin name, the protocol being to repeat the specific name in the nominate species, which would be Motacilla flava flava for the Blue-headed Wagtail but the Yellow Wagtail, a sub-species is Motacilla flava flavissima. Similarly, the other yellow wagtails named above are all subspecies with their own trinomial (three-part) Latin names.

Taxonomists can come to blows over the issue of sub-species and generally fall into one of two categories; 'lumpers' and 'splitters'. To give an example, a lumper would assert that our Carrion Crow and Hooded Crow are the same species although their plumages are markedly different. Splitters would maintain that these two crows are separate species. In my opinion it is not worth getting bogged down in this level of discussion unless it really does turn you on. Willow Warblers and Chiffchaffs are remarkably similar, differing in leg colour and the subtlest of shade but their very different songs confirm they are indeed two different species. If you are a splitter you may be aware of the large numbers of subspecies that can exist for many given species. The Crested Lark has 28, the Song Sparrow and the Yellow Warbler both of the New World each have 38, the Island Thrush 50 and the Golden Whistler (a Passerine) has a staggering 64.

So, that's taxonomy and I point out that the same principles apply right through all kingdoms of living organisms. Whenever a species new to science is discovered, as is happening all the time, it is fully described, this being submitted to and hopefully accepted by a committee of specialists and allocated its very own unique Latin name.

Until recent times no claim of a new species would be accepted without a corpse, which dare I say does not seem unreasonable. Even the best photographs may not be conclusive although birds in the hand whose DNA can be taken must surely do the job. I am just wondering, does our new DNA technology mean lumpers and splitters are endangered species?

When I was in Swaziland (now re-named Eswatini by the way) I had a lovely Turkish Van cat for ten years, who adopted me in Botswana as a kitten. He had a gorgeous soft pinkish nose, the colour and texture of spam. I loved it and he seemed to appreciate the tactile attention I gave to it. I gave him the honorary trinomial Latin name of Felis domesticus spamirostris, meaning cat, domestic having a spam-like nose. I don't think he minded.

Let's look a bit more closely at some bird names. Now I never studied Latin as a language but I did make the effort when at school to learn the Latin names of all the British birds and then later the other European species. My zeal slackened when in Africa but I picked up a hundred or so Latin names there. Whenever I come across unfamiliar words, as I do especially when reading the works of my scientific gurus Richard Dawkins and Jared Diamond, I hesitate before reaching for my Oxford dictionary. Sometimes I can guess what the word means by relating it to the Latin name of a bird. Let's say I saw the word 'glandarius'. I know the Latin name of the European Jay is Garrulus glandarius rufitergum, which translates directly as talkative, acorn-eating, rufous-rumped bird, thus 'glandarius' means something to do with acorns. If I had not known the meaning of pluvial (as in the Pluvial Period) I would work out that it had something to do with rain. This is because I know the Latin name of our Green Woodpecker is Picus viridus pluvius, this translating as woodpecker, which is green and is vocal during rainfall. Locally, the Green Woodpecker is called the Rain Bird for this reason. I have come to love etymology, the origins and constructions of words, so I am so pleased I made that effort to learn Latin names of birds – it has been very useful as of course, numerous English words have Latin stems.

Latin names of birds will be based on a range of factors, which are now considered. Many are simply based on colour as in the Robin, whose specific name rubecula denotes the ruby red breast. The Greenfinch with its binomial name of Chloris chloris denotes green as in chlorine, a green choking gas, or chlorophyll, the green pigment in plants. Blue Tits have been given the specific label of caeruleus and if you are a painter you will be aware of caerulean blue in your paint-box. The species name flava of Yellow Wagtails indicates just that – the colour of yellow. A common specific name is alba, which refers to white plumage as in Tyto alba (Barn Owl), Motacilla alba (the White Wagtails) and Sterna albifrons (the Little Tern). This is where we get the word albino from and quite probably the word albatross, a bird which we know to be predominantly white. The opposite is melanistic meaning pigmented black as in the case of Emberiza melanocephala (Black-headed Bunting) or Melanitta fusca (the Common Scoter) an almost entirely black sea-duck. Melanin is the dark pigment, which is evenly distributed in the skin of most Africans, S. Asians and Australian aborigines. Caucasians (white people) also have melanin but it is concentrated into little specks in the skin, which we call freckles and moles. When white people sunbathe the melanin in temporarily increased and spread out evenly throughout the skin.

Specific names might refer to structures such as the frequent cristatus meaning crest as in Parus cristatus (Crested Tit) and Podiceps cristatus (the Great Crested Grebe). The Long-tailed Skua bears, the specific name longicaudus, meaning long tail. The Long-tailed Tit similarly is graced by the name Aegithalos caudata. Be careful with some names that may catch you out. Typically, the generic name Puffinus does not mean Puffin but refers to a totally different family, the shearwaters. The Puffin's genus is Fratercula, Latin for little brother or friar.

Some specific names may indicate a behavioural trait. Familiaris is quite common as in Certhia familiaris suggesting the confiding nature of Treecreepers. Cercomel familiaris has the Familiar Chat's confiding nature doubly confirmed in English and in Latin. Here's a goodie – Lymnocryptes minimus (the Jack Snipe). Lymno means lake (as in limnology, the study of lakes) and cryptus means hidden. Jack Snipe remain quite still by lake margins until almost trodden on so it all makes sense.

Minimus, minuta, major and giganteus all of course refer to size and these four examples are used in the specific names of Jack Snipe (Jack is an outdated word meaning small), Little Stint, Great Tit and Giant Petrel respectively.

But now let's look at English names. Happily, all 10,900 bird species do have English names but not all animals and plants enjoy this privilege. With an estimated 350,000 species of beetles and 17,500 species of butterflies it would be a tall order to ascribe all an English name, so entomologists (insect specialists) are saddled with learning piles of Latin names instead. I bet an entomology conference would be quite a head-banging experience for a non-boffin.

Firstly, as a person interested in birds graduates to become a 'proper birder' they will appreciate that many popular bird names are in fact not really correct. For example, there is no such species as a duck, a sea-gull, a hawk, a finch or a thrush whereas there are species called Mallard, Black-headed Gull, Sparrowhawk, Goldfinch and Mistle Thrush. These collective namings may serve a purpose but one should be aware of their limitations.

Some bird species have incorrect English names that have not been altered. Bearded Tits are not even closely related to tits. They belong to the Babblers, a family of birds widespread throughout Africa. Likewise, the Penduline Tit is not a tit at all. It has its own family, various subspecies living in Europe and Asia. Mute Swans are certainly not mute. OK. They are not noted songsters but they do hiss when their young are threatened or when they're having a bad day – they are quite readily aroused. Many birds sport the names of those who discovered them, usually by blasting them out of the sky with a blunderbuss, including Schalow's Wheatear,

Brunnich's Guillemot, Savi's Warbler, Cetti's Warbler, Bewick's Swan, Sabine's Gull, Montagu's Harrier and hundreds of others. Some bird names are dedications to monarchs and titled people such as Lady Amherst's Pheasant, King of Saxony's Bird of Paradise, Lady Ross's Turaco, Prince Ruspoli's Turacao and Count Raggis' Bird of Paradise.

Some birds have misleading names with respect to their geographical location. Egyptian Plovers can be seen in Sudan, and at least three other east-African countries. Sardinian Warblers are widespread throughout southern Europe. Dartford Warblers are not restricted to a single town in Kent, in fact you would be extremely unlikely to see one there at all. They are very rare though and breed thinly in a couple of English southern counties but they flourish better in southern Europe, notably Spain. Kentish Plovers are found all along the north European and the Mediterranean coasts.

Some bird species have double-barrelled names incorporating two different birds. Examples are Eagle Owl, Curlew Sandpiper, Sparrowhawk, Harrier-hawk, Finchlark, Woodpecker Finch, Lark Bunting and Thrush Nightingale. The latter species is just as musical as its standard cousin but is restricted to eastern Europe and southern Scandinavia.

There are those birds who have been graced by subjective views of their beauty. The

Resplendent Quetzel, Superb Starling, Splendid Starling, Gorgeous Bush Shrike, Many-coloured Bush Shrike, Variable Sunbird, Magnificent Frigate-bird and Graceful Tern to name some. Names may arise due to 'personality' - Sociable Weaver and Familiar Chat, the latter (a redstart-like bird) sometimes hopping onto my dining-room table in Swaziland to gather up a few tit-bits. Happily, my cat was usually busy out hunting further afield, mostly for lizards.

I do love those birds named after the most obscure of features, their toes. What were these chaps smoking when they came up with names like Short-toed Eagle, Short-toed Treecreeper, Short-toed Lark and Long-toed Stint? I have seen both Treecreepers and Short-toed Treecreepers and I failed to see any difference in toe length although the latter does have a pale rufous wash on the flanks. So why not Rufous-flanked Treecreeper? Don't shoot me, I am just the messenger.

And then we have the onomatopoeic names such as Cuckoo, Chiffchaff, and the Go-away Bird, which is actually the White-bellied Turaco common in eastern and southern Africa. Regarding the latter, I can confirm that the bird does indeed politely tell you to clear off from its territory.

Finally, I will mention localised names. Almost every bird in Britain, and doubtless worldwide, has at least one local name. The Lapwing is called Green Plover, Peewit (after its call) Herwit or Horniwink depending on where you are in the UK. The Puffin has aliases such as Sea Parrot and Coulter-neb. When I was working in Shetland, I learned quite a few of the local names. The Snowy Owl is known as the Catyogle after its Swedish localised name meaning Cat-faced Owl. Great Skuas are Bonxies, Great black-backed Gulls are Baagies, Black Guillemots are Tysties, Shags are Scarfs and Manx Shearwaters are known as Mutton Birds, I believe this being a reference to taste. I cannot confirm this but I have actually had Cormorant for lunch, strangely twice in one lifetime. The first was indeed in Shetland but the second was on the shores of Lake Victoria in Uganda when roosting birds were battered and blown out of trees during the frequent violent storms and later gathered up by local fishermen.

Can you imagine a bird identification guide based purely on taste? One final local name I find fascinating is that for the Nightjar, locally known as the Goatsucker in the belief that they used to suck the teats of sleeping female goats. I don't think this has ever been proven but all things are possible in nature – that is why many of us find it so marvellous to study.

3. LA PLUME DE MA TANTE

Any creature today that has feathers is a bird. Some dinosaurs may have possessed feathers but that remains a matter of dispute. We are sure however that birds feathers have evolved from the scales of their reptilian ancestors. Some dinosaurs possessed feathers which evolved from the scales of their reptilian ancestors. They are strong and light and are readily impregnated with pigment to create the plumage of any bird. Some birds can use their tail feathers to produce noise during nuptial displays, snipe and woodcock being examples. Sandgrouse are unique in using their absorbent breast feathers to soak up water from far-off oases in order to take water back to their young.

Let's first consider structure. Feathers begin as mere bumps on the skin of the embryo. These develop into cones embedded in a pit, the follicle, much as mammalian hair, including our own, sprouts from follicles. As feathers grow from the base, the cells die, so the completed feathers are totally dead. They become impregnated with a tough protein called keratin, the same material as your fingernails. Once fully emerged the protective sheaths break away and the feathers unfurl and dry.

There are several types of feathers but we shall

start with the most familiar, the flight feather or primary. This has a distinct central shaft, the rachis. Attached to this branching out sideways are barbs, these barbs collectively called the vanes. Vanes on either side of the shaft will be of different widths, which ultimately aid lift. Barbs have even smaller extensions called barbules half of which have microscopic hooks while the other half has ridges. The hooks fit neatly into the ridges thus maintaining the integrity of the vanes. Preening with the bill serves to maintain this arrangement of hooks and ridges. Try this yourself. Take a primary feather and pull apart parts of the vanes. Now run your thumb and forefinger along the separation and the barbs will 'zip-up' together again, but not as well as when a bird does it. The lower end of the shaft, the calamus, is free of barbs. Most birds have 10 primaries per wing although some birds have nine or 12. Next to the inner primary are the secondaries also serving as flight feathers, again normally 10 in number although albatrosses may have over 30. Collectively, primaries and secondaries are known as remiges. Other similar feathers are the tail feathers (rectrices) which typically number 10 varying but extremes do exist. Wing and tail feathers are connected to the 'arm-bones' and the pygidium respectively. Owls have modified flight feathers to effect silent flight, by the use of downy plumes along the front of the wings. Contour feathers cover the entire body and act to streamline the whole bird. Beneath these are the down feathers, which insulate the bird. Some feathers are greatly reduced to bristles found mainly around the eyes and nostrils. They can act as sensory organs like the whiskers of a cat or as nets for catching insects as with swifts and nightjars.

Although strong, feathers have to cope with all manner of rough treatment and thus need constant maintenance. Damaged feathers cannot be repaired but they can eventually be replaced during periods of moult. A high proportion of a bird's resting time is given over to preening the feathers.

Nearly all birds have a preen gland situated at the base of the upper tail but this cannot be seen, being covered in body feathers. These structures produce fat cells, which are applied with the beak to the feathers for waterproofing and other protection. These oils may also act as antibiotics, killing bacteria and fungi. Birds inhabiting wetter environments will have larger preen glands. A few birds have no preen glands such as most ratite species including Ostriches and Rheas. Typically, a bird preens its flight feathers by closing its mandibles over the base of the feather and slowly dragging it along its length. This distributes the preen oil and zips up the barbs. Some birds may preen their mate, almost certainly a pair-bonding mechanism.

Those few birds lacking preen glands will use

alternative techniques including water-bathing, dust-bathing, anting and sunning. Anting involves the bird lying prostrate on the ground with wings and tail outstretched. This will ideally be done near an ant nest. The ants are then allowed to crawl all over the bird, which lies there motionless, seemingly in a state of ecstasy. As a child, I once approached a Blackbird assuming it to be dead. It was anting and even when disturbed seemed reluctant to fly.

The formic acid contained in ant tissues serves to kill parasites. Sometimes a bird will take a single ant into its bill and wipe it along a feather, squeezing the formic acid out of the insect as it does so. Green Woodpeckers love to ant. Again, as a child, I was lucky to witness this.

Ostriches perform dust-bathing as do many other birds, even though they may have preen glands. Ostriches will scrape a shallow depression and squat using their stumpy vestigial wings to throw dust back over their bodies. This is worked in as far as possible and then shaken out, ideally taking out all manner of creepy crawlies in the process.

Sunning demands the bird takes up the same position as an anting bird, basking ecstatically in the sun. It is thought that this may help soften the preen oils and so spread them and also help in production of vitamin D.

Those of you with birdbaths will have observed all kinds of birds bathing in different ways. Some stand at the edge of the water basin while others jump straight in. Some will try to immerse their entire bodies in water. This all goes towards cleaning the feathers. Some may expose themselves during rainfall while others, during winter, may even use snow to bathe their feathers.

When a bird moults its feathers it has to carefully coordinate this activity with other tasks in the bird's annual cycle such as breeding and migration.

The shedding of feathers is carried out in an orderly and progressive way, much like the loss of our own milk teeth before being replaced by adult teeth. The primaries and secondaries are moulted one at a time so as not to interfere with flight. You may well see this as a large raptor flies overhead with splayed primaries such as a Common Buzzard. Just the one or perhaps two missing primaries still permits efficient flight. There are, however, some groups of birds, which do lose all their flight feathers in one fell swoop. These do so in well protected areas while they wait for several weeks for the new ones to emerge and grow (see following chapter). Divers, grebes and shearwaters also lose all their flight feathers in one go. Female hornbills pull out all of their primaries once they are holed up in a tree hole by the male in the breeding season.

Moult is usually an annual event, just after the breeding season but some birds have two moults, one the usual annual moult and the other when the bird changes from summer plumage to winter plumage, usually rendering the bird a much duller individual. In some species this involves a complete colour change such as the Scottish Ptarmigan, which turns totally white in winter, rendering it extremely well camouflaged in snow-covered terrain. Albatrosses may take two years to renew all their feathers.

4. UP, UP AND AWAY...

Who knows what went on in the dreams and aspirations of our long lost Neolithic cousins. But I bet many of them would have looked up at flocks of birds and marvelled at the spectacle and perhaps wondered what it would be like to fly. In more modern times there have been a succession of individuals who have tried. This often involved strapping on a pair of home-made wings fashioned out of large bird feathers or membranes of cloth, bidding adieu to a small gathering of friends, maybe a tot of sherry followed by jumping confidently off a large building, traditionally the Eiffel Tower in

France or the Leaning Tower of Pisa in Italy. Most of these characters died in their attempts or at the very least were surely rendered wholly infirm. Those who did get off lightly still had to live with permanent embarrassment! Clearly the Greeks had pondered flight as we see with Icarus in Greek mythology. Happily, unlike Icarus with his wax and feather wings, birds do not fly that close to the sun to even singe their wings.

Flight in animals is restricted to insects, birds and mammals. In the case of the latter, only one group, the bats, can boast true sustainable flight. Flying squirrels, sugar-gliders, flying snakes and flying fish are all simply slowing down their descent by means of specially modified parts of their anatomy, such as the flaps of skin of a flying squirrel stretched between the feet.

Early fliers include the Pterodactyl back in the age of the dinosaurs (pterodactyls were not dinosaurs themselves). These had huge areas of leathery skin connecting their digits on the 'arm-bones' to the tail, enabling them to glide huge distances. They almost certainly needed to achieve flight by falling off the tops of cliffs. A pterodactyl had a wing-span of over seven metres. True flight in birds probably started with a lot of clumsy running and jumping in the early stages of evolution, but with the advent of hollow bones and lightweight feathers the inevitability of sustained flapping flight was realized.

In order to get off the ground and fly, a bird will simply lift off and sustain its flight by flapping the wings - an obvious statement if ever there was one. But that 'flapping' is extremely complex. If you watch a slowed down video of a bird in flight, you will start to notice a kind of figure-of-eight movement. Slow it down even more and you might pick up the subtle opening and closing of feathers, mostly the primaries, the final 10 feathers on a bird's wing starting from the wing-tips. Flight is possible because of the cross-sectional 'design' of the bird's wing plus its surface area in relation to the bird's weight. Fundamentally, when air above a bird's wing moves faster than the air below, 'lift' will result and keep the bird aloft. The tail is used as a sort of rudder and helps the bird maintain a course and also helps it in landing by acting as a sort of brake. A major factor permitting bird flight is the relative size of the bird's sternum or breastbone. All flying birds have well-developed breastbones (often called keels like the keel of a boat) for the attachment of flight muscles. Large flight muscles are essential for bird flight. A rough mental calculation leads me to presume it would need a breastbone the size of a large garage door for the attachment of suitably sized muscles to get a 75kg man airborne.

The largest bird today capable of flight is probably the Californian Condor. No more here on the mechanisms of bird flight per se... it is indeed complicated and beyond me to explain it all thoroughly such as how the bird attains forward momentum or how the most subtle changes of speed and direction are achieved and will not be discussed here.

Patterns of bird flight will vary greatly. There is the very slow, leisurely gentle up and down beat of herons, say, or storks and other large birds. There is the more usual fast flapping of most birds that we observe. Some birds use gliding as a way of saving energy. This becomes obvious during migrations of birds of prey along with cranes and others passing over a narrow sea strait such as that of Gibraltar or down at the Bosphorus between European and Asiatic Turkey. Some birds flap vigorously and then 'glide' but with wings fully closed, creating an undulating flight, characteristic of woodpeckers.

Buzzards will soar above at great heights as they prospect for potential food, their primaries splayed apart to catch up-draughts. Kestrels can include hovering in their flight, remaining motionless while they face into a wind as they observe below.

A hummingbird will hover before a flower as it sips nectar from its host plant, some of these amazing birds beating their wings 20 up to 80 times per second. Some sunbirds of Africa do the same but not with such rapid wing-beats.

Some kingfishers will hover and gannets do so

before plunging down to catch a fish. Being good physicists, these fish catchers even allow for refraction of light in water easily demonstrated by observing a spoon placed in a glass of water, giving rise to the spoon appearing to be bent.

When resting up on a houseboat on the Dal Lake in Srinagar, Kashmir, I observed a pair of Pied Kingfishers on and off throughout the day. In the morning they dived into the water at a fairly shallow angle. As midday approached, the angle would get steeper and at midday they would dive from directly overhead and (you know the rest) in the evening they would dive again at a shallow angle but this time from the opposite direction. This demonstrates a knowledge of refraction and the apparent tracking of the sun.

A Harrier will 'quarter' over an area of grassland or marsh in search of prey, which will incorporate different types of flight, mostly buoyant with the wings sometimes gliding, held in a shallow V until making a sudden flip as the bird pounces on its unsuspecting lunch. Albatrosses can glide for days with barely a flap. They gain height using the wind and distance using gravity. Characteristically, they will glide, say to the north, then switch through a right angle to the east, then back to north, switch again to the west and so on. Very little energy is used and they can wander the oceans with ease – one albatross in fact bears the name Wandering Albatross which has, together with another two species been sighted in British waters. If there are any prizes for flight agility, I would definitely award the Bat-hawks, which as their name implies, catch bats when on the wing, sometimes demanding an almost 180 degree switch. This must seem extremely difficult in our own eyes. I had to remove a flying bat from my lounge in Swaziland. I did so by throwing a towel up at it. It worked eventually but it was no mean feat. Descriptions of flight patterns may be used in Field Guides to aid a birder to identify a species.

Flightlessness is more common than some may think. Firstly, there are the 18 penguin species. Then there are five species of ratites (the Ostrich, Emu, Rhea, Cassowary and Kiwi). The Kiwi is a resident of New Zealand and of course New Zealanders are affectionately referred to as Kiwis.

The Dodo, a large bird related to pigeons and confined to Mauritius could not fly and was tragically clubbed to extinction by Portuguese sailors when they called in on the island to collect fresh water (see Chapter 21).

Many of Hawaii's extinct species (and there are indeed many) were flightless. Today, we also have the Flightless Cormorant, Flightless Rail and the New Zealand Wren. One bizarre creature is a species of parrot, which is the size of a large cat, green, flightless and nocturnal called the Kakapo (down to just a few pairs) in New Zealand. Flightlessness has often proved to be a precursor of extinction and if we are not careful will continue to be so.

So, we have standard flying birds and we have the non-flyers. What about those in between? Yes indeed. A chicken trying to escape you will flutter up to the roof of its coop but that is it. Certain groups of birds become temporarily flightless once a year including some ducks, notably Shelduck and Common Scoters, which moult all their flight feathers in one go and thus cannot possibly fly. They make a pre-moult flight to islands off the north coast of Germany and having moulted their primaries and secondaries, sit it out for a few weeks knowing they are safe enough there until new feathers grow through.

Flight might be used in courtship displays. Raven pairs 'tumble' together in flight, free-falling from a height and somersaulting close together as they descend. A Common Snipe will fly up high and then take a rapid dive down to where a female observes, or perhaps more correctly, listens as the bird creates a distinct drumming sound by holding outward its two outer tail feathers. You can supposedly simulate this by putting two short feathers at either end of a cork, attaching a piece of string and whirling it around your head, but I clearly would never have made a good snipe.

The Pennant-winged Nightjar has two

extended secondary wing-feathers, being without vanes barring the tips, which are white and probably serving to attract. Surprisingly, I found one of these birds in Swaziland sitting on my classroom windowsill one morning as I went to my first lesson, it being reluctant to fly off. I picked it up and took it across to a thicket where it flew down landing a few metres away from me and completely disappeared, so excellent is a nightjar's camouflage. Our European Nightjar is heard to make audible claps with its wings as they come together on the upstroke, almost certainly part of a nuptial display. Male wydahs among many bird species perform aerial displays and skylarks hover way overhead, singing away so as to broadcast their territorial domains.

A Green Heron makes an umbrella out of its wings, holding them overlapping over its stooped head as it feeds in shallow water. This creates an area above the water where the bird's reflection cannot be seen or at least fish can be seen (probably both). Various geese and Mute Swans may have cause to run at you honking (or hissing) with wings outstretched, making them appear larger and thus more intimidating. And no... a swan cannot break a person's leg with its wings, the hollow bones being far weaker than any human leg bones. This urban myth is just that, rather like a stork having delivered you your baby!

CLIVE DENBY

5. SEE ME, SEE ME NOT...

I touched on plumage in the opening chapter but I shall go into more detail here. In a nutshell, a bird's plumage is for it to be either seen... or not seen. Many sexually dimorphic bird species wherein male and females have different plumages, the males will often have their own distinctive colouration contrasting markedly with that of the females. Examples include some of the finch family, buntings and some true thrushes like the Blackbird. In other species the females will appear as rather washed out versions of the male as in the Stonechat and Common Wheatear. The females of some dimorphic species are basically dull brownish, well demonstrated in ducks, pheasants and some passerines. Juvenile birds, maybe fairly nondescript or speckled until the first moult.

It takes some birds like gulls between two and four years to reach adult plumage according to species. Some birds exhibit polymorphism wherein two or three colour variants may occur within the one species such as the Tawny Owl, which may have a brown phase or a grey phase. Skuas have phases and the Arctic Skua has a light, an intermediate and a dark phase. Fulmars also have a light and dark phase. Some male birds develop special nuptial plumage just before breeding, in order to attract a female but this may be lost after it has performed its function.

Gaudy feathers may be augmented by modifications of some feathers. These, however, are expensive to maintain in terms of energy and such structures may be an impediment to the bird's manoeuvrability as in some whydahs, widow-birds and bishops. Exceptions are the birds of paradise and hummingbirds which retain their lavish plumage throughout until the annual moult, a fact I find quite inexplicable. Most species of rollers have the brightest part of their plumage hidden until they fly. Their nuptial displays involve flying down (often from telegraph wires) to the ground 'tumbling' as they do so and revealing beautiful cobalt blue shoulder patches. The male birds of paradise and the hummingbirds may use iridescence in addition to their gaudy plumes to attract mates. Such feathers may appear to change colour depending on the angle from which they are viewed. If you wish to know how this works then I refer you to a physicist. This even occurs with the familiar Magpie some of whose black feathers will show an iridescent greenish-purple sheen at certain angles.

A wide range of birds have permanently extended feathers, which may serve to attract. Head plumes are seen in some heron species and egrets, Crowned Cranes and Great Crested Grebes. Extended feathers on the heads of birds may form crests, some prominent as in Hoopoes and Lapwings while others are more subtle as in Crested Tits and some larks. The 'ears' of the Asio genus of owls are tufts of feathers, which almost certainly have nothing whatever to do with hearing.

Plumage may also be used to provide a bird with camouflage. The Bittern with its ginger and brown striped neck will be excellently camouflaged when the bird squats with head and neck held boldly erect in a reed bed. Owls and nightjars have particularly cryptic plumage. The latter, even though it has just been flushed and landed a few metres in front of you, completely disappears as it blends in perfectly with the old bracken of heathland or leaves of the understorey of a wood. The Spotted Creeper is superbly camouflaged as it sits on a lichen-covered branch. Ground-nesting birds are generally very well camouflaged when sitting on eggs and remain unseen until you are right upon them, such as Ringed Plovers. Ground-nesting birds such as Ringed Plovers are generally very well camouflaged when sitting on eggs and remain unseen until you are right upon them.

Some birds may adopt an alternative type of camouflage as the season changes. Ptarmigans, which are species of grouse, will moult after the breeding season to a winter plumage, which is almost totally white. This is for the purpose of camouflage in the snow-covered hills of

Scotland and mountainous regions of Europe. Birds that spend much time creeping around in the undergrowth tend to have drab plumage, maybe because they have little opportunity to flaunt bright colours. However, I add here that the African Pitta seems to be quite an exception. I caught a very brief view of one of these undergrowth dwellers (about three seconds!) on an island in the Ugandan section of Lake Victoria – a stunningly beautiful bird, which looks like it has been designed by an imaginative primary school pupil.

Camouflage is used of course to prevent birds being seen by a predator. But it is also used to reduce the chance of a bird being seen by its potential prey. Snowy Owls are white as they live in snowy regions but they are apex predators and I cannot think of anything that preys upon them. It seems logical then that these owls are white to allow them to approach rodents and other prey species without being seen. The same principle applies to Polar Bears and Arctic Foxes.

The very opposite of camouflage is having plumage that can more dramatically be exhibited... when necessary. The Sun Bittern is a somewhat cryptically plumaged bird but employs a shock tactic when it is threatened. It opens its huge spread of wings to reveal two highly conspicuous eye-spots, which must surely have some effect in scaring off a would-be predator. This sudden presentation of eye-spots is also used by some of the larger moths, a case of convergent evolution.

Aberrant plumage is any plumage that is abnormal. This will have come about due to poor diet or it may be a genetic defect where certain pigments are lacking. Albino birds lack the pigment melanin, which means the bird is totally unable to produce colours on the feathers, these simply remaining pure white. Any bird can be albino ranging from male peacocks with their fine outgrowths of back feathers (not the tail feathers as commonly believed), penguins, crows, blackbirds, swallows, owls, ducks and more. Albino birds are, for the most part, totally white and have pinkish eyes, due to the blood vessels at the back of the eye providing that splash of pink. Some albino birds may possess orange or yellow feathers in those parts where such coloured feathers would normally be, due to the presence of carotenoid pigments. You may see birds with patches of white in the plumage. These are generally mistakenly referred to as partial albinos. They are not partly albino but leucistic. Such birds will have normal coloured eyes and some of their feathers will be of normal colour for the species. Leucistic birds do possess melanin but are unable to assimilate it fully in the feathers, probably I suspect, due to lack of a specific vitamin, which would act as an enzyme. American Robins seem particularly prone to both albinism and leucism.

Albino birds are able to reproduce if they can manage to attract a mate but that may be problematic as some conspecific birds may not recognise an albino of its own species and may even strive to kill it. Leucistic birds have more chance of reproducing. The young may well not have any plumage aberration if both the parent birds harbour recessive genes for the trait. We rarely see albino birds as they normally die very soon after fledging and leaving the nest. Apart from being prone to attack by other birds, they are weaker individuals and less able to survive. An albino bird's feathers are much more likely to break due to lack of melanin. Also, and probably even more important, is that albino birds are almost blind and so have little chance of making headway in life. Having white feathering may also reduce the bird's ability to retain body heat. Naturally white birds including swans, some geese and egrets are not albino and fulfil normal lives.

The opposite of albinism is melanism where an excess of melanin renders a bird much darker and near-black in plumage. All classes of vertebrates can be albino. Recently on TV I saw a group of four lion cubs, all pure white. These were captive beasts and might manage to survive but in the wild such creatures would have limited lifespans experiencing severe limitations when hunting. Some humans are albino.

At university our departmental librarian, a

chap in his twenties, was fully albino, complete with pink eyes. He could read only by placing a book just a few centimetres from his face. In Africa I have seen quite a few albino people. These go through a really tough time as their skins burn up under the strong sunlight. They often chose to wear wide-brimmed hats and needed to apply various creams and lotions. Their poor vision was clearly a huge problem to endure.

In Botswana, which could get outrageously hot (at times the tarmac on the roads melted) I had an albino lad of about 14 years of age as one of my students. His skin was forever blistering and I really felt for him as he was clearly going through agony. He was much respected by his peers who clearly were sympathetic to his plight and this was pleasantly surprising, as several African countries are quite intolerant of human aberrations. In parts of Africa, and probably elsewhere, witch-doctors will use human albino organs and parts in their muthi medicine, a sort of voodoo practise. One African country I lived in had a markedly higher level of albinism than others. I heard that some societies in Africa will put down albino babies at birth but cannot verify how widespread or common this is. Where it does occur will be because of the belief that the child has been bewitched in some way or that it is a punishment from God. There is widespread persecution and murder of albino humans in East Africa, notably Tanzania, where their body parts are held at a premium. A special Tanzanian organisation has been formed purely to protect albino people. Even in places where they are afforded some protection, albinos may be isolated from and shunned by society.

The bright and colourful feathers of some bird species are used by various tribes-people as adornments. In New Guinea the plumes of birds of paradise may be worn, especially about the head and in Africa I have seen the feathers of turacos, rollers and egrets used for ceremonial dress.

6. PACK UP YOUR TROUBLES...

How do they do it?

How does a Barn Swallow, which nested under your eaves in suburban Hemel Hempstead complete its nesting here, then set off in September to migrate way down into sub-Saharan Africa, often as far down as South Africa, then spend the African summer down there (our European winter) and do the same trip all over again the following April?

But there is more. That Swallow will not just fly to Hemel Hempstead but it may well locate No. 27 Elizabeth Crescent where you live and nest under those very same eaves. If this is not blowing your mind already, consider those young birds, which fly after their parents have left and so find their own way down to their wintering grounds. Many young birds will return to the same site where they were hatched. Imagine huge flocks of these birds making their way across the English Channel down through France and Spain, across the Straits of Gibraltar, then skirting down the western coast of the bulge of Africa and then down across Central Africa and proceeding even further down to Zimbabwe, Malawi, Swaziland, Botswana and even South Africa.

We have talked about swallows. But scores of bird species undertake these mass migrations, notably warblers and members of the thrush family such as Wheatears, Redstarts, and Whinchats, and also martins and Common Swifts and indeed any other of our summer visitors. Many wader species move down from their breeding grounds in the northern temperate regions and travel huge distances southwards. Here is the point to mention the amazing feat of the Arctic Tern, the world's greatest traveller. These birds migrate from their breeding grounds above the Arctic Circle (66 degrees north) down to the other end of the Earth where they winter well below the Antarctic Circle (66 degrees south). This means, with the return journey, these birds are flying well over 20,000km every year. There are several different migration routes taking birds from different parts of Europe and Asia down to different parts of Africa, India and other areas in SE Asia. Even some hummingbirds undertake lengthy migrations, an example being the Rufous Hummingbird, which moves from Mexico up to Alaska every year. Ringing has filled out a lot of the former mysteries but there is still so much we don't know.

So, how oh how is all this planetary movement of birds possible?

Preparation is essential. Migrant bird species have to fuel up for the journey. They spend time in a given area feeding voraciously and thus accumulating fat reserves, these being deposited in fat depots spread around and within the body. Birds may double their own weight during this pre-flight period. This is what some of the birds we were catching in Ladakh were doing and weighing birds was part of our programme.

Any re-traps we got of our own birds some days later would give us an idea of how these birds were progressing with their fattening-up periods. Grouping into flocks of normally fairly solitary species may also be an important precursor to migration.

Some migrating flocks of birds are so huge that they can be picked up on radar scanners.

During the Second World War, radar stations were picking up strange visual blips on their screens and for a while these were a total mystery. They were called 'angels' for lack of any other explanation but they turned out (much to the relief of those running the war effort) to be massive flocks of migratory birds.

Today, radar techniques have been so refined that, to some extent, birds making up these flocks can be identified.

How do birds know the way?

To find the way means you have to have an end-point in mind before setting off. Then they will need to navigate not by GPS systems but by using heavenly points like the stars (the Pole Star is very important), the sun and the moon, allowing and compensating for their celestial movements, both real and apparent. They also use the Earth's magnetic field and evidence of magnetite in the skulls and retinas of migratory birds have been found, basically proving they do indeed have inbuilt compasses. Having compasses is stunning in itself - knowing how to use them is something else indeed. During the day they may follow visible surface features like rivers, valley systems and other fixed landmarks (flying-by-wire as a pilot would say).

Physiology plays a role too. Birds have the ability to use inhaled air extremely efficiently. In short, they cycle the same breath intake twice. When we breathe, we only extract about four per cent of the oxygen available, whereas birds can up this considerably. Obviously, such a technique must be of enormous benefit to birds flying in rarified atmosphere. Having hollow bones keeps the birds' weight to a minimum.

En route, the birds may feed, either by coming down to Earth or by feeding on the wing if their diet and presence of aerial insects permits this. They have to deal with bad weather, birds of prey, the guns and traps of some southern Europeans who like to eat small birds cooked up in pies.

Many birds in southern Europe are caught by liming, which involves putting a sticky lime solution on to bushes and so trapping birds in their thousands. The nursery rhyme Alouette is all about a French bloke plucking a skylark (Alouette is French for Skylark) having trapped it and now preparing to have it, along with other birds, for supper.

In much the same way as many people believe archaeologists go on 'digs' in the hope of unearthing ancient pots of gold coins (laughable to most archaeologists and irritating to others) then there are those that hold that ornithologists' raison d'être is to spot 'rare' birds. True it is a bit of a buzz to see a rarity but if that was all there was to it then 99 per cent of a birdwatcher's time would be futile.

Twitchers of course love rarities. They are a chance to get one up on their competitors. Most twitchers go out on January 1 in order to clock-up as many birds as possible. This readily dispenses with a lot of the common stuff so they can settle down to the real business of contacting 'hot spot' sites (this used to involve phoning Nancy's Café in Norfolk but today I guess it's the internet) and then perhaps wangling days off, doing car-shares or even chartering small aircraft. Most would not hesitate to whizz off half-way up country to see a Subalpine Warbler in Britain.

When I was wardening on the Ouse Washes in 1977 during my university long holiday, a Great Reed Warbler turned up in a reed bed just 2km down the road from us. The reed bed was part of someone's garden by the way. I did go down to see it but was horrified to witness my first-ever frenzy of twitchers standing round the reed bed periphery all with telescopes and tripods, and the more hopeful even had cameras, some with a year's salary worth of telescopic lenses and filters. There must have been at least 30 people. I went back to the warden's house feeling quite awful. Not because I had not seen the bird but because what I had heard about this bizarre twitching phenomenon was actually true. Happily the bird had moved on the following day.

In 1971 when working on the Snowy Owls in

Shetland, Digby, one of the other wardens and I saw a male Red- flanked Bluetail (he actually found it first). Digby managed a few pretty poor camera shots but they were, collectively at least, conclusive evidence for our report to the local bird group's rarities committee. We did tell Bobby Tulloch, the then Shetland RSPB representative who was our immediate boss but that was it. We were spared any onslaught. Not that we wanted to keep this bird to ourselves. Not at all. It never really occurred to us and at that time the twitching craze had not really taken off.

In 1969 I had the first Red-rumped Swallow for Essex. I was not even going to report it as solo observers rarely, if ever, have their records accepted, quite reasonably so. When I heard that two such birds had been seen in Yorkshire on the same day I sent in my report, which was accepted. I doubt however I would have travelled far, if at all, to see a Red-rumped Swallow in Britain as I had seen loads of these in 1969 down in southern France.

Let's consider the meaning of 'rare bird'

Rare birds are much more likely to turn up either during early spring when birds are migrating northwards or in autumn when they are going south again. A bird may be globally, nationally or even locally rare due to its natural geographical distribution. Many island species have been rare from the outset such as the Chatham Island's Robin. They were never common in the first place due to their reduced spatial range. Many rare birds have become so due to environmental changes such as Corncrakes and Cirl Buntings and Stone Curlews, which have suffered due to modern agricultural practices.

Some birds have become rare through hunting or over-harvested as a food source such as the poor old Dodos on Mauritius, which being flightless, were so easily clubbed to death, gathered up and salted by travelling Portuguese sailors, culminating in the birds' ultimate extinction. Passenger Pigeons in North America once filled the skies numbering millions and were not given a second look. If any of these were seen today perchance then plane loads of twitchers would descend on the United States. Not that Passenger Pigeons were in any way special. They are extinct of course but I hope you get my point. Rarity is what really matters with the twitcher mentality. How many twitchers would go on a special holiday to see Harlequin Ducks and Gyr Falcons and then come home to write poems about them? And of course why should they? But again, it is rarity that generally matters.

Harlequin ducks are actually not rare... in Iceland. I have been to Iceland as part of a glacial survey team when I was doing my 'O' levels in a tech' college in 1973 and I did indeed see Harlequins and a single glimpse of a Gyr Falcon. I did not feign sickness and, with a group of strangers hire a Cessna to go up to Iceland to see these birds. But I must be fair here too as to have done so would almost certainly not have caused any discomfort to the birds. My objection to many of these characters arises when I hear of them dragging crop-fields with ropes, standing around for hours preventing a hungry lost bird from feeding, trampling regardless across farmers' fields and even worse tactics that I chose not to believe, they were so awful. I believe that such behaviour is practised only by the minority.

Enough of migration although I do want to say something about Bird Observatories in the following chapter.

7. A BIRD IN THE HAND...

Bird Observatories, unlike bird reserves and sanctuaries are concerned with the monitoring of bird migration and do so both by systematic observation and more importantly, ringing of migrant species. Observatories located around British coasts currently number 19 (at the time of writing). The first was set up by Ronald Lockley on the island of Skokholm, which lies off the SW coast of Wales in 1933. Here, as well as the ringing and biometric data collection, intensive studies were made of several bird species including Storm Petrels and Razorbills.

Lockley spent much of his life following an

arcadian existence on small islands living very simply and writing books on his life and family and the birds who shared their lives with them. I have read about six of Lockley's books and they are each a treat, especially as I am myself a committed 'insulophile' were there such a word. He spent many years living, farming and birding on Skokholm.

In the '50s and '60s other observatories were set up, each providing a wardens' house, basic furnishings, food allowance and a small salary. The lives of these wardens was and is close to idyllic but like all things 'idyllic' there are often accompanying hardships although more easily borne by those who care little of excess comforts. One of the excitements of working at an observatory is that the through-flow of migrant birds will vary from day to day. After a few days of little happening you may witness what is called a 'fall' of migrants, a sudden influx of birds of one or two species that will remain just for a few days before moving on. I witnessed such a fall on Bardsey in 1968 when hundreds of willow warblers occurred overnight and the bushes were heaving with these intrepid travellers.

We had similar influxes at our Himalayan ringing site but these were mostly of altitudinal migrants, which had moved down from the scantily vegetated mountain slopes, which soon would be buried in snow - such birds as Guldenstadt's Redstarts (larger and a lot more chunky than other redstarts) and also Brown and Robin Accentors (see chapter 27).

Of the current 19 operating observatories, two are on the Scottish islands of Fair Isle and North Ronaldsay. Bardsey Observatory lies off the Lleyn Peninsula of N Wales, where I have stayed twice. Copeland Observatory is situated on the Northern Ireland coast while Cape Clear Observatory sits on an island off the SW coast of Ireland, another which I have visited. The Calf of Man is a small island lying off the larger Isle of Man, which sits off the English coast in the Irish Sea. Other observatories include Gibraltar Point, Isle of May, Spurn, Holme, Flamborough and Portland Bill where Simon, our stalwart ringer/ornithologist in Ladakh had worked for a while, necessitating his living in an old lighthouse.

Without doubt the most prolific observatory in terms of migrant birds is Fair Isle, officially part of the Shetland archipelago although lying some way off to the south surrounded by one of the roughest sea areas in Britain. It is worthy of special consideration. Between 1905 and 1911 a chap with the evocative name of William Eagle Clarke visited Fair Isle regularly to cover the annual spring and autumn migration periods. He clocked up 207 species, which was at that time more than half of the birds on the British list. Today, that list stands at an impressive 641 and is maintained by the British Ornithologists' Union. Being a product of his time, Clarke collected numerous specimens by shooting them and did not use ringing techniques.

In 1948, George Waterston purchased Fair Isle from a Shetland dignitary and set up Fair Isle Bird Observatory Trust. In the ensuing years several building refurbishments were carried out, the last completed in 2010. Fair Isle Bird Observatory was destroyed by fire in March 2019. The company that was rebuilding it went bankrupt in 2023 and it is scheduled to reopen in May 2025. From April to June and August to October the warden and his assistants carry out regular very organised daily censuses as well as the trapping and ringing of birds. By very organised, I mean done in such a way that repetitions of sightings by two people, say at any one time, are avoided as much as possible. Looking at photographs the accommodation seems pretty smart for a bird observatory and visitors go there every year to stay for a few days or even more. Despite my own five periods in Shetland, I never got to Fair Isle. In those days sea-crossings were not to be relied on and could be quite precarious operations. I expect today's visitors arrive mostly by small planes.

Like all observatories, Fair Isle takes on an assistant each year and some of these later graduate to become chief wardens. Reading the lists of past wardens and assistants just recently I see that many have done successive stints of three to five years, perhaps reflecting what a wonderful existence it can be. Coincidentally, when working through this list I noticed the name Paul Harvey who spent some years on Fair Isle in the '80s and '90s. Racking my brain I remembered that a Paul Harvey was one of various birders who came out from Southampton to join us for a while at our own ringing hut in the NW Himalaya in 1981/2. I have since confirmed it is the same chap.

The reason I love islands is that they are a whole world and you can soon forget there is anything else out there. I am not a Luddite but I do like the simpler life. Most of the islands, which have observatories have just a handful of residents, including rather elderly folk who were born there and perhaps a young couple going for 'the good life' experience and escaping the proverbial rat-race. In most cases, visitors to these observatories flock in each year and they too stay in basic yet comfortable accommodation. Their own daily bird observations are included at the end of each day when, traditionally after supper, everyone gathers into the lounge as the warden works through a species list. As each species is called, visitors throw in their own offerings. These may not always be readily accepted as I once witnessed when I was staying on Bardsey Island at the Observatory for two weeks in 1968. These evening recording sessions are referred to either as 'log' or, the one I prefer 'call over'.

The wardens on Fair Isle oftenoyste use Heligoland traps. These are large walk-in funnels made of simple wooden frames and fine-mesh chicken wire. These are set up on what little vegetation cover there may be, sometimes just grass with the odd bush, and birds are 'driven' into these funnels by a walking warden or two or perhaps from visitors. At the thin end of the funnel is a catching box where any migrants are trapped, removed and processed. This process is fully explained in chapter 27. The main problem with Heligoland traps is that being used in windy environments, they need some fixing up before the beginning of each spring season.

Fixing battered Heligoland traps was precisely my job during my second visit to Bardsey in 1986 when I was doing my PGCE at Bangor University. Having completed a wooden boat building apprenticeship from age 16 to 20 I had become a sort of carpenter as well although there is not a single right-angle in a fishing boat. Whilst on Bardsey, in addition to mending the large Heligoland, I repaired a small hide situated on the beach just above the tideline. Here one could secrete oneself and a close friend (and I do mean a close friend as it was so small and snug) and observe just a few metres away Turnstones, Purple Sandpipers, Redshanks, Oystercatchers and other waders. The hide was extremely low and you were almost sitting on the ground when in it. It had to be emptied of wind-blown sand two or three times a season. I had to write a geography assignment for my PGCE so I took the opportunity to gather up as much info' as I could, enabling me to pull together a passable treatment of the history of Bardsey and the hardships of remote island life. Bardsey was 8km out from the peninsula and the crossing was treacherous. Several years after an earlier visit in 1968, I heard that the regular boatman had drowned on a rougher than normal crossing. I was therefore dreading my crossing in 1986 but by then the boat was a lot more than an open soap-dish so my fears were allayed.

Coming back to call-over time in the evenings, I implied above that a visitor's sightings were not always received without some further investigation. I recall, on my first visit of 1968 a rather elderly and somewhat tweedy gentrified lady reporting a Barn Owl. Now, Barn Owl had not even been called out... it never had been. Warden George Evans (I can see him now) made extra vigorous and more urgent sucks on his pipe, he fidgeted and seemed quite put out. No one else had seen a Barn Owl that day or any other day during my two week stay but at the time it did not strike me as that unlikely. Barn Owls are probably one of the most cosmopolitan birds so an adventurous individual would not have surprised me unduly. However, George was not having it and somehow managed diplomatically but forcibly to move on after spending about 20 minutes on this one bird. I am certain the Barn Owl never entered the observatory logs. As I said in the previous chapter, solo observations of highly unexpected bird species are very thorny affairs and seldom successful. I believe that in the name of integrity of the written record then this seemingly cruel unwritten law is warranted.

Many thousands of birds are ringed every year at our collective observatories. The biometric data collected while the bird is still in the hand is very valuable indeed and has taught us a huge amount. This will continue to be the case. But bird-ringing is of its best value when those marked birds are recovered elsewhere, and these are in fact referred to as 'controls'. The information that this can provide is obvious enough. Dots on an international map showing where a particular bird was ringed and where it was recovered tells us how far that bird has travelled, in what period of time and the minimum age of the bird. It helps to give us the geographical range of the bird if we can detect trends in these recovery incidents. Any recovered bird will have its number noted and the bird is released.

Sometimes, these aluminium rings become illegible if they are many years old but most will outlive the average bird. When recoveries are found whether at an observatory or simply a ringed dead bird lying on the pavement by a dog-walker, the finder is informed where to send the number. In the UK I assume the rings still bear the logo 'Inform Brit mus', this being the British Museum. The post office know where to send your letter. I found a dead ringed Greenfinch in my school playground in 1963 and sent in a report. A slip came back two weeks later telling me who ringed it, when and where. My Greenfinch had not been that adventurous and was ringed just the previous year within 20 miles of where I found it. I did better with a Puffin when in Shetland. The bird had remained within the Shetland Islands but what was interesting was its age. It had been ringed in 1970 and I had found it fairly freshly dead (oiled) on a beach, 12 years later. This is surely quite a good age for a bird, which has to endure many months away at sea every year, being tossed about in powerful storms.

A final and sad point is that when I was on Bardsey, I learnt that lighthouses can be very powerful attractants to migrating birds and many end up killing themselves as they repeatedly batter themselves against the lighthouse lamps. I have seen awful photographs of hundreds of small migrant birds being collected up in a wheelbarrow the following morning. I think Trinity House, the organisation responsible for British lighthouses has attempted to improve this situation by various technical adjustments. I do hope so indeed.

The history with Gulf oil and gas drilling masts and rigs is quite different. Hundreds of tall masts are lit up at night with extremely powerful lights to warn shipping and aircraft. Like moths to a flame, migrating birds approaching these lights become disoriented and end up actually being drawn to them. This results in them smashing into the lights and gas flares in their thousands. The oil industry seems to be impervious to remedial action and little is being done about this although I would love to be corrected.

Trying to close here on a more positive note, many birds that land on oil rigs around the UK are briefly 'adopted' and tended by sympathetic crew members enabling exhausted birds to have a good feed before continuing their journey. The birds may not be disoriented but totally exhausted and so are capable of completing their journeys having been well-provisioned by caring people.

8. TABLE FOR TWO...

We can put birds into four main categories with respect to feeding. Carnivores eat just meat, insectivores just a particular kind of meat - insects, herbivores eat just plant material and omnivores eat all of the above in varying proportions.

Examining the beak of a bird, its relative size, shape and structure, can give a good clue to which feeding category it may belong. Hooked beaks clearly suggest the ripping open of dead flesh as in hawks, falcons, eagles, buzzards and the smaller shrikes. Long, thin and often delicate bills will be those of insectivores while granivores (further specialised herbivores) will have shorter but stouter triangular bills such as finches and buntings, which feast on seeds. An extreme example we can find in Britain and nearly all of Europe except most of Scandinavia is the Hawfinch (a bird I am never destined to meet) with an absurdly massive bill for cracking open fruit kernels, especially cherries.

Other particular herbivores may have their own term such as frugivores, which specialize in eating fruit. A perfect example would be the Guacharo or Oil bird of northern South America, which roosts and nests in caves but comes out to feed in droves purely on olives, wax palm and avocado fruit during the evenings. The nestling birds have such an oily flesh they are actually used as lamps by local people, burning them with wicks pushed down the throat turning them into candles. Omnivores may enhance their chances of survival by being switching predators. If the going gets tough they can adjust their diets. Good examples are Magpies and European Jays (both members of the crow family) which can dine on acorns and other seeds and fruits but will not hesitate to take fledglings and eggs as well as insects and small reptiles. Fish catchers will have relatively long bills such as kingfishers, gannets and cormorants.

Highly specialised fish eaters like pelicans have expandable sacs of skin under their lower mandibles that can hold several fish at a time, usually caught by a group of cooperating birds, which shoal fish into shallow water and scoop them up. Herons will eat fish as well as reptiles and amphibians and even young birds such as Moorhens. They possess a very special tool. This is a sort of nail-file structure on the inner side of one of its toes. It is used to clean its bill of congealed slime and fish-scales.

Flamingos feed not on fish but algae, molluscs and larvae, these being caught by filtering out the food from the inverted bills, which are filled with water as the birds stoop down to feed. It is pigment in a flamingo's food that keeps the bird pink - those in zoos tend to become whiter as they are not fed on their normal diet.

After completing a two-year teaching contract in Kenya I got a short-term post with the Kenyan Wildlife Service to help make censuses of the Greater and Lesser Flamingos, which move around and 'graze' different shallow Rift Valley lakes in turn. Watching these birds feed in their hundreds of thousands is awesome indeed.

If you studied in detail over time say, a large mature tree, you may record several bird species flitting about amongst its foliage - but look even closer. After time you will see a trend. Some bird species will be restricting themselves to the upper reaches of the tree, the canopy. Others will be foraging in the middle layer of the tree while yet others will confine themselves to the lower parts. This reduces competition amongst birds as different zones of the tree will produce different foodstuff. There will be caterpillars, larvae, fully-grown insects, spiders, beetles, perhaps woodlice and a whole load more. There will of course be some overlap here but by and large these smorgasbords are separated thus enabling greater diversity of dining customers. That's in the tree, but what about on the tree trunk itself?

Walking through a wood or even in your garden you may see a Treecreeper jerking its way up a trunk and another time you might observe a Nuthatch doing likewise. But is it likewise?

Is there a difference of strategy? Again, there is no hard and fast rule here, but generally there is a trend. A Treecreeper characteristically starts at the base of a tree trunk and works its way upwards, probing the cracks in the bark with its delicate curved beak as it searches for small invertebrate titbits. Then it will fly diagonally down to a neighbouring tree and start again at its base and again work its way upwards. This of course continues as the bird feeds. Nuthatches do actually go up and down the tree trunk but do both equally well. They even add to their acrobatic repertoire by walking along underneath the branches. Studies have shown that these two arboreal species feed on different species of organisms (this avoiding direct competition) given as I say, a bit of overlap. I am sure both would not be able to resist a nice juicy grub, but I bet you those grubs would be of different insect species. You will appreciate that to cater for these food preferences both bird species have very different bills, each being best suited to their own diet, the Nuthatch possessing a straight thicker and more robust beak. For such reasons it is very difficult to look after an injured bird. What do you feed it on?

A Great or a Blue Tit relishes grubs and caterpillars but these will be mostly of different species. There is an added complication here as well. A bird feeding itself may not feed its young on the same food. This is because their young will require differing ratios of food classes (carbohydrates, proteins and fats) as they develop. They may not possess the mechanical ability to break down various foods or they may lack the chemistry (the digestive enzymes) to break down tough leathery beetles say or a thick-skinned caterpillar.

Speaking of the specificity of insectivorous birds reminds me of when, as assistant warden on the Ouse Washes RSPB bird reserve in the summer of 1977 a chap drove up to the warden's house and presented me with a Common Swift. It had a broken wing, which hung forlornly downwards. I immediately heard the death knells ringing. I explained to the chap that a swift with a broken wing is effectively a dead swift as they feed voraciously on particular flies as they spiral around in the heavens with beaks agape. There is no way you could go and find these same flies, let alone the quantity you would need. A grounded swift will not crawl about trying to feed... there is nothing for it to feed on. Seeing the chap's rather horrified face, I had to lie to him. I told him I would do what I could and he left feeling only slightly better. I dispatched the bird shortly after he had left.

Now we know from the age of two that ducks are birds that just sit around on the water and we know of course that they have all evolved to eat white doughy bread. But what really of ducks' feeding strategies? Once again, in nature's way of reducing competition between species they have evolved different palates and consequently different ways of collecting their food.

Ducks fall into two main categories with respect to feeding. There are the surface feeders and the diving ducks. Surface feeders, which predominantly frequent marshes and shallow ponds include Mallard, Wigeon, Gadwall, Teal, Pintail and Shoveler. As their name clearly indicates, these birds will simply feed on food material close to the surface, this action known as dabbling or some will do what is called 'up-ending,' pivoting their bodies through 90 degrees and sticking their heads under water so as to feed on stuff just below the surface.

Diving ducks do indeed take the plunge including Tufted Duck, Scaup, Pochard, Goldeneye and Ferruginous duck. These will have totally different food requirements to surface-feeders. Diving ducks can stay under for around half to one minute in my experience, re-surfacing some way from the point where they dived. We might mention sea ducks here. Long Tailed Ducks, Common and Velvet Scoters and Eider Ducks are strictly maritime except of course in the breeding season and these birds essentially have to dive for their food.

A further group of diving ducks include the Red Breasted Merganser, Goosander and Smew, collectively known as 'sawbills'. Their distinctive bills with serrated mandibles are perfect for hanging on to slippery fish. Some ducks will take down sand or fine gravel while feeding. This is to provide mechanical purchase in their digestive tracts in a structure known as the gizzard, which serves as a grinding mill, breaking down tough cellulose cell walls of plant material. When wardening on the Ouse Washes we would ensure that suitable depots of such material was available to the numerous ducks that either breed there or congregate in their thousands in the winter. Other birds also use this technique.

I have on a number of occasions in Africa seen Ostriches standing erect with clearly visible snooker ball sized lumps slowly descending down their necks, due to swallowing rounded stones, which aid mechanical digestion in their gizzards. It is believed that the dinosaurs, which fed on extremely tough-skinned tree ferns and other vegetation had large gizzards in which stones were lodged to aid in their digestion. Bacterial colonies in the guts of herbivorous dinosaurs and today, some birds, help chemically break down the cell walls of plants. These specialised bacteria possess the enzyme cellulase, which digests cellulose. If we had cellulase bacteria we could invite our friends round to eat grass. Cows, however, do accommodate cellulase wielding bacteria so we eat them instead.

Many birds of prey swallow their food whole and may even feed their young on whole rats, mice, small birds and snakes. I have witnessed an African Fish Eagle in Ethiopia shoving a large fish about 30cm long down the gullet of one of its chicks. On a human scale this would be like watching Pierre on the next table in a Parisian restaurant slowly pushing a whole baguette down his throat. They will not have gizzards though but have a different system. Their digestive systems are mechanically and chemically contrived to sort out the bones, feathers, beaks and feet of their prey items. These indigestible parts are then neatly packaged up into thick cigar-shaped pellets, generally between two and five centimetres long, which are then regurgitated. You will see plenty of these around such birds' nest sites. In addition to birds of prey such as hawks and falcons, other birds produce pellets including shrikes and herons.

When working in a government school in North Botswana in 1995, I discovered, as I did my morning runs, that a pair of Spotted Eagle Owls were nesting in a disused and derelict cattle station. I immediately had an idea although not original by any means. I approached my four most enthusiastic biology students and asked if they might be interested in entering the Science and Maths Fair of Botswana Schools, which numbered well over 100 participants. I showed them the site and explained the methods from the daily collection of pellets to their analysis, data collection and presentation. After that it was largely up to them.

The tutor was obliged to maintain a hands-off approach throughout as much as was practical. Once gathered, a pile of about seven or eight pellets were taken each day to my biology lab to which my team had its own key, although I was allowed to supervise them on occasion. The pellets were measured and weighed and then immersed in freshly boiled water. Before your very eyes the fur and feathers would float to the surface, while the bones, beetle carapaces (wing-cases), beaks, feet and claws settled to the bottom. No chemicals whatsoever were used in the separation process. The bones were lightly bleached to make them nicely clean and presentable (although they were always 100 per cent stripped of any meat) and it also made them a bit healthier to handle. Reference to a bone collection enabled the students to identify mammal bones and I sometimes had to help with identifying bird species, which was easier if there was a skull or even just a beak. Otherwise I would make an intelligent guess because owls are only likely to take ground-feeding birds like pipits, wagtails and larks. The students reassembled as far as they could the bones to represent whole animals and mounted them on board although of course each pellet was not representative of any one particular meal.

I made a large hinged wooden presentation-board for the students and we took it down to the capital Gaborone on judgement day. The headmaster who was against the project from the start due to superstition refused my much earlier request for a truck and at the last minute I had to make a mercy-dash in a state of inner turmoil to borrow a pick-up from a local brewery for the day. With the student's excellent bone, fur and feather presentations together with informative text and a couple of maps they took first prize in the ecology section. I had recommended the students handwrite the displays as I thought this would have added something to their work (I was later told by one of the judges that this had indeed helped favourably in the judgement process). I was so proud of them and I got them T-shirts with Spotted Eagle Owls emblazoned thereon and they too were proud when they appeared in the local press.

One of the student's parents had refused permission for her daughter to do the project on grounds of superstition about owls being witches of the night but I charmed her round. I enjoyed seeing her happy face at the awards ceremony and she came over and thanked me personally. I must just tell you this. One surly old bugger, a real plum-in-the-mouth headmaster complete with shooting-stick, having peered closely at the display, waved a dismissive hand and declared loudly that the bones were made of plastic and that it was a fraud. I pictured there and then a small busy band of people in a workshop in Gaborone manufacturing plastic mouse bones struggling to satisfy a booming market. (What a plonker, don't you know!)

There are those raptors (birds of prey) who feed exclusively on fish, the African Fish Eagle and Osprey being good examples. Also Pel's Fishing Owl found in east and central Africa and closely related to Verreaux's Eagle owl is entirely a fish feeder.

Okay it's not a bird but I find it most fascinating that the Daubenton's Bat, which can be seen in the UK regularly quarters just above the surfaces of rivers, scooping various insects up from the surface as opposed to the more characteristic aerial feeding of bats. These bats use their back feet and extended tail membranes to pick up their prey, located by echo-location.

Before leaving birds of prey I want to mention Snowy Owls but in particular a pair of Snowy Owls I (along with three other wardens) watched continually throughout the breeding season on Fetlar, Shetland in 1971. Their main food is a guinea-pig sized rodent, the Lemming. However, there are no Lemmings in Shetland so it was to be interesting to ascertain just what the owls were feeding on. A fuller account of that project is given in Chapter 25.

Some birds of prey will resort to scavenging, especially if the going is tough while others use it as a way of life. Of the latter, vultures are the most well-known. These will rise up on thermals so as to allow them a panorama where they can visually locate a carcass. They descend down, sometimes while the lions say, are still tearing off great swathes of meat. Vultures will noisily squabble over a nice juicy (or perhaps not so juicy if it is long dead) carcass.

There are four species of vulture in Europe and many more throughout Africa and they occur in all other continents apart from Antarctica. Vultures play a very important ecological role as decomposers. Look at some pictures of various vultures - pretty ugly yes! This is because of the prevalence of bare skin on the head and neck region. This has a clear function. Vultures feed largely by thrusting their heads into the bellies of dead zebra, wildebeest and would get caked with congealed blood were there feathers. This would not just be grossly uncomfortable but a good means of contracting bacterial diseases.

The Marabou Stork is even more grotesque. Hardly the choice of a national bird although Serbia does have the Griffon Vulture as its avian icon. Bolivia has gone for the Andean Condor, also a vulture, which has a wing-span of about three-and-a-half metres. Although facially ugly, these birds are indeed most majestic in flight and so have come to grace postage stamps, banknotes and such.

Continuing with vultures there are two species that come to mind, which sometimes incorporate quite unique ways of securing a meal. The Bearded Vulture, also called the Lammergeier found in the Pyrenees, plus a few other European sites and also the Middle East, Central Asia and parts of east Africa, notably the Ethiopian Highlands, has a remarkable habit. It flies up to a considerable height in order to drop large heavy bones down onto rocky ground. This may not always work but the idea is to break open the bones to access the nutritious bone-marrow. I presume that this rather hit-and-miss method may need some additional support with other foods but it is just yet another amazing example of nature trying every trick in the book. I have seen quite a few Lammergeyers but have never witnessed the bone-dropping spectacle.

Another bird which is really a highly specialised type of vulture although not of that family of true vultures, is the Secretary Bird, which is endemic to Africa. These fantastic looking birds of the Savannah grasslands have extremely long legs which, unlike those of many other birds of prey are not feathered, but totally bare. This means they can, in relative safety, go about killing snakes by jumping up and down on them. I have seen this just the once but it is a regular practice, I gather. Incidentally, they are called Secretary Birds owing to the plumes of long feathers on the backs of their heads making them resemble early scribes and secretaries who would put quill pens behind their ears. They do also feed on other reptiles and are also keen on rodents.

A final note on vultures. When holidaying in Tanzania in 1993 an Australian traveller and I decided over a few beers to put vultures to the test. We had seen White-backed Vultures spiralling up on a huge thermal the day before so we met up and did our deed. We found a site below where the birds had been spiralling and were doing so again that day. We both lay down on our backs some few metres apart. Arms outstretched and remaining as still as we could we did this for 25 minutes until the heat forced us to abandon this somewhat unscientific experiment. Probably the birds had larger or more tasty food in mind or perhaps they knew we were bluffing. After all, do vultures really look down on moribund animals waiting for them to die? I now doubt it as staying up there in the air takes energy. So why not wait on the ground nearby instead? But of course vultures hunt mainly by using their sense of smell. I guess I had watched too many cowboy films in my past.

Let's look at other rather specialist modes of bird feeding. Some birds are parasites, maybe not totally although pirating other birds' shopping baskets is typical of Skuas (called Jaegers in America). I have seen these on many occasions in Shetland waiting to fly up to an incoming Puffin say, which has a beakful of fish, maybe seven or eight all hanging out of the sides of the bird's laterally flattened beak. The skua (either a Great or an Arctic Skua) will harry the targeted bird, forcing it to drop its catch. The skua will stoop down and capture at least part of the catch before it even hits the sea. Apart from stealing the food itself, skuas may force a bird to regurgitate its food while still in flight and again the skua will catch the yucky stuff before it touches down in the sea.

Symbiosis is another technique incorporated into some birds' feeding methods. It is a strategy, not necessarily about feeding, where two different species or even classes of animals work together to each other's advantage. There are also symbiotic relationships between animals and plants, pollination being a splendid example. Perhaps one of the best known animal-animal symbioses is the habit of honey-guides (small birds with rather dull plumage of which there are several species in Africa) commandeering the physical strength and dexterity of mammals to prize open a bee's nest. The mammals will be either Honey Badgers (Ratels) or, in more recent times, humans. On locating an active hive, a honey-guide will fly off to find a helpful assistant and guide it back through a process of fluttering and anxious twittering to the site. Having taken what it needs, the benefactor leaves the bird a generous chunk of honey and wax-laden comb.

In parts of Asia, fishermen will use captive cormorants to help them catch fish. He will sit on his canoe-like boat with a cormorant by his side. The bird is tethered on a string and also has a metal ring around its neck. The bird dives down and catches a fish but is unable to swallow it unless it is small enough to pass the constriction in the throat created by the ring. It has no choice but to offer up the larger fish to its master. I suppose this is a rather weak form of symbiosis because if the cormorant were free in the first place it would be catching fish for itself. I think a better term here would therefore be exploitation.

In Australia, on a three month visit in 2010, I witnessed a party of about a dozen pelicans gathered around the outdoor filleting table in a small fishing port. This saved the fishermen a daily clean-up job and the pelicans were suitably dined. It was also clearly quite a local attraction.

Of great interest to me are the Scarlet Macaws of SE Peru. These birds are very fond of a particular kind of fruit and gorge themselves in great feeding orgies. The one problem here is that the fruits are highly poisonous. Not to be outdone they still eat the fruits. But... then they fly off together to a nearby cliff face made of a kaolin clay-type substance. This the birds scrape off with their powerful beaks and swallow. It seems that this serves as an antidote to the toxin. Would you dare to sprinkle arsenic on your chips even when you knew there was an antidote available? However, there is another theory suggesting the clay contains minerals which compensate for low sodium levels in parts of the tropical rainforest. Whichever is correct, it is actions like these in the natural world that make the whole evolutionary process so utterly mind-boggling.

9. HOME SWEET HOME…

If your dictionary gives the definition of nest as 'a bird's home' then it has probably been written with crossword compilers in mind. I am sure most of us know that no bird lives in a nest. A temporary structure built for the retention of bird's eggs and young while they are developing seems to be a far more acceptable entry. So many of us are interested in birds themselves and we find the amazing variety and beauty of their eggs quite overwhelming, to the point where people collect them. Collectors make a pin-hole at each end of the egg and blow out the contents and set the eggs in trays half-filled with fine sawdust. But how often do we give a thought to nests?

From the ceiling of my lab at my school in Ethiopia hung seven very different nests, all made of grass, some resembling wide bottles, some having a long entrance tunnel and some a short one, some having horizontal entrance holes while others were more placed to the bottom of the nest. All of these were disused weaver birds' nests I had either collected from my numerous trips to the Rift Valley or been given by a student. Each was a total masterpiece. Each of over 60 species of weaver bird, all occurring in Africa, build distinctive nests. Neither man nor machine could learn how to assemble piles of grass into such complex, neat and durable structures.

A weaver has just two simple tools, his feet and his beak. To me, a weaver bird's nest is one of the marvels of the natural world. I say 'his' because it is the male weaver birds who build the nests. I have spent time watching these birds collect material for their nests. Often they would fly some distance to collect just the right species of grass yet an individual can construct the whole affair in about three days. Not infrequently, the hard-working male has to build a second nest if his female is not enamoured with his first attempt...

How shall we approach this hugely

diverse subject?

Let us consider sizes of nests, the materials of which they are made and possibly lined with and the locations where they are placed. The smallest nest is made by the smallest hummingbird of the Americas, the Bee Hummingbird. This will not be any larger than a British 50 pence coin and yet large enough to rear two youngsters, the usual number. Such a delicate nest will be made largely of feathers and spider webs with an outer coating of lichens. It is often placed along an exposed branch with little attempt to hide it in vegetation. I have never visited the Americas so I have not seen these myself. I have, however, seen what is almost certainly the largest nest. This was an enormous piece of avian architecture placed high up in the fork of a tree, measuring around three metres across and probably about a metre deep. This was just near our school in Addis Ababa, Ethiopia and belonged to a member of the heron family, the Hamerkop. These all brown birds, one quarter the height of a Grey Heron have thick crests of feathers growing back from the head, giving them a sort of pterosaur-like appearance.

Fortunately, for these birds all African people, wherever these birds occur, revere them and believe to harm them will bring misfortune and to have a pair nesting on your land will bring good luck. One reason the Hamerkop's nest is so huge is that it is re-used and added to each year. Most birds will build a fresh nest every breeding season but other herons and various crow species in particular will repair their old ones, in Britain as early as February.

Rooks are a good example and their evocative clamouring calls can be heard in February as they refurbish their previous year's nests. Many birds of prey re-use and repair old nests, including the Golden Eagle, a native of Britain, which can end up with an enormous structure, a couple of metres in diameter.

Nesting materials are extremely varied and will obviously be made of nearby materials. Nests may comprise just a few pebbles strategically arranged on the ground; a simple shallow scrape in the ground lined with just some strands of vegetation, a predominantly grass affair, which is open at the top (the archetype nest), and then we have the much more complex weavers' nests already mentioned. Then there are fairly large structures made of twigs such as those of Rooks and other members of the crow family including Magpies. Magpies build nests in the shape of a vertical ellipse placed high and often exposed in a tree. The Long-tailed Tit builds a beautiful nest made of mosses, lichens, hair, feathers and spiders' webs giving the nest a sort of silvery colour. Because of the nest shape these birds are sometimes called 'bottle tits'.

Many birds such as Willow Warblers build

a grass nest on the ground. Reed and Sedge Warblers weave their deep cups around two or three tall reed stems. Penduline Tits build a sort of weaver bird shaped nest, which has an entrance tunnel, the nest suspended from a twig, hence the name 'penduline'. Swallows and House Martins build nests made of mud, water and saliva, attaching them to the upper walls of our houses and also inside barns.

The Edible Swiftlets of Indonesia and Malaysia build nests purely of saliva. These are built in caves and are collected by local people who steam them in water to make 'bird's nest soup'. In some areas these are now farmed in special boxes and it has become a thriving industry. I have been told that bird's nest soup is extremely limpid and tasteless and requires some cheering up by the addition of spices and other flavourings. Some water birds will make nests of aquatic vegetation, which floats on the water surface although it will have some sort of anchor to prevent it drifting off. This is typical of grebes. Interestingly, grebes will cover their eggs with aquatic vegetation when not incubating.

Some birds will accept our offerings of artificial nests in the form of nest boxes. Tits, Nuthatches, Eurasian Robins, Kestrels and owls will all take up such man-made garden furnishings.

Various species will give their nests a lining of softer more protective materials also making them more comfortable for incubating birds.

Song Thrushes will line their nests with wet mud, which solidifies and no further lining is added. Blackbirds also make a mud lining but this is further lined with grasses.

At this point I am going to tell you a story. At my international school in Ethiopia the music teacher was the incredibly vivacious and exuberant Helena, who hailed from my own English county of Essex. She was the eternal optimist and nothing would suppress her outgoing nature. One morning she bounced into the staffroom announcing that her knickers had been stolen from the line. She seemed quite flattered by the fact. That was it… for a while. Then Maureen, one of the primary section teachers gave the same announcement a few days later but with considerably less joie de vivre. A week later Helena revealed a further knicker theft and this was followed by Lindsey's same misfortune. By now, us chaps in the staffroom were feeling a bit nervous as one of us must surely be a suspect. This all died down and life resumed normality with respect to female undergarments. Months later our maintenance man was doing a roof repair on the school hall and this demanded the removal of a sheet of corrugated iron. Under this he discovered a large pile of grass and rags. On closer inspection he found and excavated five pairs of knickers and brought them proudly to the staffroom, having been aware of the earlier events. This old nest was that of a pair of Red-winged Starlings who had clearly adorned their nest with the underwear. Being brightly coloured with flowery designs and light enough to carry off, they had used the items to line their otherwise twiggy nest. All three ladies lived on campus, so it all made sense. Helena even decided to re-introduce her underwear to her wardrobe. How relieved we male teachers were at this discovery.

There are quite a few bird species, which go in for nest adornment and perhaps the most impressive nests and associated platforms are those of the bower birds of Australia and New Guinea. The males will clear a patch of ground and erect a tall bower structure, generally anchored to a couple of thin trees. Around the approach to the nest (it is a walk-in structure) he will deposit bright colourful objects. These may be natural such as flowers and fruits, feathers of other birds (Bower Birds themselves are notably dull brown) and beetle wing-cases, the insects caught specially for this purpose. They may also collect man-made articles including bottle tops, buttons and bits of coloured plastic such as wiring. He will then perform his display act in order to secure a female for the season. Having done so, he will continue to bring in new eye-catching material throughout the season, doubtless reinforcing the bond. This is all quite understandable but with our Ethiopian starlings, why the birds added colourful material to the nest, which would have been in darkness, remains a mystery.

Some birds build no nest at all. Guillemots and Razorbills lay their single eggs directly on to a shallow ledge, maybe only around 20cm wide. The egg is suitably tapered so that it rolls in a tight circle when moved. Even so, there must surely be some losses. Some waders such as Ringed Ploves lay their eggs on bare pebbles and shingle. Such birds rely purely on egg camouflage to protect the eggs. On my regular walk round Lake Langano in Ethiopia a pair of Kitlitz Plovers had laid eggs just above the lake margin. I had to be very careful to note the location so as not to tread on them.

One group of birds, the Megapodes, which are chicken-like birds of Australasia do not incubate their eggs at all! Some bury their eggs in mounds of rotting vegetation, and by careful adjustments of the pile they can regulate the interior temperature. Some species do much the same but using mounds of sand, simply relying on the heat from the sun to do the job. Another method is to lay the eggs in burrows in areas where geothermal heat will serve the purpose. Megapode means 'big-feet' and these they need for their mound control, removing or adding material as necessary to maintain the correct temperatures throughout the day.

Sand Martins, European Kingfishers and bee-eaters will each make a burrow into a sandbank, laying their eggs in a bowl-shaped chamber at the far end and, miraculously, the bird excavates so as the tunnel slopes slightly downwards towards the entrance and so prevents the nest chamber becoming flooded. A Kingfisher's burrow may be 50cm long. Some birds such as puffins, shearwaters and wheatears use abandoned rabbit burrows.

Birds may either nest as a solitary pair or may group together in colonies. Some colonies may number thousands of birds such as penguins, gannets and flamingos. A colony of Sociable Weavers collectively builds a huge condominium, a single grass affair, which has a multitude of separate nest entrances. These are the largest structures in the bird world, sort of avian blocks of flats. I once counted over 80 nest chambers in the one structure when birding in South Africa.

The location of birds' nests is extremely varied. If you see a bird's nest in the fork of a large tree just about anywhere in Britain and Europe, it is likely to be that of a Mistle Thrush. Some weaver birds build their nest suspended from a tree over water for added security. The Guacharo (a type of nightjar) of South America nests on ledges in caves. Some owls use holes in trees as do some ducks such as Goldeneyes, Buffleheads and Carolina Wood Ducks. Crevices in rocks and small cavities behind tree bark may be used as in Razorbills and Treecreepers respectively.

Quite a few birds of prey, notably Kestrels and Peregrine Falcons are becoming more urbanised and will nest on tall buildings, crane derricks, rigs and radio masts. I recall reading as a child a case of a pair of Blackbirds building a nest under the bonnet of a chap's little-used car. He was considerate enough to adjust his travel arrangements... hats off to him! There are other instances of birds nesting in such places as to disrupt daily human activities. Great Tits and Blue Tits have nested in post boxes, which were then declared 'out of service' by the Post Office until the young had flown.

The nests of most birds will last through the season requiring little attention whereas others may need constant repair work because other birds may steal the material (as with adjacent pairs of Gannets and Cormorants) or the nests get buffeted around in windy conditions.

The act of nest building may serve to reinforce the pair bond in certain species.

10. SUNNY SIDE UP...

Organisms reproduce either sexually or asexually, an example of the latter being the simple budding off from the parent of a new baby organism. Sexual reproduction invariably involves the fusion of two gametes, the female egg (ova) and the male sperm in the case of animals, and pollen in the case of plants.

Numerous invertebrates lay eggs and all five classes of vertebrates have representatives which lay eggs. Some fish, amphibians, reptiles and all mammal species give birth to live (viviparous) young. In the case of the latter, Duck-billed Platypuses and Spiny Echidnas are the exceptions and lay eggs. All bird species lay eggs, which only start to develop chicks once they have left the female's body, provided they have been fertilized. The development of the bird embryo occurs when one or both of the parents incubate the eggs.

The actual mating of birds is a very brief affair indeed, generally taking but a few seconds although the courting may have gone on for some days. In some species various activities serve to continually reinforce the bonding between the parent birds such as food-offering, preening and bill clapping.

I never collected birds' eggs as a child (as

did many schoolboys in such times) but I did have a modest collection, which I swapped for a Meccano set. I recall wondering then just how the patterning on a bird's egg was achieved as it could hardly have been 'stamped' onto such fragile structures.

The egg starts out as a single cell and is fertilized as it passes down the oviduct. Its development is triggered and controlled by hormones. Cell division continues apace while membranes and the yolk form, the latter being a food source for the growing embryo. The egg-white mechanically protects the embryo and also supplies it with various proteins. The incubating parent will occasionally turn the eggs, probably to ensure that the developing embryos get a fair share of these essential proteins. During development the shell forms as calcium carbonate ($CaCO_3$) is laid down around the outer membrane. At the latter stages of egg formation the patterning will be deposited with the exception of birds, which lay white or creamy eggs.

Many of the larger non-passerines have unpatterned white eggs and hole-nesters including owls and kingfishers lay likewise having no need for camouflage. Most of the ground-nesting non-passerines such as sandpipers and plovers lay heavily marked eggs, which affords them camouflage. The markings on most of the smaller birds' eggs range from just a few spots to a high density of spots giving a blotchy appearance as in Blackbirds' eggs. The Yellowhammer's eggs have markings, which are said to resemble writing thus giving the bird the localised name of 'scribe' or 'scribbling lark'.

I am unsure why most passerine species lay patterned eggs when they are well hidden in nests. Surely the bright blue black-spotted eggs of the Song Thrush must be quite visible from above when the parents are off feeding. The pattern of markings on any given egg is generally recognisable as belonging to a particular species with only little variation. However, some colonial nesters like Razorbills and Guillemots show a huge variation in their colouring and marking thus enabling the parent birds to recognise their own eggs on the cliff ledges.

Even unfertilized eggs will be laid by the females as is testified in millions of households at breakfast time everyday. Just occasionally you might see a little dark speck in the white of an egg – this is the part which develops into a bird and neither the white nor the yolk do so (a favourite question asked by school children). Only a single chick may grow in any one egg – I once believed that a double-yolker meant the egg would have been twins, but not so.

The number of eggs laid in any one clutch or brood varies from just the one to over 15 in some game birds. Many passerines lay four or five eggs and wading birds characteristically lay their four eggs with all points directed towards the centre of the nest scrape. Some smaller passerines like tits may have more than twice as many eggs. Clutch size within the same species may vary according to latitude.

I recall reading that after the severe European winter of 1962/3 when some fish-eating birds were decimated, those same species had larger clutches the following breeding season to compensate for the losses. The same happened with species like Long-Tailed Tits and Goldcrests.

The shape of eggs is also varied. These range from near-spherical, again as in hole nesters like owls and kingfishers to the exaggeratedly pear-shaped eggs as in the larger cliff-nesting auks. Most eggs are shaped in between these two extremes, more like the standard hen's egg we put in our morning egg cups. The texture of egg-shells may be rough and chalky as in Cormorants, oily and waterproof as in ducks and heavily pitted as in Ostriches and other ratites. The smallest egg is, not surprisingly, laid by the smallest bird. The Bee Hummingbird's egg weighs a mere half a gramme while that of an Ostrich weighs around 1.5kg, which is a staggering three thousand times heavier!

How long does a bird have to incubate its egg?

This will be anything from nine days to nine weeks according to species. Smaller birds will generally have shorter incubation periods, the shortest recorded being that of the White-eye (a close relative of the Old World warblers found in Asia and Africa) of nine days. Typically a tit, flycatcher, finch, thrush or warbler will need around 10 days to two weeks whereas larger birds such as woodpeckers require longer and may incubate for three weeks. Medium-sized birds of prey will sit for four to five weeks while larger species may require even longer such as eagles. Ostriches incubate for about 42 days. The incubation period of the Emperor Penguin is about 65 days, which it achieves by placing the single egg on top of its feet (the longest is the Wandering Albatross at 78 days) and covering it with a brood patch, a small area of bare skin on the lower abdomen. In some species just one sex incubates while in others this is shared. Ostriches will allow several females to lay in the same nest, called 'creching' so they may end up with over twenty eggs in the one nest. That the incubating bird can cover all of these in one go is most remarkable.

Free-loaders, who will happily feed on a clutch

of birds' eggs, include: skunks, racoons, mink, otters, stoats and weasels, foxes, rats, mice and feral cats. These are all high on the list while predation by other birds may include gulls, crows and Harrier-hawks. I once saw the latter hanging deftly onto a weaver's nest as it yanked out the young but I have been informed that these raptors will also take eggs.

Birds' eggs also formed an important part of a hunter-gatherer's diet and to this day the San people of the Kalahari will take certain bird species' eggs, especially those of Ostriches. Some birds will take other bird species eggs but not primarily as food. These are the brood parasites, which include Old World cuckoos, honey guides and cowbirds. The female will lay a single egg in the nest of a 'host' species and either that same bird or the developing young parasite will eject the eggs of the host. The foster parent instinctively adopts the young as its own and feeds it to maturity, even though in the case of the Cuckoo the provider will be dwarfed by the growing chick. I have a photo on my wall of a parent Reed Warbler feeding a half-grown young Cuckoo, demanding that she stand on its head to do so! The parasitic females will lay eggs resembling those of the host species. Common hosts of the European Cuckoo are Meadow Pipits, Dunnocks, Pied Wagtails and Sedge Warblers, all of which have similar sized eggs.

Coming back to egg collection, this once widely

accepted hobby has been illegal since 1954. A later Act in 1981 banned the ownership of birds' eggs, no matter how they were obtained or how old they were. In 2018 in Norfolk, England a chap was found with a collection of over five thousand eggs including those of many rare species. He was forced to give his collection to the Natural History Museum in Kensington and was sentenced to 18 weeks in prison. The RSPB stated during the case that egg collecting was today extremely rare.

When I was wardening at the Shetland Snowy Owl breeding site in 1971, I was fully aware that we were protecting the crown jewels of the egg collecting world. I am sure they may have fetched a hefty price being the rarest possible eggs around at the time. And of course, the rarer the egg the higher the black market value and the higher the value the more sought after the eggs became.

Finally, having mentioned bird's nest soup in the chapter on nests, the image of hundred year old eggs springs to mind here. I have checked on the net that these eggs, much favoured by Chinese connoisseurs, are closer to one hundred days old and have been preserved by being soaked in various salt solutions. From what I read about their palatability it seems hardly worth the risk of a possibly fatal dose of botulism.

CLIVE DENBY

11. WHO GOES THERE...?

We have five senses: sight, hearing, smell, taste and touch. What about bird senses? Which of these senses do birds possess? Does navigation by the stars and sun count as an extra sense? Does the relative importance of particular senses vary between birds? Let's consider these questions – there may be a few surprises.

Generally speaking, a bird's eye is much the same as ours structurally, although they are not so globular, being thinner and more elliptical. The colour of birds' eyes are many as I once saw in a taxidermist's workshop; he had to replace the eyes with those of glass or plastic.

Our own visual field is that area before us in which we can see is about 120 degrees, although that includes peripheral vision. That of birds varies between different families. Different breadths of field are determined by the position of the eyes within a bird's skull. Ducks have eyes on the sides of their heads and they can see as much to the fore as they can behind at the same time. In fact, the two fields even overlap, meaning that ducks do not have a blind spot. This obviates the risk of predators creeping up behind them. We do have a blind spot, which is located at the place where the optic nerve leaves the eye and travels to the brain.

Owls have excellent forward vision, their eyes being placed on the front of the head but they have a huge blind area behind the head. This is another example of a trade off. Owls need to be able to catch small rodents in total darkness and so have well-developed frontal vision at the expense of hind vision. Most owls are nocturnal and face hardly any risk of a predator stealing up on them but Eagle Owls have been known to dine on some of their smaller cousins.

All birds have binocular vision, enabling them to see in 3D and most can move their eyes independently. Probably all bird species can see colour. We know this because the retinas at the backs of their eyes contain special cells called cones, which are used in all those animals that possess them to appreciate colour. We have cones of course but Fido, your faithful companion, has no such luxury. Similarly, bovines (cattle) do not possess cones, so if you are charged by a raging bull it won't be because you are wearing red clothing.

The ability to see detail (visual acuity) is high in birds of prey (eagles, buzzards, hawks) and considerably better than our own. The Passerines (perching birds) are known to have fairly low visual acuity, probably not as good as ours. Some birds can see a wider spectrum of light than us which enables them to see colours in nature that we are unable to. A white flower to us may appear brightly coloured to a bird which can see UV light, such as hummingbirds and some sunbirds. This can also benefit migrating birds as UV light can penetrate cloud and so allows birds to still see the position of the sun, even on the cloudiest of days.

As in our own case, the ears of birds have two functions, hearing and balance. As with eyes, the ears of a bird are much the same 'design' as our own with outer, middle and inner ears, the latter containing the semi-circular canals which control balance. The outer ears are placed just below and behind the eye and not on top of the head. The 'ears' of Long-eared and Short-eared Owls are almost certainly nothing to do with hearing and probably serve some nuptial purpose. In nearly all birds the aperture of the outer ear is enshrouded in feathers and in some birds these outer ear coverts will have slightly different plumage and thus may provide us with identification features. This is well demonstrated in the Yellow Wagtails. Vultures and Marabou Storks have bare unfeathered heads rendering the outer ear apertures visible. Some of the most impressive feats of hearing occur in the order of owls. A Tawny Owl can, after some period of listening, approach and pounce on a small rodent in pitch dark. This is done mostly by hearing and not vision as is commonly believed because owls do have rather large eyes. When a Tawny Owl is weighing up the location of its prey it will move not its eyes but its entire head, slowly getting an accurate fix. This is aided in some owls by a prominent facial disc, a more or less circular arrangement of dense feathers on the face, which serve as a parabolic reflector and concentrate sound to the outer ear. Barn Owls have very clearly marked 'discs' which are actually more heart-shaped than circular. Those owl species which dwell in high latitudes can actually hear rodents under half a metre of snow.

Echolocation is a highly specialised form of hearing where a bird emits pulses of sound (which we can hear as clicks in the case of the Guachuro) in front of them as they fly. As the pulse returns to the bird in the form of an echo, its brain informs the bird of what objects are ahead. This system is used by Cave Swiftlets and Oil Birds, both of which roost and breed colonially in dark caves. So refined is the process that birds do not collide in flight.

Smell is particularly important to some birds, such as vultures searching for carrion. Experiments on albatrosses have shown that these birds are able to detect smells of substances in the sea over many kilometres. Petrels and shearwaters are of the same order as albatrosses and they too use smell, notably to help locate their nest-burrows, especially at night. The olfactory (smell) receptors are located in the nasal cavity at the base of the upper mandible, although Kiwis have theirs on the tip of their beaks as they find earthworms by probing in the sand along New Zealand beaches at night.

Until recently I fully assumed that birds could not taste, being as so many swallow their food whole. However, that is not the case. Most birds have a very good sense of taste for various reasons. Waders probing for invertebrates may well use that sense. Insectivores need to know if their prey item is poisonous or not. Some insects develop toxins taken from the plants they feed on thus giving them some protection from birds. This is true of the Milkweed Butterfly. This insect contains a strong toxin in its tissues obtained from the food-plant whilst still a caterpillar. A bird eating one of these butterflies will find the taste abhorrent and will not try the same trick again. Of course that unfortunate butterfly is dead but it certainly works for the species as a whole. Carrion eaters such as some crows need to be able to determine if food has become toxic due to putrefaction although I expect smell must also play a role. This is why I find it surprising that gulls can get botulism from our landfill sites due to the decay of organic material.

Still in the early stages of research is the ability of birds to home in on the Earth's magnetic field to aid its migratory navigation. Some birds do definitely possess crystals of magnetite in their skulls and beaks, which would clearly serve no other purpose than the utterly complex system of using the Earth's magnetic field to aid navigation. This, together with the location and apparent movement of stars and the sun and making all the necessary computations still remains one of nature's great marvels.

I have somehow come to believe that migrant birds may delay their movement if the conditions at the target area are unfavourable. An example might be a cold spell in the UK preventing birds in Scandinavia from heading southwards in winter. If this is true then a most remarkable sense indeed must be in operation and I would very much like to know more of this.

12. E = MC²

It is a stunning coincidence that I have just watched Dr Jane Goodall being interviewed by Stephen Sackur on BBC's Hardtalk. By 'just' I mean two hours before I arose and got on with this chapter. The main theme of this will be to emphasize that birds do in fact exhibit a high degree of intelligence. Dr Goodall stated in the interview that nobody can spend a long time with an individual or a group of animals without coming away believing that these are not just dumb creatures responding to stimuli and working entirely on instinct.

Dr Goodall was criticised by some of her scientific peers most unfairly that she was 'wrong' to name the chimpanzees she was studying, as it was unscientific. They claimed that some of her other actions were likewise. I agree with Dr Goodall, you can scarcely study any mammal or bird in depth without witnessing some signs of intelligence and actions that cannot simply be written off as instinctive. I wish to draw on several examples that I have witnessed all of which clearly demonstrate intelligence.

The first goes back to when I was a schoolboy and maintained a bird table for about five years wherever my family was living at the time. Of course millions of us have witnessed the same but it was this that set my mind onto bird intelligence. Once I had done the pre-paper-round early morning re-stock of my bird table, birds would appear within seconds or maybe just a couple of minutes. They had learnt that this particular food supply should appear at around that time. Most would head straight for their preferred food, the tits going for the hanging bacon-rind or the peanut wire basket, the finches would settle on the table itself to gather up the grains (I used Swoop wild bird food), and Fieldfares and Redwings in the winter would go straight for the large apples I had impaled on inverted nails. In the early years I would stock the table all through the year until I learnt that it is neither necessary nor advantageous to feed birds during their breeding seasons. Even so, most birds would still come to the table. As adult birds, they knew full well what their young required. But were they allowing laziness to overcome their instincts as the bird table reduced the need for widespread foraging? It is difficult to know and suggesting laziness in birds might possibly be rather anthropomorphic but other more reliable examples of intelligence follow.

Again, as a boy, my family would have our milk delivered every morning to our doorstep by the obligatory whistling milkman. During the 1962/3 winter when I brought the milk in (one of my allocated tasks) the tops had often been removed and cream pecked off, some of it dribbling down the side of the two bottles. This was of course the work of Blue and Great Tits. An individual of one of these tit species must have been the pioneer and was then copied by others, ultimately being taken up by both species. That habit swept all over Britain and I would bet that it started independently in separate pockets rather than radiate out from a single focus. Could that be written off as instinct? I very much doubt it. It was nothing less than intelligence, it had to be. Sadly the morning 'milko' is virtually extinct, milk being bought in supermarkets these days.

My second topic is Snowy Owls. I think few could have solidly studied a pair of Snowy Owls as those RSPB wardens who monitored the breeding pairs of owls which nested on Fetlar, Shetland between 1967 and 1975. In 1971 I was one of four wardens who ran a 24/7 watch covering the entire breeding season of two Snowy Owls on Fetlar. Every time either of the sitting birds left or returned to the nest, every time they stretched their wings, in fact every time they did practically anything, was all recorded in the wardens' log. From the outset, the very fact that these birds were attempting to breed so far south where there are no lemmings, their main diet, suggests to me intelligence. Surely they were really going beyond their instinct as they must have been aware that their favourite prey was absent before breeding commenced. They had made a choice to give it a go as apart from lack of lemmings and the dearth of rabbits the habitat was fairly typical for this species and there were plenty of nutritious birds for the taking.

I wonder if a pair of Snowy Owls had met up just some way further to the south, say in the Scottish mainland (where they do sometimes turn up), would they still have attempted breeding? I doubt it, as there would be little similar in the habitat and the possibilities of raising a brood were close to zero. The owls had made a choice. Am I to be lambasted for saying a bird can exercise choice, above all of its instincts? Choice, to me, indicates intelligence.

I need to step for a moment out of the bird box for my third example of intelligence because it was that demonstrated by none other than my cat in Swaziland. He never acquired a proper name as I never got further than 'Puss' although he did respond to it, so I guess it did serve as a name. Just to outline ten years of notes I made on Puss I share the following. Firstly, he adopted me when I was in a garden bar in Botswana with friends. He worked his way round all five of us, still a kitten but on his second circuit he clambered up onto my shoulders. I had made quite a bit of extra fuss of him. He sat there for well over an hour purring in my ear. Having checked with the bar manager I learned he was a stray so I put him in my canvas shoulder bag, which I used when I was on my motorbike. He showed absolutely no signs of resistance as I put him in the bag and drove five kilometres to my home. That to me was his first display of intelligence. He had chosen the 'fuss-maker'. He spent the first six months of our relationship in Botswana. I fed him sometimes on butcher's meat and sometimes on tinned catfood. This was OK for a while but then I noticed he would not eat solid foods but take them off somewhere. He then brought back to the house a very pregnant female, clearly expecting me to take her in as well. I was prepared to have one cat and he would shortly be relieved of his testicles but I did not wish for an entire family. With the female out of the house (I did not know where) I started to provide more solid food items such as a slab of liver or a medium-sized fish. Puss was without doubt taking these to his female, or if you like to his genes. I started wrapping up what I called 'nibblies' which were small biscuits specially prepared for cats. I wrapped them in squares of net curtaining and smeared them slightly with wet cat food forming a tennis-ball sized bundle and soon got him to take these to his female and subsequently kittens. This became a regular habit. That struck me as pretty smart. When Puss and I went down to Swaziland I used to leave a window ajar for him, day and night. Occasionally, Zandile or I would forget to re-open the window, closed only during a storm. If he was inside the house trying to get out, he showed signs of attempting to open the window, doubtless having seen me. I then went out of my way to show him and after a few weeks he could do it. If he was outside he would either bang on the window with his bottom (one could never hear it of course) or he would go to the next room (my study) and catch my attention at the window there. So, the problem was in one place but the solution was elsewhere. That to me displays intelligence.

If I sometimes slept on, say a Sunday morning, Puss would sometimes wake me up by standing on my chest and licking my face, often my nose. This was almost certainly to stir me into getting him breakfast. Instinct – I do not think so. Puss, like many cats showed us his trophies before eating them. On more than one occasion, he caught a large lizard, maybe 25cm long and, having eaten just the head, would hide it under our bed, found only weeks later when we could smell the rotting corpse. As we ferreted about under the bed he would slink away fearing a verbal scolding. During thunderstorms he would hide under the bed but I once put him in the wardrobe when I found him visibly shaking with fear. It was much the same when celebratory rockets were going off for various events. He soon learnt to open the wardrobe door and even more remarkable half close it as he bedded down amongst our clean bedding. Once when he was accidentally locked in the house and Zandile and I were both out working, he purposefully pooed in one of my plimsolls so as to avoid soiling the carpet. I hugged him for doing so as he cowered when I entered the house, telling me immediately that something was up. That's enough of my cat but I include it here to provide my own reasons why I know he was a highly intelligent creature. Intelligence demonstrated by mammals, to me suggests there ought to be some level of intelligence in birds, both of which arose from common ancestors.

Returning to birds, when wardening on the Ouse Washes RSPB bird reserve in 1977, a male Song Thrush would sing its proverbial heart out from a telegraph pole right outside the warden's house. It would weave into its own repertoire the songs of Reed Warbler, Wren and even the calls of waders like Redshank. Sedge Warblers themselves are known to mimic other bird songs. Why should a bird do this? If it were instinct then surely it would be more widely practised both within the species and by other species. I believe it to be individuals choosing to do so, again implying intelligence although I do accede there might be a predisposition of certain species to imitate others. If mimicry is instinctive then why don't all Song Thrushes mimic other birds instead of just some individuals doing so?

While living in Swaziland, immediately outside my back door was a fine stand of Canna Lilies. These are from South America. There are no sunbirds in Swaziland with the correct length of bill to reach down the corollary tube to get at the nectar or pollen of Canna Lilies. One species of sunbird common in my area had developed the habit of stabbing its way through the base of the red inflorescence, a sort of Caesarian entry to the nectar chamber. This did not help the plant so it could not be called symbiosis. How did this habit start? Surely, an enterprising individual happened on the technique and it was learnt by others of its species. This has to be intelligence!

Greenfinches outside my window today in Britain fly straight on to vertical peanut wire-mesh feeders. This they have undoubtedly learnt from tits. The required upright feeding stance required comes naturally to tits but the Greenfinches have had to copy and learn. I have seen Starlings trying this technique recently with zero success.

Am I just being anthropomorphic with all this? I think not. Anthropomorphism irritates me as much as the next person and I dismiss it as sentimental gush. Having said that, I do agree that the distinction between such silly sentiments, intelligence and instincts can sometimes be tricky. I admire those who have attempted the study of animal behaviour (ethology), such as Niko Tinbergen a Norwegian biologist, who did a lot of work on gulls, and German Konrad Lorenz who made extensive studies on geese (See Reading List). Yes, these studies were actually looking at instinct but it is essential to recognise innate behaviour before claiming that some actions are chosen and thus due to intelligence. I am far from up-to-date and not well read on bird behaviour but I fully expect that great inroads have been made with respect to avian intelligence.

Experiments with members of the crow family have shown that a bird will take water from a container until it can no longer get its bill down far enough. It will then find small pebbles, which are dropped into the container, thus raising the level of the liquid and so permitting the bird to drink once more. Again, this has to be intelligence.

I can hear some saying, "Oh yes, but we know crows can be intelligent."

Well if that is true then so must other bird families be intelligent. I refuse to believe that some groups are smart and others are stupid. They are all possessing intelligence but some more than others. And how much work has really gone on in bird intelligence research? How much is missed on a day-to-day basis? It is not a coincidence that those who spend time studying any one bird will witness some acts of intelligence. I recommend the reading of David Lack's monographs on Robins and Swifts respectively, birds which he studied in great depth and the books now British natural history classics (see Reading List).

Does forward-thinking suggest intelligence? I believe it certainly can. Migration itself is forward-thinking. "If I have some good meals and stock up on fat then fly so far in such a direction I will come to a place where my favourite food stock is to be found in abundance."

Did it start like that...? We can never know.

That migration must now be firmly entrenched in the genes for migratory species is certainly the case.

What about food storage?

"Now, there are lots of acorns around at the moment and soon they will be gone. If I hide some then I will have a store for the winter."

Such may have gone on in the mind of a Jay. Today, all Jays do this. Is this another milk-top example where a pioneer 'thinker' has let loose what becomes a habit among their own species?

Many birds store food but there are others who probably could store food if they so wished. Is it just waiting for that spark of initiative (intelligence) to set the machine running? There is a more immediate form of food storage, shown by Red-Backed Shrikes and their cousins. Having caught an item of prey, a shrike may impale the dead creature on a thorn, it serving as a 'larder' it can draw from later. This action of hanging meat gives the shrikes the name of 'butcher birds'. I agree that all individuals of the species may practise this but I cannot detach this from some degree of intelligence, at least in its formative stages.

Birds are said to evacuate areas where a natural disaster is about to occur, such as an earthquake or a violent volcanic eruption. It is possible that they 'feel' the event coming, feeling perhaps subtle vibrations coming from deep down in the Earth. Or are there other signs that the birds detect? Are they using intelligence here? Will we ever know, for such experiments would be complex indeed and would vary among different species.

And then we can present these arguments in reverse... How many of our own (and other mammal) actions are attributable to instinct? Having recently read Dr Desmond Morris's superb book called Manwatching, it seems that so many of our actions such as hand movements, leg positions, facial expressions or entire body aspects can be explained as instinct.

I maintain to the last that there is indeed a spectrum covering instinct to learned behaviour and even spontaneous decisions made by birds, the latter two requiring intelligence. This is not because I 'want' birds to be intelligent because they fascinate me. And there are few of us indeed who do not find birds fascinating.

I close here in the knowledge that there will be many who do not share my view that birds are able to show varying levels of intelligence, some to a high degree. In the meantime, I must go and change my budgie's library-books.

13. DO NOT DISTURB...

There was once the widespread belief that Barn Swallows in Britain hibernated in the mud at the bottom of ponds throughout the winter. Daft maybe in the light of modern knowledge. But let's just consider what almost certainly brought about this attestation, even by some of our more learned scholars of the day. At the close of summer, swallows congregate and can be seen each day lining up on telegraph wires or on the branches of trees. The birds tend to do this near water as many of the insects they feed upon fly around just above the water of lakes and rivers. Even in the earlier part of the season people noticed that swallows were often near water as they needed this to make the cement for their mud-nests. So, there came the day when they saw a whole row of birds sitting on the wires or in the trees but next morning there was none. Hey presto – vanished. While seeming to us today to be an absurd notion, was this any more absurd than explaining that these little birds weighing no more than a pencil had flown off the previous day and started a journey across the English Channel, down through France and Spain into Africa, all the way skirting the Sahara and thence onward as far southwards as Zimbabwe, Malawi or even South Africa? And then of course to make the same journey in reverse the following spring. Which theory would you have gone for? Impossible to say now of course as you know the truth but I think it would have been reasonable to give each of these possibilities some consideration without fear of ridicule.

We know now of course that hibernation is the preserve of mammals. Not so fast, as they say. Some fish species, some amphibians and reptiles also go in for these naps, which last a whole winter season. And birds? Remarkably yes, but just the one. Why should one species of bird out of 9,200 known species on Earth opt for hibernation as a survival strategy? I can give no answer here as I simply don't know.

A North American species of nightjar, the

Poorwill which lives in the western states of California and New Mexico is well proven to undergo true hibernation during the winter, instead of migrating like its cousins. Just prior to hibernation the Poorwill's metabolism goes way down to levels that barely keep the creature in the land of the living. The bird's normal temperature is around 38°C but drops to about 20°C. The respiration rate falls such that it becomes undetectable. The heartbeat rate, normally 130 beats per minute goes down to around 10 bpm. The hibernating bird will fit snugly into a hollow log or maybe a patch of grass prior to nodding off. The main upshot of hibernation is that it uses minimal fat, which has been accumulated prior to hibernation.

The Common Nightjar, which we see throughout nearly all Europe (except Scandinavia) makes the effort to fly south down to Africa every winter. So why doesn't the Poorwill pop down to central or South America? Well, it is simply using an alternative strategy – that is the way of nature as it tries every trick in the book. I doubt that the biochemistry of the Poorwill's hibernation is the same as that of the mammals and I further expect each are examples of convergent evolution. OK, so only one bird fully hibernates. Are there other strategies?

Imagine you are a very small species of bird, which feeds by hovering in front of flowers in order to sup the pollen and/or nectar. You need to work flat out all day just to stay alive or else your body temperature will fall to fatal levels. What do you do at night? You can hibernate... but just for the night. In the morning you will awaken from a deep sleep and start all over again, repeating the process over and over.

There are well over 300 species of hummingbirds living in the New World and most of these will need to beat their wings about 1,200 times a minute (20 times per second) enabling them to maintain a fixed position as they push their bills down the corolla tubes of flowers. I suspect that it may be difficult for such small birds to accumulate sufficient fat reserves to undergo long-term hibernation, but on a day-to-day basis it is clearly possible. This period of deep short-term sleep is called 'torpor' and the bird is said to enter a 'torpid' state. While not advisable, if one picked up such a torpid bird it would remain in sleep. The states of torpor will doubtless vary between species and conditions. Birds which use torpor include many of those which rely on a non-stop supply of insects. Young swifts can arrest their development in the nest if the insect supply becomes unreliable due to bad weather. The sun-birds are the African equivalents of hummingbirds although they tend to be larger and the diversity of species is a lot lower. Some of these, along with Speckled Mousebirds, also an African species, use torpor. Some European tit species, if they are small and with high metabolic rates, can slip into nightly torpid states.

Quite a few other small species can reduce their body temperatures substantially on a nightly basis, such as Treecreepers in Europe and the Chickadees, which are the North American equivalent of tits. Frogmouths (another species of nightjar), some small owl species and larger birds like the Road-Runner all employ torpor when conditions demand. Any bird going into a torpid state must be well-hidden as obviously it becomes extremely vulnerable. Following a night of torpor, a waking bird may exhibit a shivering action and take up to an hour to fully awaken.

While not the same as either of the above, I will mention huddling here. This is the practise of birds, generally of the same species, forming tight huddles, which serve to conserve heat during cold nights. In Britain and Europe, Long-tailed Tits, Wrens and Goldcrests all use the huddling technique, the latter sometimes forming globular masses of birds. Those species of penguins which live on the Antarctic ice-sheet will employ huddling, birds on the outside later being allowed ingress towards the interior while others take their place. Altruism indeed! (Or just more instinct...?)

Interestingly, NASA is researching potential torpidity in humans as space scientists move towards sending crews to Mars. This would, to be effective, need to last for between 90 and 180 days. It would certainly cut down on the crew's daily requirements and would obviate the need to take along a good book.

14. WHY AM I HERE?

If you are a birder living in Britain and regularly cover your patch (your stamping ground) you soon get to know which birds to expect, the ones you are likely to see on any birding session. If you take a holiday then you may have the pleasure of seeing some new birds depending how far and in which direction you travelled. If you live in Liverpool and go off to East Anglia for the first time for a break then you might hear Bearded Tits 'pinging' in some reedbeds. If your place of residence is on the east coast of Essex say, then a visit to Cornwall might well reward you, if you scour the coastal cliffs, with Choughs, rare members of the crow family restricted to a few British coastal sites in the south west peninsula and Wales. You like these sightings of new birds and decide to really take off for a week to the south of France or Spain. There you will see Bee-Eaters, Rollers, Hoopoes, Black-winged Stilts, Short-toed Eagles and loads more, birds you just don't see back home.

Well that trip to the Camargue was certainly worthwhile and gave you about 40 new species. Next summer you are going to the USA so you start to mug up on what you might see. The USA is a hell of a big place so it has several different Field Guides to cover all the species of birds occurring there. So, let's say you are pouring over your new field guide to the Birds of the eastern USA. You will notice something interesting. There do not seem to be any birds you are familiar with. Even the warblers look different. That's because they are different. They are all New World warblers while you have been used to seeing Old World warblers in Britain and Europe. The American Robin is quite a different creature from the European Robin, which sits on your garden spade handle and graces your Christmas cards. Yes, they are of the same family but are each of a different genus and therefore also different species. With all the new stuff you are going to see in the States it is hard work to keep up with it all. You return with your burgeoning notebook, eager to tell your neighbour, also a keen birder, all the birds you have seen. Well he, as it happens, took off for Kenya last week and is having the same sort of experience. Most of what he is seeing is new but he does see some birds with which he is familiar. You may well have seen more new birds than he is going to. The Americas are a very long way from the joined continents of Europe and Asia and so whole separate assemblages of birds have evolved, either side of the Atlantic.

Many birds you can see in Europe you may see in Africa, partly because many of our summer breeding species fly down to Africa for the winter. Birds summering in Europe however, do not usually venture across to North America, if at all. Your neighbour and yourself compare notes after the holidays and you both decide to go to New Guinea next year together so you each get another field guide. Such a trip would produce some amazing sights including various birds of paradise (closely related to crows) with the males wearing their gaudy plumes and head-dresses. All the birds you see there will be new to both of you and your neighbour, many birds being endemic to New Guinea (occurring nowhere else).

A trip across the Torres Straits to Australia will have required that you buy yet another field guide as once again most of the birds are different. A few introduced species may be familiar but apart from those, just about everything will be new. So, we speak of a bird's geographical distribution and the study of the distribution of animals and plants is called Biogeography, a module I took when I was at university.

The world's land masses have been ordered into six major zoogeographical biomes, each characterised by their respective assemblages of animals and plants. This is not to say that these assemblages are totally exclusive to each biome, but broadly speaking they do each have their own particular groups of organisms. These biomes are: the Nearctic (North America and Greenland), the Neotropical (Central and South

America), the Palaearctic (Eurasia, Middle East and N. Africa), the Afro-tropic (the remainder of Africa), the Indo-Malayan (India and SE Asia) and Australasia. Some authorities add a seventh biome, the Oceanian to include New Zealand and South Pacific Islands. The Nearctic and the Neotropical are together termed the New World while all other biomes collectively form the Old World. There are very few bird families, which occur in both the New and Old Worlds.

Let's look even closer. The Old World flycatchers make up a large family comprising well over a hundred species, all of which are confined to the Old World. The New World, however, has its own complement of flycatchers of a totally different family, which has hundreds of species, none of which occur in the Old World. Much the same can be said for Old World and New World Warblers with both different families restricted to their own biomes. Thrushes form pretty much an Old World family although it does have a few New World representatives such as Blue-birds (which incidentally never were seen over the white cliffs of Dover). Some members of the finch family are to be found in both the Old and New Worlds. Bird families found only in one biome, the Neotropical, include the wood-creepers (46 spp) and the spinetails (70spp). Also unique to the Neotropical biome is the huge family of ant-birds, which themselves are split into a number of genera: ant-wrens, ant-shrikes, ant-creepers, ant-catchers, ant-thrushes, ant-pittas and ant-birds proper. (It seems it might be tough going for ants in South America with over 200 species gunning for them).

Elsewhere in this book I stressed the importance of all organisms bearing scientific names and quoted the American Robin as being a different species to the Eurasian Robin. Quite a few families of birds contain species which have been confusingly named. For instance, the New World Warbler family has 10 species of redstarts, which share only the name with redstarts belonging to the Old Word thrush family and are not closely related.

So much for the spatial distribution but what about time. Many of the species of living organisms living on Earth today may well not have existed in times past, and here I am using a geological time scale.

Birds came onto the world stage during the Jurassic about 180 million years ago. Since then new species have evolved and some will have become extinct. The reasons for their extinction may be due to climatic change, to competition from other species or during the last seven to 10,000 years due to the hand of man after he became a farmer and started changing the environment to suit his ever demanding needs. It is a rolling programme and what we can see today is like a still in a film.

Why do birds end up where they are?

By far the main reason is not so much the movements of birds but the movements of the land masses on which they live. Sounds a bit fantastic yes! Let's go back a bit to 1912. In that year German meteorologist Alfred Wegener made the observation that when one looked at a globe then the eastern coast of South America would fit quite snugly into the western coast of Africa (try it, it's fun). He looked more closely and found similar close-fit scenarios, given the odd tweak and maybe partial rotation of a land mass. He was able to back up his story by the distribution of a certain type of plant called Glossopteris. This he found to exist in Antarctica, Australia, Africa and the southern parts of South America. This was indeed odd and could only be explained if those continents had once been a single land mass and Glossopteris grew at a single centre. Sadly, Wegener was somewhat ridiculed by many of the scientific community for making this ludicrous and unprovable suggestion. He was asked for a mechanism driving this movement of continents – he could not come up with one and died without his due glory. In the late 1960s and early '70s came a whole deluge of research and proofs that the continents were indeed shifting and what's more a mechanism was found. The core of the Earth, a sphere of nickel and iron about the size of our moon undergoes alternate crystallisation and de-crystallisation. This generates heat... a great deal of heat which in turn sets up powerful convection currents, which rise and fall through the mantle of the Earth's interior. If you make jam you may notice how there is an upwelling of froth from the centre of the saucepan and then a lateral flow outwards followed by movement of the froth down the sides, indeed a convection current. That on a global scale is what we have and it has been calculated that it is enough to explain the movement of land masses. The world's land masses are not just one land mass. There are numerous cracks running through them rendering the crust of the Earth to be made of a score or so of separate 'plates'. The edges of the plates are known as plate margins or plate boundaries and here is where the action takes place. Most plate boundaries lie beneath the oceans. However, some are manifest on land. Some adjacent plates push together (converging plates), some pull apart (diverging plates) and some glide laterally past each other as in the now famous San Andreas Fault making a land presence in California. This plate movement is very slow (understatement) around two to 10cm a year. If you are wondering how on Earth we can possibly know this it is actually rather simple and there is more than one way.

We can set up a laser beam, which travels across a plate boundary. From timing the sending and the receiving of these beams to special stations we can calculate the distance between each station and of course these timings will change due to the moving of continental land masses (continental drift).

Another method is to take star sightings from different parts of the world, also pinpointing specific places on the Earth's surface. A bit of trigonometry tells us the distance between any two points. The two methods are mutually supportive. When I learnt all this stuff doing A-level Geology, my heart really went out to Alfred Wegener.

You may see maps showing what the world looked like way back in the Carboniferous, the Devonian or perhaps the Eocene periods. How can we do this? In the same way that a weather forecaster can know what weather is coming in a few days time using known air-mass locations, temperatures and speeds, geologists can predict what the world might look like in say, 50 million years time. They know the current speed and direction of various plates and can thus fast forward the 'film' to suggest what future world maps will look like. They can just as easily rewind the 'film' back to past geological periods. If we go back far enough we can see that South America, Africa, India, Australia and Antarctica were once all one land mass centred more or less over the south pole. This supercontinent has been named Gondwanaland. Its counterpart to the north where North America was joined to Eurasia, we call Laurasia. As each of the two super-continents broke up all of the living organisms living on them also drifted apart, riding the plates as passengers. There came a point when this separation of organisms led to the evolution of new species.

I know they are not birds but let me use the example of marsupials (animals with pouches). It is generally known that marsupials live in Australia but they also occur (just a few species) in South America, having gone off their separate ways as Gondwanaland broke up. It is by chance that Australia took off with most of the marsupials and that South America took just two or three. The birds in Europe and Asia show variation but it is more of a slow gradation from type to type as these two continents are in fact joined. Look at a globe – this will enable you to fully appreciate the true sizes of the continents and their relative positions, something not really achieved on a two-dimensional map. The gulf between North America and Europe is absolutely huge and even birds do not cross this formidable barrier, which is of course the Atlantic Ocean. North America and Europe have been separated for so long that their respective species can no longer interbreed and thus the avifauna (birdlife) in each is totally different. Australia drifted away from Gondwanaland (undergoing a bit of rotation as well) and took with it as passengers a whole host of bird species and now after millions of years of isolation it harbours an almost unique species assemblage of animals and plants. The study of all this continental wandering is called plate tectonics and just about my favourite part of geological study. I followed Geology to A-level and I loved teaching it as you could open up with outrageous suggestions and then slowly unfold how such is possible and how in the end it all makes sense.

When teaching, I asked students loads of questions but occasionally I would throw in a real teaser, sometimes leaving it with them until a couple of days later to hear their answers.

One (of many) was, "Why don't Polar Bears eat penguins?"

Answers ranged from the predictable jokes about chocolate bars to the more feasible biological offerings. Only a few students got this right. The answer is that the two species never meet, never have and never will. Polar bears are in the north polar region and penguins in the south polar region with the exception of just under half of the penguin species occurring in South America, Africa and Australia. This reminds me of when, as a child, I saw a painting in a large stately home showing a young Horatio Nelson slaying a polar bear with a spear.

Witnessing this event in the background was a load of penguins. I mentioned this fact to the lady of the house (whom my mother was working for as a domestic) and she was most indignant that this upstart precocious child should cast aspersions on her cherished piece of artwork. So, my point here is that penguins are not found in the Arctic. Those niches are taken by the auks (Puffins, Razorbills, Guillemots) in the northern regions although this family still retains the ability to fly. Polar bears evolved from the Brown Bears of the northern temperate forests, slowly adapting to the frigid treeless wastes of the Arctic. There was no way such a mammal could have evolved in the extremely distant and isolated continent of Antarctica and there was no nearby mammal from which to evolve.

Let's look at the Sahara. What is your image of this place? A vast expanse of majestic sand dunes maybe, which is the most usual image held by most people. The Sahara today has a surprising amount of different habitats including areas of forest, grassland, sparsely vegetated scrub down to bare rock-strewn expanses and of course sand dunes. However, sand dunes make up just 10 per cent of the Sahara. But even more surprising is that the Sahara once supported vast swathes of Savannah type grasslands and these grasslands in turn supported all of the megafauna (large mammals) currently living to the south. How do we know this? Cave paintings in a number of sites in the Sahara depict hunters spearing elephants, antelopes and gazelles and there are paintings of rhinoceros and hippopotamus along with zebra and giraffe. It is known that a great period of drought was responsible for drying out of the Sahara so its demise was not due to tectonic forces but climatic.

Britain was once in the tropics but I would not expect all of my readers to readily believe this. Britain has coal deposits, lying under millions of years worth of rock strata.

Coal is formed from ancient tree-fern forests, which have been inundated by lakes and rivers. There, when the trees died and fell they became buried in sands and compressed to form that stuff we burnt in our fireplaces and of course our power stations, which fed the National Grid with electricity. (On September 30, 2024, the UK's last power station making electricity from coal – Ratcliffe-on-Soar in Nottinghamshire – closed). The conditions for coal formation are entirely tropical and British coal formed as we moved across the tropics to where we are now. The period when this was happening we call, not surprisingly, the Carboniferous. We can say the same about coral limestones. Once Britain had plenty of these. (While the UK doesn't have tropical coral reefs, it does have cold-water coral reefs, which are facing declines due to climate change, pollution, and fishing practices, and are a priority habitat under the UK's biodiversity framework.)

Corals live only in warm shallow tropical seas. Both of these examples are obeying the geological principle that the present is the key to the past, known as Uniformitarianism. Conditions needed for coal formation and coral formation in the present day must have applied also in the past.

So, all this wandering of continents results in them passing through different climate belts and as they do so, plants and animals have a choice – they adapt or die out. If you look at a natural vegetation map of the world you will see that particular types of vegetation occur in bands across the world map. These latitudinal belts give rise to the separate biomes.

Now, in addition to the birding holidays you enjoyed earlier in this chapter, you are going to travel around the Earth following the equator. You will be provided with transport across the three oceans you will need to traverse. You may be excited about all the new birds you will see as you proceed. You will certainly see quite a variety as you move from northern South America, across to central Africa and then to Indonesia. But, you will have made the entire journey travelling in just the one biome, the equatorial forests. Consequently, the bio-diversity will not be as great as you may have expected. Now you need to repeat this journey

(OK wait until next year) starting from the North Pole down to the South Pole. This time you will be crossing all the lines of latitude and thus crossing all the different biomes. You will be on ice as you leave the North Pole and then a bit of sea crossing. Then you will pass through Tundra, vast expanses of swamps and lakes where the sub-surface soil is frozen (permafrost). Next you will start to see stunted trees and these will become taller and denser so now you are walking through the vast coniferous forests of the northern temperate regions. Then you will come to bands of deciduous forest followed by extensive open grasslands called the Prairies in North America and the Steppes in Russia. From there you may cross a huge and laborious stretch of desert. Finally, you will enter the luxuriant dark tropical rainforests and hack your way through to the equator. So what happens next? Well, you will do much the same again, only this time in reverse order until you end up crossing the ice of Antarctica to the South Pole. All these different latitudinal zones are biomes, which are really global habitats. Each will have its own assemblage of animals and plants.

In addition to his treatise on the evolution of birds, Charles Darwin devoted two chapters to bird distribution in his classic work, On the Origin of Species.

15. IS IT, OR ISN'T IT?

I briefly mentioned subspecies in an earlier chapter. I need to refer to them again here in this chapter of problem species. Marsh Warblers and Reed Warblers are both distinct species but look remarkably similar in the field. The geographical range of the Marsh is Central Europe with just a few birds nesting in Britain. The Reed Warbler also inhabits Central Europe but extends its range to include much of Southern Europe and it breeds throughout most of England and Wales. Peterson's Field Guide indicates leg colour as being diagnostic and helping to separate the two species and yet goes on to say that the Reed Warbler's leg colour is variable. The roundedness of the head is pointed out as a further identification feature and yet this seems altogether indiscernible in the plate showing these two birds even when juxtaposed. The Marsh does have a slightly shorter thinner bill and this can be seen when viewing two adjacent illustrations. But in the field where you have no such comparison... I remain sceptical. And the one bird is described as being 'more olive'. I am not sure I know what 'olive' actually looks like and again, without juxtaposed comparisons, such a statement is unhelpful. Let me stress here I am not berating this field guide – it was my bible from a very young age and continues to be so for European birds. The songs are different between the two birds and the wing formulae show different relative lengths of some of the primary feathers. My question here is, why are these two species distinct species and not subspecies? The subspecies of the Yellow Wagtails all have much more marked differences in head plumage than the two warblers and yet are classified as subspecies.

Willow Warblers and Chiffchaffs can be problematic unless seen at close quarters. The dark legs of the latter are supposedly diagnostic as are the songs of the two birds. However, once again the field guide tells us that the legs of the Chiffchaff may sometimes be pale like the Willow Warbler's. In the hand an expert ringer can identify these birds by the wing formulae of each, the Chiffchaff having slightly shorter blunter wings. I fully agree that the two are separate species but I remain confused when birds showing greater differences are grouped in the same species.

The Marsh Tit and the Willow Tit together make up another problem pair. One has a glossy black cap while the other's is dull or matt black. One does show a little bit of white in the closed wing and these birds are regarded as full blown species and not subspecies. On my morning paper round as a teenager I used to pass a thicket every morning which had one, other, both (?) of these birds. I never really convinced myself sufficiently about the 'texture' of the black cap and as both have much the same distribution in Britain and both are attracted to much the same habitats, I never resolved this problem. To this day I don't know whether I have seen both or just one of these bird species. I suppose I could have sorted it giving the matter more dedication but, at the risk of shocking some of my readers, I simply was not that bothered as I was never one to maintain bird lists except when I started bouncing around Africa.

The same goes for Temminck's stint and Little stints. During an 'Ornitholidays' birding trip to Lake Neusiedl in Austria our leader pointed out a Temminck's stint. And as fortune had it, a Little stint also obliged us with an appearance. The man pointed out the different leg lengths of the two species but again, how would one make this comparison when seeing just the one species? I do not dispute the leader's identification – he was a greater birder than I – but on my own I would have not had the confidence to delineate the two birds.

Bluethroats are spread throughout Eastern Europe, sparsely at a few locations in Western Europe and also Scandinavia. In the latter, it is the Red-spotted Bluethroat which occurs while all other European birds are the White-spotted form. The Red-spotted is the nominate bird with the White-spotted as a subspecies. It was the Red-spotted form we were catching in Ladakh (see chapter 26).

I saw my first Hooded Crow when I worked on Fetlar (see chapter 25) but was to be denied noting it as a new species, as the Hooded Crow is a subspecies of the Carrion Crow. There is considerable difference in the plumage of the two birds yet they are rated as sub-specific.

In East Africa I never did sort out Little and Slender-billed weavers. The field guide gave the former as preferring Acacia woodland while the Slender-billed opted for riverside vegetation. Riverside vegetation in east Africa has a good chance of being Acacia scrub so habitat proved no useful guide. The females of these two birds are inseparable and the males have only the bulk of the bill to render them each a name. With no two different birds to compare, I could never confidently identify these two separate species.

There are quite a few other examples I could quote. My own reservations on what constitutes a species or a subspecies is not, I prefer to believe, due to my own ineptitude. Many ornithologists have raised the same questions and birding colleagues even fall out over such issues, so hotly are various opinions defended. I am unable to ascertain how much advance has been made in DNA analysis of bird relationships but I imagine that as time passes we shall learn a lot more. I have yet to read a clear explanation of what criteria are used when placing birds into species or subspecies. Is it plumage, song, habitat, geographical distribution or combinations of these? We know full well that adaptive radiation will lead to minor differences within species, leading ultimately to speciation given sufficient isolation over time of two different populations. So, all subtle variations between separate species and subspecies are merely initial stages in the ultimate separation of one into two species. Are they not all like the stills in a film, each capturing just how far along the change spectrum the birds have travelled? I find the question of subspecies interesting but not sufficient for educated academics to publicly slag each other off in scholarly papers as has been the case in the past.

CLIVE DENBY

16. A LOOK ON THE DOWN SIDE...

While there are so many positive aspects to birds, it is a sad fact that they can also render considerable disservice to man. I will consider three main ways this occurs: crop destruction, transfer of disease and bird strikes.

Birds cause damage to crops at all stages ranging from the sowing of seeds, the emergence of saplings and ripening. Here I use the word 'crop' to embrace grass and cereal crops, leaf crops and fruits. According to one UK government report, 63 species of birds were listed as having some detrimental effects on our crops. I am wary here though that there is a gradation between mild damage through to total devastation. Wood Pigeons, Grey Partridges and House Sparrows rank highly on the destruction list in the UK. But let's think globally and move further afield.

The Red-billed Quelea, closely related to weavers and sparrows lives over most of Africa from the Sahel right down through Sub-Saharan Africa. These undertake regular seasonal mass movements in search of new feeding grounds. Flocks can be, and often are, huge, sometimes numbering millions of individuals. It is possible to hear the collective wingbeats of these enormous flocks.Some post-breeding populations have been estimated to contain up to one-and-a-half billion birds. The Red-billed Quelea is the most numerous wild bird on Earth. They feed chiefly on the seeds of grass crops and cereals, including barley, wheat, millet and sorghum. Understandably, this species has earned the name 'Africa's feathered locust' and certainly the devastation can be equivalent to that done by huge swarms of locusts. Over Africa as a whole these infestations of bird pests can be borne to some extent but to villages and individual farmers they can be a death knell. Some attempts to reduce this bio-hazard range from simple scarecrows to spraying and to the more drastic use of fire bombs (doesn't that too damage if not obliterate the crops?).

Returning closer to home, non-cereal crops such as oilseed rape are the delight of Wood Pigeons and fruit farmers have come to dread the damage that can be caused by Bullfinches devouring the buds of fruit trees. Grey Lag and Pink-footed Geese have greatly increased due to the fall in persecution and these are now having a large impact as they feed on winter wheat while in their wintering grounds. Brent Geese have increased well over ten-fold since the late '50s and now they have moved inland away from their traditional salt marsh sites to feed on winter wheat and oilseed rape. The advent of winter-sown barley in Britain means that in early summer there is a rich source of food for granivorous birds. Various methods of bird scaring have been tried in rural Africa but these tend to be ineffective. I have witnessed, in East Africa, children spending their entire day standing in a crop field (often maize) banging sticks noisily on saucepans to stop birds from settling. It is a sad and desperate sight indeed and almost entirely without success – even birds can only be fooled for some of the time.

So much for crop damage, what about disease? In recent times we have become aware of animal-transmitted diseases like swine-flu or bird-flu (avian flu) where the cause of the transfer of the disease has not always been confirmed. Even so, the supposition that avian flu caused by a virus started up in South East Asia was almost certainly the case, caused by humans living in close contact with domesticated fowl. Indeed, a whole basket of human diseases have arisen since the agricultural revolution seven to 10,000 years back when we started domesticating animals. I have seen in Ladakh, India, rural villagers living in the upper level of their wattle and daub houses while chickens, cattle and other livestock live below at ground level. This is great for the transfer of heat to the upper chamber but equally efficient in spreading nasty microbes. Birds can spread several diseases which affect us, due mainly to their droppings harbouring pathogens including bacteria, viruses, fungi and other parasites. It is worrying indeed when diseases start to cross the species barrier as is happening today and of course well exemplified by Covid-19, currently bedevilling the planet.

The first known incidence of bird-flu was in 1997 in Hong Kong while another outbreak occurred in Vietnam in 2004 when one-and-a-half million poultry had to be culled. More than a dozen different types of bird-flu are recognised and given the mutation rate of viruses in general there will surely be more in future. One type occurs naturally in wild waterfowl but this can spread easily to domestic poultry and later passed further down to humans. Once again this is a disease contained in faeces.

Pet shop owners and individuals who choose so unwisely to give their budgies a pair-bonding kiss are certainly inviting a nasty respiratory disease called psittacosis. It is also called ornithosis or parrot fever. It can be spread by more than just parrots and budgies – pigeons, hens, ducks and gulls, are also prolific spreaders. I became aware of this disease as my schoolfriend's Dad owned a pet shop and went down with psittacosis, suffering pneumonia-like symptoms. He recovered but it knocked him for six for sure and left him permanently drained of energy.

Grain for poultry food has been infected by pigeons either through faeces or dead birds, this causing Newcastle disease, a virus, which can affect poultry and humans. In the USA droppings from Red-winged Blackbirds provide an ideal medium for the growth of fungi whose spores cause histoplasmosis in humans. The huge increase in gulls, roosting on reservoirs have elevated bacterial levels including that causing salmonella. Candidiasis, a fungal infection, is another disease spread by pigeons to humans and paratyphoid is yet a further pathogen passed on to us. Reading through the literature on bird/human transfer of disease, pigeons are constantly recurring as the bad guys. Surely those keeping pigeon lofts must be particularly prone to diseases. Others susceptible to disease, caused mostly by infected pigeon faeces include chimney cleaners, bridge inspectors, roofers, demolition workers and maintenance staff all of whom may inadvertently come up against festering masses of pigeon poo. In 2001 over 500 high school students became infected after faeces-laden soil was rotavated by a school maintenance worker. The largest ever outbreak of histoplasmosis occurred in Indiana in the late 1970s. Over 120,000 people became ill after a building was demolished. Air ducting is also an excellent way of distributing pigeon faeces dwelling pathogens.

Pigeons are found in many of the world's city centres and are often encouraged by people unwisely feeding them with scraps. Apart from the risk of diseases, pigeon faeces also disfigure buildings and in quantities can create a horrible slippery goo on pavements and windowsills. These feral pigeons have been bred from the wild Rock Dove, a bird of inland and coastal cliffs of Europe. The birds have adapted well, having tall (cliff-like) buildings to nest on and loads of people who get some pleasure out of feeding these 'rats with wings'. Trafalgar Square in London has more than its fair share of feral pigeons and Horatio Nelson underwent a cleaning programme some years back (I bet he appreciated it too). Quite a few attempts have been made in recent years to reduce these pigeon populations. These include the erection of special nesting structures where the birds can be concentrated - sort of honeycomb affairs. I don't actually see how this works as pigeons are not colonial nesters by nature. Also, the removal of eggs from nests and replacing them with dummy eggs is being used. Contraceptive chemicals have been put down but no poisons per se as these tend to be non-selective, killing more than just the 'target' organisms. One natural control, which is emerging is that provided by the pest birds' natural predators. Peregrines just love a nice pigeon and they have increased hugely of late. I do not hide the fact that I believe feral pigeons to be a menace and that their numbers have reached outrageous proportions. Let me close this section on pigeons by relating a short anecdote.

When doing a short-term job for the RSPB on Golden Plovers in Wales in 1982, my colleague and I were asked also to keep an eye on a Peregrine's nest just outside the village where we were living in a very wet and leaky caravan. At the end of the season, we visited the nest to collect some pellets. Littered all around were the red legs of scores of feral pigeons, over half of which had rings on. We kept that quiet to prevent any local pigeon-loft owners from finding out as they may well have tried to form a vigilante group to control any future Peregrines.

A further hazard presented by birds is that of bird strike. This is the term used for flying birds having collisions with aircraft, both large and small. It is an unfortunate coincidence that in locations that are suitable for airports (expansive flat areas close to but outside cities) are also conducive to the siting of reservoirs and landfill sites. So it is that gulls now congregate around airports and can be a huge risk. Most bird strikes occur during the day during take-offs and landings - strikes at altitude are indeed rare. Damage may be slight with just a dent or two but a large or even medium sized bird flying into a jet engine can do enough damage to down the aircraft. Birds may also smash the glass screens of aircraft. A single bird strike event may involve a solitary bird or an entire flock. A strike by a single vulture flying at 12,000m in Africa has been recorded.

Over 13,000 bird strikes take place every year in the USA, most causing very limited damage such as dents to the fuselage and wings. Canada Geese are particularly prone to flying into aircraft and it is not difficult to imagine the damage just one bird might do to a jet engine. The first strike was recorded in 1905 when Orville Wright (of the Wright brothers) encountered a flock of birds and one was killed. The earliest human fatality was in 1912 when a pioneer aviator collided with a gull, which jammed the control cables. The plane crashed into the sea and the pilot drowned. The greatest loss of human life by bird strike was in 1960 when a craft flying from Boston flew through a flock of Common Starlings. The plane crashed into Boston Harbour with 62 deaths out of 72 passengers. In 1988 when I was teaching in Ethiopia an Ethiopian Airlines plane sucked a few pigeons into both engines during take-off causing a crash killing 35 people. In 2019 a Ural Airlines aircraft from Moscow incurred a strike. The plane crash-landed and 70 people were injured.

Attempts to eliminate bird strikes at airports include flying a bird of prey along the runway prior to take-offs and landings; playing the calls of birds of prey, playing the target species' own alarm calls and using machines, which emit loud bangs. Again, I am wary of the effectiveness of these methods. Certainly a loud bang will scare a flock of birds up into the air but there they will simply become a scattered confused mass not necessarily far removed from the runway. It is hard to believe that a few small birds weighing no more than 50 or so grammes apiece can destroy a jet engine. But this they certainly do and I have heard it said that even a coin thrown into the nacelle of a jet engine is enough to effect considerable damage. I was very aware of this when looking down at a runway just prior to take-off in Khartoum, Sudan to see a Coke can as we taxied past it!

During my late teens there was the ongoing debate as to where to build London's third airport. There were several proposed sites bouncing around, as the NIMBY (Not In My Back Yard) brigade kicked these suggestions around like a political football. Living in Essex my birding mates and I used to frequent the saltmarshes on the Essex coast ranging from Walton-on-the-Naze to the north of the county to the north Thames saltmarshes to the south. One of the proposed sites was Maplin Sands. Obviously, we were alarmed as this particular site is very important for wintering birds providing rich feeding grounds for all manner of wildfowl and waders. I recall a newspaper article written by a councillor stating in a totally couldn't care less manner that "the birds could find somewhere else to breed". His cavalier thoughtless attitude was compounded by his crass ignorance, believing that the concern was for the birds' breeding site and not feeding site. Happily, he was hauled over the coals for this inexcusable blunder. But Maplin won the day and it was, after much deliberation, decided not to build the airport there. Why? Not for any conservation reasons, rest assured. Local and national bird and other wildlife organisations managed to convince enough councillors that the risk of bird strike would have been colossal and ongoing. Short of exterminating the birds, bird strike would have been the norm.

I have a story that I was hard-pressed to know where to put it but I did so want to include it in the book. I think here is the best place. We have considered how birds collectively may adversely affect humans. But there was once an individual whose tale should be told. When undertaking our bird migration research in the Himalaya (Ladakh) I collected, on the weekly shopping trip to Leh, a bottle of methylated spirits used for lighting our Primus stoves. The shopkeeper meticulously wrapped the bottle in several layers of newspaper. Having returned to our base-hut I chose to scan the pages of the paper, the *Hindi Times*, I believe. There was an article telling of a man who was riding alone on his scooter when a lakh (Hindi for large bird of prey) flew overhead. The bird was carrying a long snake. As it passed right over him the bird dropped the snake and the bemused reptile fell across the man's shoulders. The man immediately panicked and hurled himself sideways off his machine into the path of a sizeable military truck. All this was witnessed by a scooter-rickshaw driver travelling behind him. The man died. Perhaps the most bizarre aspect of this event is that the snake was not even a poisonous species and it must surely rank as the ultimate bad-luck story.

17. RUNNING THE GAUNTLET

When I taught the module in the International Baccalaureate (Geography syllabus) on Man and the Environment I had a mnemonic to help students recall five major topics. AHIPO was my mnemonic, which stood for Alien species, Habitat destruction, Islandisation, Pollution and Overharvesting. Today, I would have to increase that list to seven main categories, adding Climate Change and Illegal Trade in Wildlife, which I hope have found their way onto later syllabuses. Let's work our way through some of these.

Alien species of plants and animals have been introduced from their places of origin to different lands and rivers all over the world. The Victorians were great introducers and it was fashionable to fill our gardens, parks and zoos with exotic species. They were not the first however. Early settlers of foreign lands took with them familiar birds to comfort them and remind them of home. Thus the House Sparrow travelled the world following wherever the British went. Birds were also brought back home from far-off lands. Pheasants were probably brought in by the Normans from Asia, primarily for sport and ultimately the pot. Little owls were introduced during the late nineteenth century. The Peacock, a species of Indian pheasant, almost certainly came to Britain via the Romans to grace our parks and private estates. In the above three examples of alien introductions, they all seem to have settled down with native species with no adverse effects on either side, although Peacocks never really did run wild. In many cases the introduced species would have simply faded away as they failed to fit in to their supposedly similar environment. Many, far too many, have had disastrous effects and a patient dedicated naturalist could write volumes on this alone.

If you mention Hawaii to most people they will mentally conjure up images of long sandy beaches and adjacent forested mountain slopes teeming with loads of beautiful birds, butterflies and other creatures and of course, twangy guitars - a perfect holiday venue indeed. About half of Hawaii's plant species today are aliens having been introduced while at the same time many have perished as a result of the new competition. Numerous bird species have become extinct, particularly those which were flightless and were thus already vulnerable. Humans, in the form of sailors, explorers and prospecting traders landed in Hawaii to collect fresh water but doubtless they stocked up on many fruits of the forest. Many decided to settle in this volcanic island group. But, and worse still, were the ships' stow-away passengers, rats and mice, which were introduced accidentally and without concern, and goats, pigs and domestic pussy cats introduced intentionally for those who intended to stay. All of these alien species wrought havoc on the indigenous bird populations, especially those nesting on or close to the ground where nests were constantly raided of eggs and fledglings. The goats would eat just about any form of vegetation and could denude areas of bush and forest in very short periods being quite capable of clambering up into trees and shrubs.

A whole swathe of bird extinctions followed human peregrinations around the world and many of those in the Red Data Book are there because of this. The Red Data Book is a list indicating the level of rarity and thus potential extinction in three classes; animals, plants and fungi and is maintained by the IUCN (International Union for the Conservation of Nature). It is sad but obvious that this list grows from year to year. Closer to home, the Ring-necked Parakeet, which has escaped from aviaries now flourishes in parts of Britain and NW Europe. I recall when I spent a year in Brussels seeing and hearing parties of these birds coming in to roost at nights. They are very pretty but not, in my book, welcome. It has been suggested that these birds are a threat to Tawny Owls having the same nesting requirements, holes in trees. Whether introduced bird species compete with native species for food, territories or nesting sites or maybe that introduced species may like to eat native species of birds then decimation of the latter is inevitable.

I confessed earlier that I had a cat in Swaziland for 10 years. I grew very fond of him but always felt terrible guilt when he caught a bird (he preferred rodents and lizards) and did my best to talk him out of it. Feral cats, those domestic ones that have become wild, do untold damage to ground-nesting birds. When I was working in Shetland on Snowy Owls in 1971 (see chapter 25) feral cats were just starting to become a problem, although I never saw one.

Habitat destruction, our second topic, is a vast subject. Let's just look at ways in which we do this, either directly or indirectly. In the name of agriculture we drain swamps and wetlands, fill in ponds, remove hedgerows to create larger fields (easier to operate large machinery like combine harvesters) and we plough up grasslands, which were until then rich meadows heaving with plant diversity and all its dependants. We clear-fell great chunks of tropical rainforest (TRF) to turn them into hamburger factories, currently rampant in the Amazon. We cleared away lots of different habitats in Britain for the totally unnecessary and hugely expensive HS2 rail project. We may divert rivers to irrigate our crops, reduce flooding risk and to facilitate easier navigation.

One might argue that agriculture creates habitats but this is fickle. Nearly all of our crops are grown as monocultures, where a single crop is grown and woe betide any formerly native plants, which try to make their way back in. A whole cocktail of herbicides is available to prevent this. Consequently, many birds have suffered. Monocultures are also injurious to the soil as the same crop demands the same minerals each season, finally depleting the soil fertility and altering its mechanical properties. This necessitates our application of fertilizers, largely nitrogenous compounds. When these flow into rivers through overland flow or throughflow, algae will grow furiously to a point where it blankets the river in parts and de-oxygenates the water, killing various invertebrates and fish and ultimately all those birds that feed upon them.

As we increasingly urbanise our populations we build houses, schools, hospitals, airports, roads, railways and a whole lot more. This will seriously alter drainage patterns and so lower water tables all around as water cannot infiltrate through concrete. I have heard it said that when a motorway is constructed, around three times the width of the road itself is damaged as we clear the way for secondary features such as feeder roads, drainage pipes, motorway services and more. A similar or even worse situation is set to arise with the building of HS2.

Islandisation was a word I picked up from

an ecological textbook, which I used at university. I think it might better be called forest fragmentation. A single road might be driven through a huge area of forest, followed by another and then another, perhaps this time traversing one of the former roads. These roads open up the forest so loggers, mineral prospectors and ranchers have easier access to their proposed spoils. Loggers have to build roads just to haul out huge fallen trees thus the problem becomes compounded. TRF so abounds with tree diversity that a single hectare may hold over 600 species. This means if the logger's target is Mahogany there may well be hundreds of metres before the next Mahogany tree appears. This demotes all other species to unnecessary 'weeds' and many are destroyed as the target trees fall on them and are dragged from the forest. Consequently, the forest is fragmented into smaller and smaller parts until in some areas only isolated pockets remain. These small areas may be too small to continue to support various bird populations. A good example I saw in Sir David Attenborough's programme Life of Birds was the Ant Bird. It feeds on what its name suggests but these small ground-hugging birds are loath to pass to adjacent tracts of forest taking them out in the open. Even though they can fly they restrict themselves to their foraging areas. There are many other examples where fragmentation of forests is hammering bird populations.

Pollution, topic no.4 is another very serious cause of bird decline. Farmers distribute toxins in the form of herbicides, fungicides, bacteriocides (and doubtless other more specific 'cides'). Some may use broad-spectrum poisons, which kill just about anything. There is a wonderful highly influential but very depressing book published in 1962 by American Rachel Carson called Silent Spring (see Reading List) referring to the marked demise of songbirds in the American countryside due to toxic pollution. It became a classic read as the public became more enlightened. And as the public became more concerned, politicians and industrialists had cause to tremble as there is nothing more powerful than public opinion. We learned words like 'organochlorines' and a new meaning of the word persistent. The latter means that a certain chemical remains in the environment for a long period and works its way through a food chain, becoming more concentrated as it passes along to the top predator. Once there, or even before reaching the top predator, the poison is concentrated enough to kill.

In the '60s in Britain we became aware of the plight of Peregrine Falcons whose numbers fell dramatically. What was happening is that the incubating birds were inadvertently smashing their own eggs. These eggs lacked a shell or at best they were very thin and the contents was precariously contained in the translucent membranes, which adhere closely to the inner sides of the shells. You can see this clearly when you tuck into a boiled egg at breakfast time. This problem was traced to DDT, a highly potent broad-spectrum pesticide. For those who might want to roll its full name round the tongue DDT is an acronym for, wait for it – dichlorodiphenyldichloroethylene. The chemical interfered with calcium metabolism and affected not only Peregrine Falcons but North American Brown Pelicans. DDT was subsequently banned (but is still sold to developing countries). Think of the number of schoolkids and military personnel who were liberally sprayed with this stuff in days gone by in order to de-lice them. DDT was never used in Antarctica and yet it has been found in the tissues of penguins, having entered oceanic food chains. This shows just how persistent DDT is. Public awareness led to certain pesticides being banned, some were weakened while others were modified in various ways to reduce the carnage such as making pesticides, which only affected the target organism or those which were biodegradable meaning they broke down shortly after deposition. Murdering birds does not win votes

Heavy metal does not just refer to bands like Iron Maiden and Black Sabbath. The heavy metals include elements such as cadmium, mercury, lead and chromium. These can all be rather nasty if released into the environment and allowed to enter food chains. Mercury poisoning was detected in Japan in 1956 and was attributed to a chemical factory discharging contaminated water into nearby rivers. This went on to kill several thousand people along with their domesticated livestock and wild mammals and birds for several more decades.

The lead shot used in shotgun cartridges and the weights pinched onto anglers' lines are made of lead. In the UK in 1987 anglers' lead weights over a specified weight were banned and a harmless substitute used. This was good news for swans and other water birds, which accidentally took up this highly toxic heavy metal, perhaps when taking in sand and grit for use in their gizzards. However, it went only part of the way to solving the problem. In 2019 (31 years later!) this was taken further but still some fishermen's weights and wildfowlers' shotgun pellets are made of lead. The EU is ahead of the UK on this legislation. Computers contain all four of the heavy metals mentioned above and each of these too are very dangerous if they enter food chains, demanding that we take great care in the disposal of these items, ideally recycling them.

We may also cause bird demise indirectly, through upsetting food chains in other ways. Billowing smoke from our factories, power stations and vehicle exhausts is dissolved in rain as raindrops absorb sulphur particles. This forms weak sulphuric acid and thus we have 'Acid Rain'. This is denuding some forests in northern temperate regions where trees die from the top down and is called 'die back'. The sulphur dioxide does damage to the stomatal cells on the leaf undersides, which allow entry and exit of essential gases. Acidity is measured on the pH scale of 1 – 14, 7 being neutral, 6 down to 1 is acidic and 8 up to 14 is alkaline. The scale is logarithmic meaning that each level goes up or down by a factor of ten. Thus river water of pH 5 is ten times more acidic than 6 but a pH of 4 would be 10 x 10, a hundred times more acidic. Many lakes in Finland, of which there are thousands, now have pH values of 4 to 5, which is quite frightening. The oceans are becoming more acidic and this is bleaching coral by killing off the algal component of coral reefs. These reefs have been likened to rainforests in terms of biodiversity and biomass productivity. With bleaching follows fish diversity decline, which in turn means the decline of all those birds that feed on fish. All this increase globally of acidification in the environment reduces plant production and ultimately affects all those dependent upon it. We are only just beginning to understand just how disgracefully polluted our oceans are by plastic waste. It is utterly sickening to see this on TV news and documentaries and one wonders how on earth it got to this stage. Much of this will hang around for centuries and even when it does break down there is still the residual microplastic residue, which can harm those that live in the oceans.

Still discussing oceans, what about oil pollution? Tankers are generally too large to safely ply the seas and oceans with their deadly cargo (this is something to do with tanker size and wave periodicity and that's all I am saying – ask a physicist for more details). The Torrey Canyon tanker grounded onto rocks in Cornwall, UK in 1967 when I was 17 and I was utterly horrified at the death-toll of sea-birds. Eleven years later the Amoco Cadiz caused another huge tanker spill, this time off the coast of Brittany, France. In March 2025 the US-flagged Stena Immaculate, carrying 220,000 barrels of jet fuel (made from crude oil) was struck by a German cargo ship in the North Sea. Such terrible events are headline news for weeks and thousands of seabirds perish or have to be put down as a consequence.

There are many spills which don't make the newsdesks yet if you walk along an area of coastline, before long you will find an oiled bird, maybe a Puffin, a Guillemot or perhaps a gull. There is a problem with oiling of birds. It seems that some seabird species when under water fishing look up to see a dark patch. Up they go, heading straight for the slick, believing it to be a shoal of fish. That is it. No matter how little oil a bird gets on its plumage it is likely to die. This is because all waterbirds have special preen glands at the base of their tails. These contain an oily substance which when rendered on their feathers during preening confers waterproofing. The first time an oiled seabird tries to clean itself it transfers slick oil to its preen gland and so blocks it. Eventually the bird loses its waterproofing and can no longer float.

Other, more localised poisoning of birds includes that nasty disease called botulism, a severe form of food poisoning. This affects several gull species as they increasingly scavenge our waste food at landfill sites. Putting down snail poison so your lettuces will grow to maturity will kill Song Thrushes and others who feed on the snails. When in Lesotho I witnessed the aftermath of the spraying of a widespread infestation of cut-worms, which affected at least the capital Maseru. Our school playing-field was heaving with these little caterpillars. Fortunately, the school could not afford to poison them. Even so, the city council could afford to spray grass-edged walkways, parks and other public places. Over the course of one week as I walked down to my local bar at the end of each working day, I must have seen at least a dozen dead birds, mostly thrushes but also two African Hoopoes and a couple of crows. I was in no doubt whatsoever as to what had killed them.

Overharvesting is simply taking more out of a resource than that which is allowed to replenish itself. Humans have been overfishing for a very long while and certain fish stocks have dwindled and even totally crashed. The final collapse in 1993 of the Atlantic cod fishery was due to overfishing in the once highly productive Grand Banks of Newfoundland for the previous 20 years. These fish-stocks have, even today, not fully recovered since remedial action was enforced. Healthy fish populations are essential to numerous birds of many species and they too have suffered as a consequence of overfishing and this becomes all the more noticeable at breeding times.

The illegal trade in wildlife is a booming industry in which hundreds of species of animals are smuggled from one part of the world to another. Attempts to prevent the catchers and the smugglers are often futile. Attacking the markets is probably more effective here although rampant corruption can very much put the lid on that approach. The ongoing fad for bush-meat is also taking its toll but here again, this is taking place in largely rural parts of developing countries meaning that little is achieved to stop it.

When I was in Botswana, Mopane Moth caterpillars festooned the foliage of Mopane trees. These are misleadingly called Mopane

Worms. They are gathered up by the bucket load every season, largely by young children in attempts to boost family incomes. Children would bang on my door to ask if they could take my Mopane Worms. I enforced a policy stating they could take what they could reach and no climbing was permitted nor indeed, one child standing on the shoulders of another as they tried on me once. I tried my best to explain the obvious but I fear it fell on deaf ears.

Climate Change is really something else and something that I will only mention briefly here given the broad scope and enormity of this subject. Far better scientists than I, largely specialists in matters climatic and meteorological, will churn out books and more books together with scientific papers on the possible implications of this global phenomenon. At present we cannot possibly know of the consequences of this now unstoppable scourge but it is without doubt the greatest threat we and all our fellow creatures have ever faced. That it is man-made is now irrefutable and even the most ignorant and powerful politicians will have to acknowledge it if they want to keep their jobs. As I write this on November 8, 2020 we learn that US President Donald Trump has been deposed. He, the leader of the 'free world' did not believe in climate change and took his country out of the Paris Climate Accord. The incoming president (Joe Biden) was to reinstate the USA into this oh so important international pact to reduce carbon emissions. (On January 20, 2025, shortly after his second inauguration, President Trump signed an executive order to withdraw the United States from the agreement for a second time.) Climate change is far from new. What is new is our widespread awareness of it, both by the public and scientists. Getting governments on board may be a bit more challenging. But Climate Change is dogged with problems. Even climate specialists cannot agree on the matter. Put 20 climate scientists into a room and ask them to write a thousand word summary of the problems and you will have 20 differing accounts. There will be overlap but there will be as much disparity or more. Surely it is time to install climate-change ministers along with numerous specialist scientists in world governments – scientists who will be listened to!

We cannot say for sure when this man-made climate change started. Well it didn't really start at any identifiable time. It simply grew slowly at first from around the middle of the eighteenth century, the start of the Industrial Revolution, which occurred predominantly in Britain. Then with the world hungry for power to run its myriad machines and vehicles, ships, aircraft and heating for homes and other buildings it really took off and continues to do so exponentially. Much of the puff and wind of today's politicians is based on ignorance or a preference to ignore truths, which may conflict with economic interests (Trump wanting to make America great again is happy to, "Drill, baby drill.") Such world leaders cannot be blamed for ignorance but they can be blamed for ignoring those that know better. The scientists are also in part working in the dark at the moment and are floundering for answers but they are not in denial.

Climate change impinges on all aspects of life on earth and earth processes such that no single person can possibly grasp all the problems and possible solutions. It will take many specialists in the physical, chemical and biological sciences to work together to make inroads into the biggest problem the world has ever been confronted with. The possible permutations of what can happen are enormous (seemingly infinite) and nobody can claim to have even a fraction of possible remedies. And of course, knowledge is one thing - timely action is another. It is largely down to our grandchildren to sort out this bloody awful mess, which we pass down to them. What will they make of us as they look back? Attempts are being made to harness the minds of our climate practitioners and doubtless inroads will be made to implement corrective measures but it has to be truly international. We are currently (as I write) going through a resurgence of fanatical nationalism, with China and Russia becoming increasingly isolated. On February 24, 2022 Russia invaded Ukraine and US President Donald Trump is negotiating with Russian President Vladimir Putin to end this war. Since October 7, 2023 the Gaza war has been fought between Israel and Hamas-led Palestinian militant groups in the Gaza Strip and Israel. It is Israel's 15th war in Gaza, and has sparked an ongoing Middle Eastern crisis. Again, the USA is spearheading peace negotiations.

Paranoia is cropping up all over the place as countries come to mistrust others – hardly the desired setting to tackle something as big as climate change. What we are faced with today is just as serious as if an impending meteor-strike was threatening to obliterate all life on the planet. Were that ever so, do you believe that we, over 200 nations could fully co-operate to try to blast the hurtling mass of rock away from the earth? We could probably actually achieve this with our collective space technologies. But we need more than technology. It is going to be necessary for mankind to pull out all the stops, to co-operate globally and direct funds and efforts to make any appreciable headway. We have seen very little global cooperation to fight Covid-19 and in the UK we have witnessed a conveyor-belt of delay and incompetence. This certainly does not auger well in the case of tackling climate change. We have little time left for procrastination and ignoring the scientific community. One of our weapons against climate change must be education and yet more education, not just of our children and grandchildren but of those currently running the show. Can we hope for that? We have to hope but immediate action is vital.

I want to consider now those that come back with the snappy reply that "...but there have been loads of climate changes in the past and the scientists have proven that". This is perfectly true and there is plenty of conclusive evidence for this. Past changes seem to be caused by the perturbations of the earth's axial tilt. What we all need to grasp is that this time it is happening much much faster than any previous event. Animals and plants need generations (and thus time) to adapt to changes and failure to do so will be their undoing. We need people to understand that yes, a warming planet can produce extra snowfall. Seeing New Yorkers shovelling away snow in search of their cars is meat for the doubters who claim that this negates global warming. Increased sea-surface temperatures (even of just 1°C) will increase evaporation rates and that extra atmospheric moisture has to go somewhere. It falls either as rain or snow.

We need those not of a scientific bent to understand that sea-levels are rising for two reasons - thermal expansion of water as sea temperatures warm and also as the ice melts. The rapid rate of ice loss in the Arctic is occurring so fast that Polar Bears will be but a memory within your grandchildren's lifetimes. There is no continental landmass under the Arctic so what refuge will our white furry friends have?

Arctic Ice is frozen sea-water and is already 90 per cent submerged so its melting is not raising sea levels as much as thermal expansion. The Antarctic is a different ball-game. Countless trillions of tonnes of ice, made of fresh water, sit atop a continent and is thus not yet in the sea. If that lot melts (as it is doing so) then sea levels will go up to a staggering level, by up to tens of metres, depending on which scientists got their sums right. The problem is that we don't and cannot know what sums to actually do - nobody can safely predict as there are so many variables.

We also need to take our focus away from the cuddly and iconic top predators like Polar Bears. I would be too embarrassed to buy my grandchildren T-shirts with Giant Pandas on the front. They might start asking awkward questions. Of course we don't want to lose such majestic creatures but looking after the base of the food chains, the phyto-plankton and the zoo-plankton which abound in our oceans is not just preferable but essential. There is a very fine balance in operation and it won't take much to upset it irreversibly. It is upset for sure but hopefully not yet irreversibly. No one is going to wear a T shirt demanding algal rights or 'save our rotifers' but we do, collectively, need to take responsibility, to learn and to act. We have to be brave and tell our children and grand-children what a mess we are making and how sorry we are.

Politicians are generally not scientists but they can be spurred into action if there is widespread public awareness and the will is there. It is happening slowly but is action really being taken to any significant degree? I agree with Greta Thunberg and say a resounding, "No, it isn't." There does seem to be a shifting of public thought about us and our planet but it is agonisingly slow. The world is run by extremely powerful companies who are able to manipulate politicians, courts and other control bodies. The current (as I write) Covid-19 pandemic has really given us collectively a big nudge and I wonder if it will develop into a real paradigm shift where governments will have to make brave, intelligent and informed decisions. This is not just a call to learn and understand as much as we are able, it is not just a call for more recycling bins…it is one for the survival of us, Homo sapiens, and every other creature that has evolved on this little corner of the Milky Way galaxy, Planet Earth.

18. AND MAY I INTRODUCE...

That last chapter may well have proved a bit depressing so let's try to cheer things up a bit with some good news. I refer here to particular reintroductions of birds into the UK. Firstly, let me stress the word RE-introductions and not introductions. This is the re-establishment of any species, which once bred in a given location or country but has ceased to do so, normally due, directly or indirectly to the hand of man. Individuals of a species are taken from other countries and either the eggs are artificially incubated or a number of adult birds will be released into suitable habitat and left to their own devices, hopefully to form a sustainable breeding population. I shall consider two success stories, those of the Red Kite and the Great Bustard.

I recall on a birding weekend in central Wales in 1970 with a couple of friends, being quite chuffed with having had rather distant views of a couple of Red Kites. Fifty years later there are an estimated 1,000 plus pairs in the UK. These birds had long been persecuted by ignorant farmers who rated anything with a hooked beak as 'vermin', despite kites being scavengers and thus providing a service to humanity. Egg collectors took their toll, exponentially as the birds became rarer and rarer and so pushing up the street value of eggs. Poisoning, either primary or secondary also helped decimate Red Kites. The plight of this species was recognised as early as 1905 by the RSPB but it was not until the mid '80s that some definitive action was taken. The RSPB together with the NCC (Now Natural England) undertook feasibility discussions about reintroducing Red Kites into Britain. Between 1989 and 1994 a number of birds of Swedish and Spanish origin were released into both England and Scotland. In 1992 breeding in the wild took place at both release sites. This was repeated when in 1995, 11 more birds were released leading to successful breeding two years later. A third major release occurred in 1996 of 19 Red Kites of German stock into central Scotland and once again, breeding followed. This success of the re-introduction of Red Kites into Britain is all the more important as birds on the European mainland are currently under various pressures. Birds can still be affected by secondary poisoning as they eat dead poisoned rodents and power lines also take their toll. Both these issues are apparently being addressed. When I returned from Africa after 27 years away two friends took me on a 'surprise' trip to a farm in the Chilterns where an enterprising farmer was making a healthy sideline by putting out offal and other bits of slaughtered livestock. This brought Red Kites down in droves. The farmer had a contribution box at his gate. I remember feeling rather awkward about this... it seemed more like being at a zoo and bearing in mind the cocktail of chemicals fed to or injected into livestock these days, I was concerned about persistent chemicals building up in the birds' tissues. Also worthy of note is when I was in Cornwall and a Red Kite was following a tractor and plough, taking up earthworms as it went. While I never saw a Red Kite being zapped by power lines, I did witness just that when a Black Kite alighted on a cable right outside my classroom in Kenya and, with a flurry of feathers, dropped to the ground, having been killed outright.

One of the world's heaviest flying birds, the Great Bustard, became extinct in Britain when the last bird was shot in 1832. Today, over 40 birds thrive on the edge of Salisbury Plain in England (one of their earlier preferred locations) enjoying the protection from the Ministry of Defence who use the area as training grounds. Great bustards live on open grassland and farmland in Asia and Central and Southern Europe, with well over half the world population being in Spain and Portugal. Spain has an estimated 30,000 individuals. This species is highly dimorphic with the weights of males three or four times that of the females. Average weights of males are around 12kg but one

Spanish bird weighed in at 19kg. Standing over one metre tall and with a wing-span of 2.5m it is surprising just how well these birds can fly. When threatened the birds prefer to run rather than take to the air and can reputedly outrun a fox. The male birds show off their wares in a lek where prospective females gather in an arena to watch the performing birds. The male has a highly inflatable throat and can enlarge it enormously. This combined with wing displays all add to his nuptial charm as he performs. Females lay from one to three eggs and nest in loose colonies of a few birds. Males reach sexual maturity after about five years and may live a further 10. Great Bustards are true omnivores, feeding on a large range of plant material including legumes, cereals, and alfalfa. Insects, lizards, rodents and birds are also welcome additions to the diet. One might think these mighty birds had no predators but the list is long. The eggs and chicks are taken by crows, raptors, hedgehogs, rats, mustelids, foxes and wild boars while the adults may be tackled by various eagle species. The threats imposed by humans include intensive agriculture, afforestation, pesticides, irrigation schemes, road-building and power lines, the latter being a particular hazard. Birds brought into the UK from Russia by the Great Bustard Group successfully reared young in 2009/10. Considering how popular these meaty birds were as the fare of kings (sometimes scores of birds were taken for a single event) it is surprising how they were not domesticated and bred for the table instead of us preferring to introduce Common Turkeys from the USA.

Some birds have re-introduced themselves into Britain. Little Egrets were once fairly common until around the sixteenth century when they finally disappeared as a UK species. The head plumes of egrets were much sought after for the adornment of ladies' hats although this alone was probably not the only cause of their demise. In recent decades these white members of the heron family enjoyed a widespread expansion and spread across Europe into France, becoming regular visitors to Britain. They then started breeding and now nest all along the south coast and much of the SE coast. They also nest down the eastern margins of Ireland. Their expansion continues ever northward in Britain and birds are now also breeding in the New World.

Another sweeping success story of the avian world is that of the Collared Dove. Until the close of the nineteenth century this small pinkish dove was found in southern Asia from Turkey across to China and down through India. It then started to disperse predominantly in a north-westerly direction. It swept into and across Europe and was first reported in Britain in 1953. By 1956 the species was breeding and continues to flourish. Their northward expansion took them to the Faroe Islands way out in the Atlantic, north of the Arctic Circle and also Iceland although they do not yet breed in the latter. This is not a case of a bird re-introducing itself to Britain, it simply was not here before its massive dispersal.

With climate change in full swing, who can predict what substantive changes may occur in the global distribution of birds?

Reintroductions are generally fine but introductions are not likely to be. Introductions will be alien species (which we discussed in the previous chapter) and unlikely to prosper in the new environment or, alternatively, will cause bio-havoc. Even some reintroductions may no longer work as the former environment may have changed significantly.

19. GOING, GOING, GONE...

These days we hear quite a lot about extinction. Nearly every wildlife programme on TV closes with a warning of the impending threat of extinction to this or to that species. Those who delve deeper into the matter will be aware that we are not just talking about a few species, but a whole basket of living things, which may not be with us beyond the end of this century, and some may disappear well before then.

During my teaching career I became aware that some confusion existed about the precise meaning of extinct. Extinction is the disappearance of an entire species, so when we say the Dodo is extinct, we mean there is not one remaining on Earth as far as we can possibly know. If you shoot me, I have not become extinct as there are close to eight billion of my species still running around. And of course, extinction is forever, an obvious statement but one which jars on the senses when given thought. Scientists have found conclusive evidence for five major extinctions in the geological record. In every case at least 65 per cent of species living at the time were eradicated forever and on at least one occasion 99 per cent of life was swept away in one fell swoop.

Below is a table of when these mass extinctions

occurred, working from the oldest at the bottom. I made a mnemonic to help students learn the geologic timescale – *Camels Often Sit Down Carefully, Perhaps Their Joints Creek, Even On My Private Property.*

Pleistocene

Pliocene

Miocene

Oligocene

Eocene

Cretaceous   65m years ago. Major extinction killing all dinosaurs and many marine species.

Jurassic

Triassic   210m years ago. Major extinction

Permian   225m years ago. Major extinction killing 95 per cent of all animals.

Carboniferous

Devonian   365m years ago. Major extinction.

Silurian

Ordovician   440m years ago. Major extinction.

Cambrian   600m years ago. The 'Cambrian Explosion' of numerous life forms on Earth.

During the earliest named geological period, the Cambrian, there was a relatively 'sudden' flourish of organisms coming into existence. These were not merely species but whole families and whole phyla of creatures were new on the block. Until this 'event' all life forms had been unicellular simple organisms but now there were multi-cellular life-forms entering the world stage. This is rather misleadingly referred to as the 'Cambrian Explosion' (see Wonderful Life in Reading List). Obviously it took place over millions of years but it was still quite rapid in a geological perspective. Also misleading is the use of the term 'event', sometimes used in geological texts when referring to a happening, which suggests something occurring in an instant – clearly not the case here. By far the majority of all those new creatures did not survive. It was nature 'trying out' new ideas, the world a huge workshop to mess around with different 'designs' of organisms. Don't ask me how this figure is derived but it is estimated that about 30bn species lived since the Cambrian Explosion. If we take a midway estimate on the number of species extant today to be 30m then the maths tells us that 99.9 per cent of all species that have existed have been lost to extinction.

It is interesting to note that extinction is actually a facet of the complete evolutionary process. I have read that the average life expectancy of any given species is around four million years, again I know not how such a figure is reached. Darwin identified the main feature of extinction as being a gradual but continuous process, the rate of extinction being uniform with no surges or recognizable catastrophes but this seems not to be the rule.

So, what causes extinctions?

A number of possible causes have been put forward, some quite bizarre and unlikely such as things going on in outer space like exploding super-novae. Among the more feasible causes are global cooling, falling sea-levels (marine regressions), predation and competition amongst species. Common to all previous five mass extinctions was a drastic drop in sea-levels. Now, water on Earth is basically in either of two places. It is locked up as ice in the polar regions or it splashes about as a liquid in the oceans. The more usual situation is a bit of each as we have at present. During any advances of the great ice-sheets (during Ice-Ages) sea-levels must go down. Another factor which determines sea-levels is the configuration of the Earth's landmasses ranging from the single land mass of Pangea ('all Earth') way back in the Pre-Cambrian and the familiar distribution of continents we see today and which is still changing, albeit extremely slowly.

Lowering of sea-levels leads to a loss of habitats, which in turn leads to decreasing biodiversity. Exposed continental shelves, formerly heaving with life forms dry out and are subject to erosion and oxidation of organic matter that was once safely tucked away on the shelf floors. Oxidation withdraws oxygen from the atmosphere and puts in carbon. It has been calculated that the Earth's oxygen concentrations may have once dropped to below half of current levels. Clearly, all terrestrial life would have been adversely affected. The Earth has undergone dramatic cooling during a number of periods in its history as extensive glaciations reached out from the polar regions. Climate change has certainly been one of the major factors leading to extinction of species.

Additional candidates for fluctuations in the Earth's climate are changes in the convection currents circling in the mantle between the core and the crust and also variations in the Earth's orbit around its central star, the Sun.

The most recent mass extinction on Earth 65m years ago was caused by the impact of a meteorite, which had escaped from the asteroid belt between Mars and Jupiter and, having travelled for millions of kilometres smashed into our planet. Today, with several separate strands of evidence, each mutually supportive, we can be pretty much certain this is what happened. That impact would have dwarfed man's entire arsenal of nuclear weapons going off all in one go. The meteor would have vaporised and the material displaced by the collision would have taken dust into the upper atmosphere blackening out the rays of the Sun for long enough to kill off most plant-life by preventing photosynthesis. No plant life means no animal life and our favourite friends of schoolchildren, the dinosaurs, perished, having 'ruled the Earth' for 140m years pretty much untroubled. Other terrestrial life forms also perished and various groups of marine creatures went the same way, notably the ammonites, a large and varied group of invertebrates related to the modern nautilus. While the impact itself could be described as an 'event' taking some seconds once the meteorite entered the Earth's atmosphere, the extinction that followed may have taken many years. Scientists had worked out that this huge impact occurred at the end of the Cretaceous period 65m years ago but had not found the impact crater. It was just a matter of time and in 1990 this was discovered submerged in the Gulf of Mexico on the tip of the Yucatan Peninsula. Evidence suggests that it was actually a shower of meteors rather than just the one.

Throughout my teaching days it has become clear to me that young people are very concerned generally about what is happening on Earth. However, I have been lambasted by a few (mostly students' parents) for teaching doom and gloom. I taught the facts as far as we can know them. Tomorrow's leaders need to know what we are up against before any curative measures can be taken. If people get depressed about what I incorporate into teaching about environmental issues I make no apologies. It is depressing stuff. But from this comes thought and discussion, which maybe in the future will lead to substantive actions.

Once a student brought up the matter of resurrecting species by cloning, such as from the cell of a mammoth being implanted into a surrogate elephant. Firstly, this is very much a gimmick and has no real conservation value. What if we could bring back a few dinosaurs? Where would we put them? Does such habitat now exist for these creatures? And anyway, dinosaurs all died out as a result of a natural catastrophic event and not by the hand of man. Let's concentrate on looking after what we have already got.

Dr Richard Leakey and Roger Lewin in their book The Sixth Extinction (see Reading List) identify patterns in past extinctions enabling to some extent prediction of where we are heading. It is generally agreed among various scientific disciplines that the Earth is plummeting towards a sixth extinction. Life survived five extinction events so will the sixth be any different? Unfortunately, almost certainly, yes. First and foremost, the earlier five extinctions were all a part of the great ongoing cycle of life. The impending sixth extinction is entirely due to human action and is therefore preventable. We are not short of the knowledge. We are, however, very lacking in the collective will. The current extinction rate is way and above everything that has gone before and is happening at an alarming speed. Animals and plants are becoming extinct even faster than we are discovering them. Laws are not preventing the illegal sale of wildlife. Our dependence on chemicals to grow crops to feed our burgeoning numbers remains. Corrupt and ignorant politicians will continue to run the show. The rainforests continue to make a few ranchers and loggers rich as they destroy the 'lungs of the Earth'. Alien species continue to be introduced into unsuitable habitats. Millions of tonnes of plastic is dumped into our oceans every year. Coral reefs are being killed by the increasing acidification of sea water. This and more. Species cannot adapt to the rapid alterations of ecosystems let alone total destruction of habitats. By urbanisation, drainage of wetlands and widespread over-grazing leading to soil compaction and, ultimately, desertification, we are irreversibly changing habitats.

We know well enough by now that no species can live alone. All life on Earth requires healthy oceans, coral reefs, rainforests, uncontaminated water, unpolluted atmosphere and relatively stable climates in order to survive. Throw out one spark plug from a car engine and it will struggle to work. Throw away two and it won't work at all. This is the stage we are approaching on Earth and, risking quoting an old cliché, we really do need to get our act together now and actually do something to stop this downward spiral instead of spouting puff and wind at world conferences, which amount to little or nothing being achieved.

It is important to appreciate that extinction of any organism does not just mean down to the last male and female. It means down to such low numbers that the location of mates (a huge problem with Blue Whales) becomes an issue and so the creature has gone below its threshold level, referred to as a 'viable' population.

Habitat destruction is probably the greatest cause of bird decline. Once the threshold is reached then extinction will almost certainly follow unless extra-special efforts are made by us to bring about an increase of population. People talk about 'the' Loch Ness monster. If they existed at all they would have to number quite a few in order to even just sustain a viable population.

We can thank our grandchildren in advance for inheriting the mess and sorting it out!

20. THE DODO - A TRIBUTE...

The Dodo is without doubt the very emblem of extinction. This poem, written by Hilaire Belloc for children in 1896 deserves entry here:

> The Dodo used to walk around
>   and take the sun and air
> the sun yet warms his native ground
> the Dodo is not there
> the voice which used to squawk and squeak
>   is now forever dumb
> yet may you see his bones and beak
> all in the mu-se-um

Many birds have become extinct and yet the Dodo seems to have captured a place in our hearts. Its demise at the hand of man is shameful and indeed sad. First recorded in 1598 by Dutch explorers on the island of Mauritius (2,000km off the SE coast of Africa) the bird was extinct within a little over six decades. This was due to several factors: clearing of its preferred habitat, the coastal forest; the introduction of domestic animals such as dogs, cats and pigs and the careless release of stowaway rats, which are always bad news for ground-nesting birds. Crab-eating Macaques were also introduced (why?) which relished the Dodo eggs. But surely the greatest single factor was that Dodos were systematically and brutally killed by man. The Dodo was a member of the Pigeon and Dove family although was much larger than any pigeon, standing a metre high and weighing an average of 14kg. It was also flightless due to the absence of natural predators. It is possible the Dodo also lived on the nearby French island of Reunion.

From what little we can gather, the markedly fat dumpy Dodo had greyish plumage, yellow feet and a green/yellow bill. Its tail was a curly tuft of fine feathers and around its head it sported a kind of Rambo headband. Its wings were greatly reduced and remained as mere stubs. It earnt its name from Portuguese sailors who used their word meaning 'stupid'. While a bit unfair, the Dodo was rather a daft-looking bird and showed a naïve trust of humans, allowing itself to be approached and clubbed on the head, later to be salted and stored in casks aboard ships for food. Even so, various reports state that it was not particularly appealing to the palate. Its oil was, however, used as a muscle relaxant. The few remains of Dodos show that it had a gizzard, presumably to aid mechanical digestion of the stones of the fruit, which formed part of its diet. The call has been likened to that of a young goose. It was already disadvantaged in that it laid just a single egg and thus would have struggled to build up its population. Its demise is all the more ironic as the Dodo had survived millennia of volcanic outbursts and climatic change.

The bird was last seen in 1662 although some authorities put this to be a couple of decades later. All that exists today is a single head incorporated into a model and exhibited at Oxford University Museum along with a cast of a skeleton. A single skull is housed in Denmark. A few bones were found in a cave in Mauritius, a place the birds would not have ventured into so it is likely they are the remains of birds taken to the caves by escaped slaves. A lone egg may exist in South Africa although it awaits genetic confirmation to be of that species.

Lewis Carroll included the Dodo in Alice in Wonderland, reputedly mocking himself due to his awful stammer (did Dodos stammer?). Also, this allegorical bird became iconic enough to feature on coins and bank notes and as logos heading various government documents. Today, Mauritius, less than 2,000 square kilometres in area is largely sugar plantations with much of its biodiversity lost. At the time of the bird's extinction, no more than 50 people lived on the island, whereas today that has soared to over one-and-a-quarter million, sugar and tourism being the mainstay of the island economy.

The closest living relative of the Dodo is the

Nicobar Pigeon although of a different genus.

So, there it is, the oh so sad story of the Dodo (Raphus cuccullatus) who at least lives on by name and will never be forgotten.

21. HIGH FLYERS...

Swifts? Migrating White Storks? No. I want to talk about people. People who dedicated most or at least part of their lives to the study of ornithology. Pioneers who greatly added to the body of knowledge of various branches of natural history. I have already mentioned a few people who have had birds named after them but now I wish to home in on those who described, studied, collected, painted in days long gone and, in more recent times, filmed them. These trailblazers were almost exclusively from Britain or Europe while some North Americans also made major contributions. I have read a book entitled The Great Naturalists (editor Robert Huxley) which covered the lives and work of 40 distinguished naturalists, who lived from classical times to the end of the nineteenth century. Of those 40, 35 per cent were British, 15 per cent French, and 10 per cent each from Germany and Italy. Three came from the USA. We'll start by going back to times before Christ.

Aristotle was without doubt the broadest-based philosopher of all human history, covering astronomy through to zoology and many categories of natural history alphabetically in between. Born in Greece in 384 BC he trained under another of humanities greats,

Plato. Aristotle favoured zoology and one of his well over one hundred books was Historia Animalium comprising nine volumes and discussing over 500 animal species. It should be stressed here that in ancient times Historia meant research and not history, hence when we talk today of natural history we are really referring to the research or study of nature and not its historical development. While doubtless a highly superior mind, he did not always get it right. He believed that the Earth was the centre of the universe but I think we can forgive him for that. He made some inroads into the field of classification and Darwin believes Aristotle demonstrated some cognizance of the modification of species through his understanding of structure in relation to function. Darwin described Aristotle as the greatest observer who ever lived.

The Renaissance produced numerous great revolutionary thinkers in a wide range of disciplines and the Italian Ulisse Aldrovandi was one such person. He was born in 1522 and at the age of 17 embarked on studies in law and humanities. At the age of 31, he graduated in medicine and the following year he began lecturing at Bologna University. Seven years later a special chair of Natural Philosophy was created for him, clearly his favoured domain. With this he organised a public botanical garden of which he was director. He had become aware that some earlier works were not always complete or accurate in their attestations, including those by Aristotle and Pliny and he was determined to attempt to address such issues. Aldrovandi strived to identify and describe as many living things and also minerals as was possible and started to collect specimens from all over the world. The continued penetration of the Old World together with the 'discoveries' of the New World kept material pouring in for study and he used his home as an ever-expanding museum for over half a century. He also amassed numerous paintings of wildlife and had these bound in volumes. He used, wherever practical, all this accumulated material to teach his students, giving them what today we would describe as a 'hands-on' experience. Aldrovandi was a stickler for accuracy and reality and had no truck with any kind of aesthetic approach to natural sciences. Further to his collected material, he commissioned wildlife artwork and even trained painters himself. He was in his late seventies when he published his three-volume work, 'Ornithologia' and it was just prior to his death four years later in 1605 that he bequested his entire museum and his extensive library to the city of Bologna.

Another child of the Renaissance was Pierre Belon, born in France in 1517. He was an all-rounder but he marvelled at the similarity between a bird's and a human's skeleton, noting the same number of bones and recognizing them as homologous structures. His last book was A Natural History of Birds published in 1555, which was based on his dissections of around 200 species of birds.

When I started bird watching I was nurtured on the Observer's Book of Birds. In that edition, following each scientific name was an abbreviation of the person responsible for the naming and/or classification of that bird, and the name Linn appeared quite frequently. This was short for Carl Linnaeus, a Swedish doctor and naturalist born in 1707. He was eager to bring some order to all animals, plants and fungi. He was primarily a botanist although he was responsible for the classification and naming of numerous birds. I have just looked at my current Observer's Book of Birds and find these names not included in my edition. Also different is that the edition on my shelf now bears only the binomial scientific names and not trinomials. These are the Latin names written in italics after the bird name comprising two words, the Genus and the species. This system of naming was introduced by Linnaeus. In 1735 he published his Systema Naturae, which classified plants largely on the characteristics of their sexual organs. Believe it or not, his sometimes rather suggestive scientific names for plants seemed too much for those prudes of society, notably the church of course but also some of his fellow botanists. Bizarre indeed to think that one engaged in the innocent and worthy pursuit of naming and classifying plants may end up on the sexual offenders list. I recall that the Latin name of the Stinkhorn Fungus is Phallus impudicus as it does without doubt resemble the erect human male organ to the point of some detail. I am not sure if that was one of his. After Linnaeus's role as physician to the Admiralty and then Professor of Medicine at Uppsala University, he finally took the Chair of Botany, carrying out his naming and classification for the remainder of his working life. His marriage to a well-shod lady surely helped him in this pursuit. He died in 1778.

Born in the same year as Linnaeus, Comte de Buffon became a wide-ranging naturalist and produced an impressive work entitled Natural History, General and Particular. He managed to complete 44 volumes of his proposed 50. Impressive indeed.

John James Audubon was born illegitimately in France in 1785 becoming a US citizen 27 years later. He was a naturalist and artist and he both hunted and drew birds. His legacy was a magnum opus titled The Birds of America, which kept him busy for 11 years from 1827. He drew a lot of dead stuff but he succeeded in mounting freshly dead birds in a special apparatus, which conferred upon the corpses some semblance of life. His bird paintings are very identifiable as his own and are action-packed while his writings are rich in anecdotal material although some of his captions are rather anthropomorphic. Audubon did also paint live specimens. He used just about every media available to the artist and his great work comprised 1065 paintings of 489 species. It must surely remain the world's foremost publication of ornithological art. Audubon also produced his Ornithological Biography covering five volumes between 1831 and 1839, which was based on his journals. So for some years he was working on two of his great achievements at the same time. The science of ornithology was then at its embryonic stage and Audubon's work made a major contribution to its advancement, notably with respect to bird behaviour. Furthermore, his bird paintings incorporated attention to background and presented various aspects of American culture and landscape.

He was well recognised outside of his adopted country and in England he was bestowed several honours including membership of the prestigious Royal Society and the equally esteemed Linnaean Society. He flitted between Britain and the US exhibiting his drawings in the former to help finance his great projects. He harboured an increasing concern for the environmental degradation going on around him and urged the Secretary of State to set up a society to promote conservation in the US with himself as head.

In the meantime, he had gone on to work on a three-volume work on mammals of North America and this was later published by his two artist sons from 1845 to 1848, his own health by then starting to deteriorate, including failing eyesight. By 1847 he could no longer see to paint and he died of dementia in 1851. Such a huge tragedy for both him and the world of natural history as clearly he still had much to do.

Charles Darwin could scarcely escape the attentions of this book. Born in 1809, Darwin, having passed his childhood was, like so many in his day, destined for a life in the church. He spent a couple of years studying medicine at Edinburgh University and then a couple of years reading Theology at Cambridge. Neither ventures were completed although at Cambridge he demonstrated his passion for collecting insects, mostly beetles and also a love of logic, maths and philosophy. At the age of 22 this restless young man was offered the post as ship's naturalist on board HMS Beagle, captained by Robert Fitzroy. Fitzroy's main task was cartographical work in South America and his 27 metre vessel was crammed with 74 people so it was a bit crowded. Darwin shared a cabin with Fitzroy, who was a fully committed Christian. Darwin was then an agnostic.

The Beagle set sail from Plymouth in 1831 and over the next five years was to travel extensively, including crossings of the Indian and Pacific Oceans on the way home to the UK. In the early days of the Beagle voyage, Darwin's primary interest was geology. At any given opportunity, Darwin left the ship and went off for long treks on horseback into the grassy plains of South America and the Andes mountains. He explored, observed and collected as his stock of specimens on board steadily grew. In the penultimate year of the voyage, Darwin explored the Galapagos archipelago, which lies 1000km off the west coast of Ecuador and sits astride the equator. He noticed that the Mocking Birds on different islands showed differences between themselves. He made a collection of Ground Finches from a number of islands but, remarkably, did not notice their enormous variation in bill size and shape at the time. He also failed to label the different Ground Finches, which came from different islands, most surprising for one with such an astute mind. The finch bills were later pointed out to him by a colleague, John Gould, who helped Darwin with his collections back in England. He had also collected fossils on his five year journey. During the voyage he confirmed earlier thoughts about the formation of coral reefs, caused by subsidence of oceanic mountains. It was unfortunate that this intrepid gentleman should be a sufferer of sea sickness, a malady which on occasion found him prostrated on his bed as he dipped into the work of Charles Lyell, The Principles of Geology. As the Beagle sailed, Darwin sometimes read his grandfather's 'Zoonomia' wherein the first idea of transmutation of species was propounded.

Darwin's own ideas on the subject were being reinforced daily. He saw that biogeographical distributions were haphazard. Why were there no penguins in the north polar regions, no hummingbirds in Africa and why might a hawk in one continent have a counterpart in another? He recognized patterns of distribution and the similarities of species as pointing to relatedness rather than separate acts of creation. His small collection of fossils led him to consider the temporal aspect to variations between species as well as spatial. He put his mind to the length of time which would be necessary to bring about such changes and geology was providing just that by the study of ancient sedimentary rocks and the fossils they contained. It was proven beyond any doubt that the Earth was much much older than the 6,000 years ascribed to it by the church authorities, based on how many people 'begat' others, working backwards through biblical time – a case of a most unreliable and non-scientific text written by so many people and which had undergone various translations (just one example of religion holding up the progress of science). Together, with enough time now permitted, and his numerous communications with specialists all over the world, and of course his own brilliant deductions, he pulled together in 1842 the 'first sketch' of his major publication. By now, Darwin had jumped off the fence of agnosticism and landed with a resounding thump as a full-blown atheist. He could explain the diversity of life on Earth without the need of a God. Current political and social paradigms, some unrest in scientific circles and Darwin's wife Emma Wedgewood's devout Christianity all served to delay him publishing. His acute depression brought on by the death of his much-cherished daughter was almost certainly another contributor to his tardiness. A letter from Alfred Russel Wallace who was undertaking similar work in the Malay Peninsula and coming to the very same conclusions about origins of species forced Darwin's proverbial arm. Darwin's close friends, having talked him out of abandoning his work, the two amicably published a joint paper in 1858 and Darwin knew he could not sit on his hands any longer. He moved out of London to Kent where he resided with his family in the stately Down House, which today stands as a museum left pretty much as when the Darwins lived in it. This gave him the peace and quiet he craved to get his magnum opus finished. In 1859 the much-expected book was published, bearing the short snappy title On the Origin of Species by

Means of Natural Selection or the Preservation of Favoured Races in the Struggle for Life. It flew off the bookshop shelves and took the world by storm. It is still being repeatedly reprinted to this day. Note that the word 'evolution' does not appear in the title at all and I think I am correct in saying the entire work. That term was coined by another later with respect to the formation of species.

The church was rather miffed of course and I presume Charles and Emma remained on speaking terms as they continued life together thereafter. It has been rated by the scientific community as the most important and influential science book ever written. Put at its simplest, the core statement of the book is that as populations of animals and plants increase geometrically and only small numbers of offspring survive, nature will favour variations best suited to those particular conditions existing at that place and time leading to different races and ultimately new species. The first four chapters of 'The Origin' deal with artificial selection, which so clearly demonstrates the efficacy and speed at which us humans produced new varieties of domestic livestock, selecting for favoured traits such as appearance, milk production, fineness of wool, temperament, resistance to disease and so much more. He also drew upon experiments he had made on his return to England on plants and captive pigeons.

After publication of 'The Origin' Darwin had no interest in public-speaking but his champions Thomas Henry Huxley and Joseph Hooker of Kew Gardens stood up to rigorously defend Darwin's thesis, notably the former's battle with Bishop Wilberforce in 1860 at Oxford University. Darwin was then looking at other natural history matters including ants, orchids and climbing plants. He had wisely side-stepped any discussion in 'The Origin' about the emergence of man on the world scene (perhaps all in one go, this may have proved too much for the public to take on board). But deal with this thorny issue he certainly did, in his next book The Descent of Man, published in 1871. He went on to write The Expression of Emotions in Man and the Animals the following year, involving his own children in his research. His final offering to the world was his monograph on the lowly earthworms submitted in 1881, just one year prior to his death. He was given a stately burial in Westminster Abbey where his bones still rest along with those of Sir Isaac Newton. Both, in their respective disciplines, are upheld as the most complete scientists of all time.

While Darwin worked his own world patch, Alfred Russel Wallace was busy in his, doing pretty much the same as Darwin, initially in South America. Born in 1823, Wallace, like Darwin was a mediocre pupil who showed no special signs when at school. A friend and colleague, Henry Walter Bates and Wallace set off in 1848 to collect specimens in Amazonia and would also attempt to solve the mystery of the origin of species. Wallace remained for a further four years and amassed a huge collection of birds and insects. This was tragically all lost in a fire on a brig which was sailing to England with the entire Wallace collection. Undaunted, but doubtless pretty fed up, he later ventured forth a second time, then to the Malay Archipelago (now called Indonesia) under the auspices of Sir Roderick Murchison, then president of the Royal Geographical Society. He was alone this time and sold specimens to boost his meagre finances. His travels took him to numerous islands and over eight years he made huge collections of mostly birds and butterflies. He had recognised in the field the enormous difference between the eastern and western halves of the archipelago, split by what became known as 'Wallace's line' separating the Asian and Australian faunas. This turned out to be situated along a tectonic plate boundary.

The upshot of his admirable commitment was the idea that species arose through selection of favourable characteristics – in fact precisely what Darwin had also come to believe. He wrote to Darwin eventually and they collaborated on a joint paper in 1858, presented before the Linnaean Society. The two naturalists were in no way competitive and had great mutual respect. Darwin even organised a state pension for Wallace, which was accepted, unlike membership of the Royal Society, which Wallace declined. Another thing the two had in common was a waning faith. Wallace recognised the plight, which often accompanied animals after encountering man and rightly assumed that animals were not created for the benefit of man as the church, irresponsibly, wanted everyone to believe. He is today regarded as the father of biogeography and also a prime-mover of the appreciation of the relationships between organisms and their environment, this acquiring the name of ecology in the 1970s. Wallace died a year before the outbreak of the First World War.

Jean-Baptiste Lamarck is now pretty much known for having got it all wrong but I shall give him mention here as he was quite influential in his time and did at least offer a possible mechanism for the origin of species other than that by super-natural creation, as thrust upon us by men of the cloth. Born in France in 1744, Lamarck spent a few years in the military but then developed an interest in the natural sciences, particularly botany. He published his Flore Francaise in 1778 and in that used his own invention of the dichotomous key, still used today in plant identification guides. I recall having to devise such a key in an A-level practical Biology question wherein 10 species had to be identifiable.

Lamarck is credited with the word biology as a branch of the natural sciences. Surely not to his credit was his firm belief that life regenerated from primordial ooze. With respect to life forms becoming species, he proposed two laws. Firstly, he declared that excessive use and reduced use led to strengthening and enlarging of organs or weakness and diminution of organs respectively. His second law dictated that any resultant changes were passed on to offspring provided that the newly acquired characteristics had been present in both parents.

This second bit is quite humorous. Lamarckists would claim that a wrestler would pass his meaty muscles onto his children. But this second law requires that his good wife is also of a meaty disposition. I think such an unlikelihood would have slowed down the evolutionary process considerably! Similarly, Lamarck told us that giraffes had developed long necks due to constantly stretching up to browse on the leaves on tall trees. Of course there are few supporters of Lamarck today but in his favour he did acknowledge that the age of the Earth was indeed old enough for formation of new species to have taken place, a brave statement given the ruthlessness of the church who thought otherwise. So, was he implying that together with suitable conditions was all that was needed for, maybe, wine tasters to develop huge noses with flaring nostrils or perhaps the children of circus clowns to be born with red noses! By 1818 he was almost blind and he died a decade later, having published a final volume of invertebrate biology in 1822.

Moving now to the twentieth century brings me to two animal behaviourists whose works I read in my early teens. In fact, those two spent much time working together. Konrad Lorenz, born in 1903, was an Austrian zoologist, ethologist (practitioner of animal behaviour) and ornithologist. He is regarded as the founder of ethology along with his academic colleague Nikolaas Tinbergen. Lorenz worked a good deal with Grey Lag Geese and Jackdaws. In the case of the former he investigated the known phenomenon of 'imprinting' wherein a hatching precocious (already well developed and capable of walking) chick forms a strong bond with the first object it sees on emergence from the egg. Making himself that first object, Lorenz had lots of fun as a brood of goslings would follow him everywhere, both on land and in fresh water. His written works include King Solomon's Ring, On Aggression and Man Meets Dog, all of which I have read and recommend as they are well-laced with good humour (see Reading List). I recall his anecdote in King Solomon's Ring of his standing on Vienna railway station shouting loudly up to his pet parrot, which had flown up onto a roof beam and was misbehaving. After he had acquired no small audience the recalcitrant bird finally flew down from the high building and alighted on his shoulders, stroking Lorenz's cheeks with its head. Lorenz firmly believed that animals were capable of feeling many emotions that we do, as indeed do I (see chapter 13). Both he and other workers in the field of human psychology felt that parts of Lorenz's studies had relevance to the human condition but here is no place to discuss that further. Suffice to say that in 1973 he published Behind the Mirror: A Search for a Natural History of Human Knowledge. In 1973 he and Tinbergen shared the Nobel Prize in the Physiology or Medicine category for elicitation of individual and social behaviour patterns in animals.

Lorenz and Tinbergen together were instrumental in developing ethology as a fully-fledged sub-discipline of biology. Nikolaas 'Niko' Tinbergen was born in 1907. He was a Dutch biologist and ornithologist who in 1951 published The Study of Instinct. After WW2 he moved permanently to England where he lectured at the University of Oxford. His graduate students include Professor Richard Dawkins famed for his bestseller book titled the Selfish Gene and Dr Desmond Morris, author of the The Naked Ape (both of these disciples went on to produce many fine books, several of which are classics). Tinbergen became a member of the Royal Society in 1962 and was awarded a medal by the British Ornithologists' Union.

A lot of his work focused on 'supernormal stimuli' which were artificially created models larger and brighter than the original stimuli. He made a wooden male Three-spined Stickleback on which he painted unusually bright red undersides. A real male stickleback would attack this more vigorously than it would another real stickleback. He found birds more keen to sit on dummy eggs, which were larger and more prominently marked than their own eggs. In 1953, he published a monograph called the Herring Gull's World. I recall reading this when at school wherein he makes wooden models of Herring Gull heads twice the size of heads of real birds and with relatively larger and brighter red spots on the end of the lower mandibles. The chicks normally peck at these to stimulate the parent birds to regurgitate food for them and did so with much more zeal when the models were introduced.

Another field of biology is that dealing with life in the oceans, marine biology. Surely it is Jacques-Yves Cousteau whose name comes to the fore here. Born in France in 1910, he became a naval officer but later ventured out to become explorer, conservationist, innovator (he designed and pioneered the aqualung), scientist, film-maker, author and researcher. With his trusty and committed crew he sailed the five oceans in his ship 'Calypso' which became the focus for a superb John Denver song, JD being a fervent wildlife conservationist himself. The high quality footage Cousteau produced of life in the sea and delivered to our living rooms must surely be commended as an enormous contribution to popularisation of this oh so huge subject. However, it is said in scientific circles that even today we have only covered just a very few per cent of what dwells below the surface of the world's oceans.

There is one man, still very much amongst us who has made such an impact in the fields of natural history that I scarcely know how to adequately cover his cornucopia of achievements. I speak of course of broadcaster/naturalist Sir David Attenborough. Born in 1926, he spent his formative years collecting fossils in the rock formations in his native Leicester. He lived on the campus of University College, Leicester where his father was principal. His caring parents had fostered two Jewish refugee girls from Germany. At the age of 19 he won a scholarship to Cambridge where he read Geology/Zoology. In 1947 he was called up and entered the Royal Navy, serving two years. Shortly after he married Jane with whom he had two children, the son Robert taking up a lectureship in Bio-anthropology at the Australian National University in Canberra. His daughter Susan became the headmistress of a primary school. At the time of his marriage he was working as an editor of children's science textbooks. In 1952, he joined the BBC as a trainee but soon became bored and restless and considered how he might escape the confines of the studio and get out to make wildlife films. He embarked on what was to develop into a series of expeditions, which took him on animal collecting ventures to Madagascar, Guyana, Paraguay and Komodo (Indonesia). Working with a regular film crew, he would spend time with and film native tribes-people, at times himself wearing little more than a loin-cloth. Some of these people had never before seen white people, something I experienced myself when birding in dense forest on an island in Lake Victoria, Uganda where I showed them my bird field guide pictures and they gave me cormorant meat for lunch. He would return after each trip to present their films plus the exhibiting of various animals in the studio. These 'Zoo Quest' programmes proved extremely popular and each were written up in well-written and often quite humorous books. For any admirers of Sir David (and he certainly has plenty) I recommend this series of books all of which I have savoured in my early years. Never idle, he was always busy with his filming exploits and a series called Eastwards with Attenborough featured on TV, similar to the Zoo Quest series but minus the collecting element.

In 1965 as controller of the BBC, he

introduced the first colour TV broadcasts, airing programmes like Kenneth Clark's 'Civilisation', Professor Jacob Bronowski's 'Ascent of Man', Pot Black, a snooker programme shown to demonstrate this new use of colour and that revolution in British humour, 'Monty Python's Flying Circus'. It was in 1979 when his 'Life' programmes began. These started off with general treatments of global natural history with Life on Earth, the Living Planet and Trials of Life. These programmes were sweeping up huge TV viewing audiences and each was followed by a beautifully written and photograph-laden book. His programmes followed with no breaks, these covering various taxa of animals including Life of Mammals, Life of Birds, and Life in the Undergrowth, which dealt with the largely unknown field of invertebrates. His work knew no bounds and his Private Life of Plants was, predictably, a huge success, using time-lapsed photography and taking years to complete. He even took us into the ocean depths with his Blue Planet TV series, which itself was later trumped by Blue Planet II wherein the scourge of plastic pollution of our oceans really made an impact on the public and sparked off a worldwide movement to tackle this shameful issue. His plunge into the oceans revealed many species of invertebrate never before filmed and some were new to science. The Dumbo Octopus was one such creature. Again, each programme series was followed by a book. My bookshelves are graced by all of Sir David Attenborough's books and I have learnt so much in reading them.

In 1985 DA was knighted, being on that year's Queen's Birthday Honours List. He was now Sir David Attenborough. In the year 2000 he made a remarkable series of three programmes called State of the Planet. This was a kind of stock-take of the world's biodiversity followed by an outline of some of the problems facing life on Earth. The final programme covered various projects which were attempting to solve some of those problems. That series was indeed an eye-opener for naturalists, non-naturalists, and even, maybe, politicians.

In addition to narrating the programmes, Sir David has been instrumental in pioneering new camera technology and broadcasting techniques. An example was those cameras hidden about the environment such as 'dung-cam', a small tennis-ball sized camera pushed into the middle of a chunk of elephant poo or one hidden in a rotting log (log-cam). Apart from travelling the Earth laterally, he also rose to great heights in an air-balloon, where he caught with a sort of vacuum cleaner, aerial spiders kept aloft by updraughts of air. Conversely, he took us down to the ocean depths in a specially reinforced metal bathysphere. He even experienced weightlessness as he went up into the upper atmosphere and then careered down in a Boeing 747 wherein he countered the force of gravity. The aircraft, with good reason, was christened the 'vomit comet'.

Sir David has had over 20 species named after him, mostly invertebrates but also one dinosaur, Attenborosaurus and one bird, Polioptila attenboroughi, a kind of gnat-catcher. He has amassed 32 honorary degrees from British universities and in 2016 the new British polar research ship was named after him, the RRS Sir David Attenborough. I wonder if he himself can remember the over 40 awards that have been conferred upon him. His published books number over 30 and he has written numerous forewords and introductions in the works of others. Never really a politically active force, he has in more recent years been more vocal as conditions become more desperate. He recently spoke out against the carnage of albatrosses due to entanglement in long-line fishing gear. He was interviewed by Barack Obama at the White House where they discussed pressing environmental issues. This was not a publicity move for Barack Obama – he too is genuinely concerned about the plight of the planet.

Sir David has been criticised for being too soft on those who damage the Earth's fragile ecosystems but I suppose he feels his role is to educate and leave it up to the public to form their own opinions rather than be embroiled in constant battles with ignorant business folk and politicians who are more concerned with annual bonuses and votes respectively. He has also been lambasted for his failure to mention God in his programmes. Like so many enlightened people, he says he does not see the need for a creator – all can be explained by the evolutionary process. I like his logic when he relates the story of the parasitic worm infecting a child's eye as he sits on a river bank in West Africa, the worm slowly burrowing its way through the child's eyeball causing him to go blind. Sir David asks how such a merciful God may dream up and conjure up such useless but harmful creatures. Sir David has been blasted most pertinently for showing various animals killing each other. He showed nature doing its thing, warts and all. How easy it is when people are extolling God's virtues to speak only of beautiful butterflies, hummingbirds, cuddly white bears and cutely bespectacled pandas.

Sir David Attenborough has done more than any other single person to help us understand and appreciate the wonders of the world of which we are just a part, and in terms of duration of occupancy of the planet, a very small part indeed. His programmes have gone a long way in smashing the absurd idea that all other life-forms are here for us. Every single animal and plant species alive today was flourishing on Earth long before our entrance to the world stage.

I shall close this chapter of the greats by briefly mentioning the trimates. The trimates I hear you say, do you not mean primates? Indeed no. The trimates is a snappy term coined by Louis Leakey for three ladies who came into his life. These are Jane Goodall, Dian Fossey and Birute Galdikas each of whom made detailed studies of Chimpanzees, Mountain Gorillas and Orangutans respectively. Apart from sharing a common interest in the great apes, each of these ladies spent long durations with their study subjects, they each went to Cambridge University colleges and each were taken under the wing of archaeologist Louis Leakey, who did much of his work in Kenya.

Jane Goodall is an English primatologist/anthropologist born in 1934. She lived with Chimpanzees for some years and studied them for over 60, working in Tanganyika (now Tanzania). She is one of the very few people who completed a PhD without having done an undergraduate BSc or BA degree. She witnessed displays of aggression, including chimps tearing monkeys apart as well as showing deep affection and told the story without any sloppy anthropomorphism. Her legacy is the Jane Goodall Institute set up in 1977, which looks at wide-ranging African conservation issues. She has written 15 books plus a further 10 for children and is the subject of over 40 films. She is still with us aged 90. Dian Fossey was an American primatologist/conservationist and made an extensive study of Mountain Gorillas in Rwanda. Born in 1932 her life was cut tragically short when she was brutally murdered in her study hut, probably by a poacher although one of her assistants was a suspect. She had taken a PhD at Darwin College, Cambridge in 1970. In 1983 she wrote her famous book Gorillas in the Mist. Birute Galdikas was a Lithuanian/Canadian primatologist born in 1946 who studied Orangutans in SE Asia.

All of the above mentioned passionate people, together with so many more, have each left their legacies, either in the form of the written word, in the form of drawings and paintings, as documentaries and also as stuffed specimens, which are housed in our museums and private collections. There must be thousands of people working behind closed doors and out in the field working for their PhDs and thus furthering our body of ornithological knowledge. Our own work on bird migration across the Himalaya, 1976 to 1982 (see chapter 27) confirmed that migratory birds are flying over the tops of vast snow-covered ranges for hundreds of miles to move to more favourable conditions. As I write, all over the world, there will be specialist naturalists hacking through dense forests, crossing baking deserts, ascending great altitudes, diving great depths, staring down microscopes, photographing high nests on precarious tree-platforms, huddling in tents, wringing out wet socks all in the name of good science. All are carried by their enthusiasm and commitment and disregard for comfort and dry socks.

There will continue to be other pioneers – there is no shortage of ornithological research to be done, and as in all spheres of knowledge, the more we know then the more questions are raised. People sometimes say to me, "It's all been done." This is total nonsense. Take trouble if you will to stare down at a large atlas such as the Times Atlas. Look around the oceans. Those little splods you see are not biscuit crumbs, they are small islands but when you look at the scale of the map you will appreciate that most of those small islands would take several days to walk round. Look at the huge mountain ranges and the valleys between, all currently guarding their secrets. Many places on Earth are completely scientifically unexplored. The days of the traditional university expeditions are far from over. Any good expedition comes back with lots of answers but it also comes back with lots of questions. It was Einstein who said that as the circle of light expands (knowledge) then so too does the area of darkness (questions) around it.

22. COME AND JOIN MY GANG...

In these times when we hear all the doom and gloom of looming extinctions, climate change and illegal wildlife trafficking let's cheer ourselves up a bit by considering all those splendid organisations trying their best to protect the world's plants and animals. Dealing initially with those concerned directly with bird conservation, we will also consider those outfits with a broader base in the natural sciences.

From early age, most of us like to belong to clubs, where we enjoy mingling with like-minded individuals. I recall being a member of the YOC (Young Ornithologists Club), a sort of sub-branch of the RSPB that helped to put young birders in the same county in touch and I made a good birding friend, who also lived in Colchester. It was great to get the monthly magazine and to learn what was going on in other parts of the country. Then there was the Essex Naturalists' Trust and the Essex Birdwatching Society, each adding to what it was to be a birder. If any of you have children or grandchildren who are into birds or indeed any other wildlife, then I fully recommend the joining of a club.

The Royal Society for the Protection of Birds (RSPB) is the UK's largest conservation charity, established in 1889. It was started up by three ladies. Emily Williamson formed the Plumage League, which set about to ban the use of Great Crested Grebe and Kittiwake feathers for gracing ladies' hats. The other two ladies were the first Fur, Fin and Feather Folk (what splendid alliteration). These combined and rapidly grew to become the RSPB which today boasts over a million members. With more than 1,300 staff and 18,000 volunteers, it runs in excess of 200 reserves nearly all of which have resident wardens. One such told me that the annual Warden's Conference was more like the Bearded Men's conference. The wardens spend much of their time undertaking land management tasks. Many of the reserves have hides and visitor information centres. I had the pleasure of being one of three of us who erected the visitor centre on the Ouse Washes in 1977. Can I please explode a myth here? Wardening on a bird reserve is not wandering around with your bins bird watching. That might happen once a month if lucky. Most of the work I was engaged in on the Ouse Washes involved numerous land management tasks and often getting caked in sticky clay. Even so, the work was extremely rewarding and kept us mega-fit. My wardening on Fetlar, monitoring Snowy Owls, was very different and was an example of concentrating efforts on a single species. That too was so very rewarding. These two wardening periods of my life are presented in chapters 25 and 26 of this book, covering both scientific and social aspects of the work.

The British Trust for Ornithology (BTO) formed in 1933 after a meeting of minds at the British Museum (Natural History). Its primary aim was bird ringing to learn about migration routes and wintering areas. These days it is more concerned with population research. It also houses one of the largest collections of bird skins in the world and thus serves as a rich reference for modern researchers such as taxonomists and bird artists.

The British Ornithologist's Union is very much academic. It encourages the study of birds and an understanding of bird biology, ecology and conservation. It opened in 1858 since when it has produced its prestigious quarterly journal, Ibis, which publishes scholarly articles.

Moving down to a more local level, Britain has about 46 county trusts, all of which are charities. Over 2,300 reserves exist, which vary greatly in extent with respect to size and habitat. Some counties are too small to have their own trust so they amalgamate with others, such as BBONT, which is the trust covering Berkshire, Buckinghamshire and Oxford. When I was on the Ouse Washes, my actual employer was CAMBIENT (Cambridgeshire and Isle of Ely Naturalist's Trust) who supply an assistant warden every summer to the RSPB.

Some locations may become SSSIs. These are Sites of Special Scientific Interest and over 4,000 sites harbouring rare or uncommon plants and animals are managed and monitored, primarily by volunteers. These can be fruitful grounds for PhD students, who can set up experiments free of disturbance. Call me cynical, but I have the impression that an SSSI will enjoy that status only until it succumbs to a higher force. Bypasses, industrial developments, housing projects may all win the day presenting the case that it is of 'national interest'. I bet HS2 is taking its toll of such important sites.

Some private ventures have made a huge impact in bird conservation. Slimbridge in Gloucestershire comprises 800 hectares of saltmarsh, reedbeds and lagoons, providing sanctuary for many thousands of ducks, geese and swans, which include both breeding and wintering birds. Slimbridge is also extremely important as a feeding ground for waders. It was founded by Sir Peter Scott (son of Robert Falcon Scott of the Antarctic) and since then a further eight more reserves have been established in the UK.

The National Trust in Britain, dating from 1895, covers a very broad spectrum, but is largely there for the conservation of stately homes and estates. Having over 500 under its wing it must surely provide safe havens for numerous birds and I am sure each will have its token Peacocks wandering around.

As this crowded green and pleasant land becomes ever-more urbanised it is important that agriculture plays an increasing role in environmental protection. Many farmers today are proving that farming can work alongside conservation to some extent. My good friend Andy farms 400 acres in Hampshire and he now, in his later years, is putting up feeding stations and looking after rich meadowland ideal for butterflies and other insects. He has also put up owl boxes, which is a far cry from the situation less than 70 years ago when many farmers killed owls and indeed just about anything with a hooked beak. More environmentally friendly pesticides and fertilizers are being introduced and the particularly dangerous and persistent organochlorides have been phased out. Some farmers will take school trips around their farms and even give talks to local groups.

Global organisations include the WWF, set up by Peter Scott in 1961. He later received a knighthood for his services to wildlife. The WWF concerns itself with protection of wilderness areas and the reduction of global human impact on the environment. WWF formerly stood for World Wildlife Fund but today means Worldwide Fund for Nature. It has over five million supporters in more than one hundred countries and is currently involved in around three thousand projects. Its funds come largely from individuals such as bequests and from governments and corporations.

The IUCN (International Union for the

Conservation of Nature) is the home of the Red Data Book, sometimes referred to as the Red List, mentioned in an earlier chapter. Currently, 116,000 species of animals, plants and fungi fill the pages, one quarter of which are approaching extinction, including many birds.

Wetlands International based in the Netherlands is fully engaged with preservation of the world's vital wetlands and waterways which, in addition to providing much of the world's fresh water, secure habitats for water birds and other creatures. Many wetlands are drained to make way for agriculture and urban expansion so wetlands are under considerable threats worldwide.

Africa is famed for its game parks, also called national parks. These are normally quite extensive in area and serve as refuges for countless animals. Birds, which of course can freely fly in and out of the park boundaries do enjoy some level of protection as tourists cannot just wander around these reserves and generally have to remain in their vehicles. Some national parks do have resident human populations but others have moved people out completely.

Somali bandits abound in Kenya's game parks and the Kenya Wildlife Service regularly flies over the parks in search of these poachers, adopting a 'shoot to kill' policy. Most of the parks are funded by governments and employ nationals as rangers. Today, many of these rangers are ex-poachers, who know the ways of wild animals and are thus well-suited to the job. Having spent 27 years in Africa, I visited quite a few game parks although much of my birding took place in the open 'bush' so one did have to be wary at times of predators who may possibly give you a hard time. I do maintain, however, that very few wild animals will attack a human unless they feel its young are being threatened. Controlled hunting is allowed in some national parks, notably in Tanzania. The funds received in exchange for the shooting licences go back into conservation. This does make perfect sense as some animal populations must essentially be culled to control burgeoning populations. So if they have to be killed why not drag in a mindless, ruthless but wealthy hunter to do the job?

Some spectacular locations are given the label World Heritage Sites. These are places where the profundity of wildlife excels or perhaps the geology is of particular interest. To mention a few: the Jurassic Coast of southern England (famous for its fossil-laden limestones); the Grand Canyon, which has many millions of years of fossil-packed sedimentary strata stacked up like pages of a book; Yellowstone National Park (the home of Yogi Bear), Yosemite National Park (the latter three being in North America) and the Florida Everglades, also in North America and heaving with water birds and alligators. The Great Barrier Reef off the eastern coast of Australia plays host to thousands of fish species (and consequently other creatures) and the Galapagos Islands 1,000 km from the coast of Ecuador is home to Galapagos Flightless Cormorants, the Galapagos Penguins, numerous other bird species and of course the famous Land and Marine Iguanas and the Giant Tortoises after which the islands are named. There are many other World Heritage Sites.

Bird Observatories, discussed in chapter 8, deal with the ringing of birds and are not really conservation undertakings although their long-term results may have some such value such as increasing our understanding of populations.

Coming down even more locally, there are doubtless numerous school bird clubs all over the world. Although I was already quite interested in birds, it was not until one of our primary school science teachers, Mr Ewbank, set up a nature room and also took out groups of pupils in his own vehicle to nearby birding sites. Do that today and you'll have the Social Services banging on your door. He would take us after school sometimes and I remember him showing me my first Magpie, Sparrowhawk, Green Woodpecker and Kingfisher. I once took him a dead Emperor Moth (one of Britain's largest moths) in a tobacco tin for the nature room. On opening it, the moth took off and careered around the room and was later given its freedom. I recall chatting with Mr Ewbank's son, also a pupil at my school, who was not the slightest bit interested in wildlife and preferred the absorbing pastime of collecting car numbers! Wow! Did I miss out?

What of government protection of birds in the UK? Basically, all birds, their nests, eggs and young are fully protected but there are exceptions, mainly for pests, game birds and wildfowl. Under the auspices of the Wildlife and Countryside Act 1981, the various exceptions are outlined. Pests may be those who feed on our crops such as Wood Pigeons or those who constitute a health hazard. Birds maybe a real risk at airports as they may fly, individually or in flocks into a jet engine, with disastrous consequences – this is called 'bird strike' (see chapter 17). Game birds and wildfowl are shot for the pot and there are seasons when this is permissible. In Britain the wildfowling season starts on September 1 and ends on January 31. In some cases the open season dates may vary between different nations of the UK and may also differ according to species. In all UK countries no birds may be taken on Sundays or Christmas Day. Cliff, the warden on the Ouse Washes told me of a group of Italian wildfowlers who were intercepted by himself, police officers and other RSPB representatives (following a tip-off) and discovered a sack of birds including Lapwing, Fieldfare and many other non-wildfowl and fully protected species.

One of my favourite TV films is The Snow Goose where a bunch of wildfowlers in the Suffolk marshes shoot a Snow Goose, it being unfamiliar to them. The bird was wounded and taken along to a coastal observation tower by a young lady named Fritha (Jenny Agutter). The chap who lived there (Richard Harris) and her nursed it back to health. Having later migrated to the high Arctic, the bird returns the following year to the site where it was restored to health. The film was based on a book by Paul Gallico and is available online.

Coming even further down to the micro-level there must be millions of bird tables in Britain, providing sustenance to numerous birds in times of need (primarily winter) and collectively they must save unknown numbers of birds every year.

Of indirect value, museums provide an excellent educational service if they have natural history collections as most have to some extent. My favourite building in the whole world is the Natural History Museum in Kensington, London. Many teachers take their students along on day trips. A huge amount of research goes on 'below stairs' in our great museums. I have heard it said that some of the specimens brought back by Captain Cook's expeditions still await identification and classification, preserved in casks of rum. I expect many other scientific collections there are also still awaiting specialist attention, going back as far as those of Captain Cook made in the mid-eighteenth century. Whenever I shifted to my next African country, I immediately checked out if there was a natural history museum. There were particularly good ones in Nairobi and Addis Ababa and I would take students there.

Some may justify zoos as centres of education but I remain totally unconvinced. They are also claimed to undertake research and breeding programmes of rare species but a TV programme I watched tended to suggest this was greatly exaggerated. Releasing cage-bred animals into the wild is of dubious merit in my opinion and is side-stepping the main issues. When I was about 11 years old my uncle took me to Whipsnade Zoo. I sobbed profusely on seeing large formerly majestic cats pacing up and down a concrete floor and elephants swaying their heads from side to side staring out in front of them doubtless wondering how the hell life had come to this. Even at that young age, I vowed to myself never to visit a zoo again or to take my children to such a place.

TV documentaries educate us on the world's wildlife and the subtle interconnections within ecosystems. Sir David Attenborough must surely be at the top of the pyramid when it comes to wildlife film-makers and narrators. We owe so much to that fine gentleman who always remained the scientist and never fell into the trap of over sentimentality. Professor Brian Cox seems destined to be the ideal successor to Sir David as he broadens his base from astronomy to wildlife. The word 'biodiversity' can now roll off the lips of bar-room chatterers, which can only be encouraging. The place of ourselves in nature is slowly being more widely understood and appreciated and more and more of us are becoming aware of the plight of our animals and plants, with all of us living on this spaceship called Earth and many wanting to get involved. I used to teach geography and biology so I was well-placed to spread the good word and wherever possible spoke of the importance of humans being good stewards of our wonderful, and possibly unique planet.

A NOTE FOR READERS

The following four chapters 24 to 27 are personal accounts and are more anecdotal. They delve a little less into scientific matters. Chapter 24 deals with a birding excursion I was asked to lead in Ethiopia in 1988, a venture that did not go quite as planned! Chapters 25 and 26 cover my working on two RSPB bird reserves, each demanding very different approaches. The first covers the time in 1971 when three others and myself spent our working shifts staring at the rarest two birds in Britain at the time. The second relates to the summer I was wardening on another RSPB reserve in 1977, which I include to relay to some readers who may be surprised that working on a bird reserve is far from wandering around looking at birds. Chapter 27 covers four expeditions to the NW Himalaya (between 1976 and 1982) where others and myself were involved in research into resident breeding birds and more importantly, trans-Himalayan migrant species.

23. NEVER AGAIN...

The monthly field-outing of the Ethiopian Wildlife Society was coming up. The British Ambassador, Sir Michael Samuels was the society's secretary and was a good friend of the international school I was teaching in. Knowing of my penchant for birds, he asked me if I would lead it. I was so relieved that he was still talking to me as during the school pantomime just one week earlier, I had stood on his lines in one scene and completely messed him up. I agreed to lead the trip, happy in the knowledge that I had time yet to travel out to the site and check it out for bird potential. It was to be a bird watching excursion to a sizeable lake (Lake Gurfasa) 25km to the north of Addis Ababa. The lake served as a reservoir and also the reed beds were harvested annually for roofing material. There was some mixed woodland running adjacent to the lake just beyond its marshy shoreline.

Two days later I travelled by motorbike (I had a Russian Ural 650) to the lake and spent a highly productive afternoon there, seeing a variety of waterfowl, a few wader species and some woodland stuff. Several raptors also put in appearances. I don't really like birding in large groups but my visit cheered me up and I was actually looking forward to the trip in another five days' time. Martin, one of my flatmates and fellow geography teacher asked if he could join me as he had a peripheral interest in wildlife and wanted to increase his knowledge of the local area.

The day arrived. Aynellum, our live-in house assistant had made us up a substantial packed lunch. Such choices we left up to her as she knew that the three of us in the flat ate just about everything. Martin and I took just the one small rucksack equipped with light waterproofs, a field guide, notebook and of course our lunch. It was early on a Saturday morning when we all met up in the Post Office car park and boarded the hired coach. We were 32 in number and were predominantly expatriates with just a few Ethiopians, some of whom I knew to work at the British Embassy. Fifty minutes later, the coach arrived at Lake Gurfasa, the driver having had to stop and wait while a fuel station opened. Why had he not sorted this out earlier at the bus depot? It was just a minor irritation and nothing serious and in no way gave me forewarning of how the day would unfold.

It was around a quarter to nine on an overcast and slightly chilly morning. The water-bailiff was waiting there for us as he was obliged to accompany us for the duration. The coach disgorged its passengers and we all stood there huddled together like a bunch of penguins. I realized everyone was looking over at me – I felt like the Messiah who was expected to issue forth great words of wisdom. "Right," I quipped confidently, "I have only been here once before but I can assure you it's a good spot. Let's move across to that reed bed over there."

Among the assembled party was a Dr Rory Dravers, a high-up UN agricultural advisor who was to be in Ethiopia for some months. He had come to the school the previous week and given a talk on Ethiopia's potential to be Africa's bread basket due to its highly fertile black cotton soils. He had come across then as quite a character and clearly not the sort of person with whom to mess. His 'daughter', although I think the relationship was cosier than that, had come along to do some sketching and was to seek out her first pitch. Armed with her folding seat, she asked Dr Dravers for the shoulder bag he was carrying, which contained her materials. Not having another bag, Dr Dravers asked if he could put his lunch-pack in someone else's. I readily responded, passing him my rucksack, eager to secure the friendship of this fellow thespian. Martin, in the meantime, was still on the bus ministering his kindly attention to an elderly lady who was feeling 'a bit wobbly 'and in no way was field-trip material.

I intended to keep a record of the day's sightings as I had been asked to write the trip up in the Embassy monthly magazine, which bore the awful nationalistic name of 'The Bulldog'.

The pen I had brought along was stuck fast between a seat and the side panelling as I had used it to try to dislodge a small scorpion, noticed en route. It was probably not deadly but I would have felt better having removed the creature. I was thus without a pen.

Seeing my plight and pre-empting my question, the Ambassador held out his own pen and said, "You can borrow this Mr Denby but do take good care of it – rather special don't you know."

I took it gratefully and refrained from asking what was so special about it, although I did note the engraved wording, 'for slippery Sam on our twenty-fifth.'

As we arrived at the reed bed, I began to speak, "Now at this time of year I would expect to…"

At that moment I was drowned out by the horrendous noise of a nearby chainsaw. It lasted for about 15 seconds, then stopped. Catching my puzzled glance in his direction, the water-bailiff informed me, quite cheerily I must add, that a bit of selective felling was going on in the nearby forest. The chainsaw resumed its cacophonous roar and was followed by a deafening crash of what must have been a substantial tree. I turned to my loyal flock and said it was pointless trying to see anything at that spot and ushered everybody on to the open lake.

As we progressed, I stopped to point out a small party of Yellow-Billed Duck.

"Are you sure Mr Derby?" asked a very rotund

lady. "Their bills don't look very yellow to me."

I politely, but emphatically assured her of my identification.

A little further round the shore the same lady started complaining about the marshy conditions underfoot. I stared down at her footwear, which might have been better suited to an office party. Casting my eyes around, I saw a few more old dears who were equally under-dressed for the occasion. Rather irritated, I stressed that lake shores did tend to be a bit boggy, which is why I had sensibly donned my wellies.

Shortly after we were nearing another patch of reeds and I heard a rather unfamiliar grating noise. It then struck me. "Ah, some species of crake I expect – I doubt we will see it but I know crakes to make that sort of noise." We stood still but the noise grew louder. The crake was heading our way. And then the noise producer revealed itself. There was no need for binoculars as it stood well over a metre-and-a-half tall and was only 10 metres away. There before us was an almost naked man, his 'manhood' scarcely concealed by his minimal loincloth, carrying a large scythe, a sharpening stone and a broad grin. So much for my crake. I consulted the bailiff who told me that once a year the local people were allowed to cut reeds to repair the roofs of their huts. By now I was dearly wishing I was somewhere else – anywhere but here with several hours yet to go. This feeling was reinforced as I noticed that the party was starting to fragment. Less than half the people had binoculars and most of them seemed oblivious of my role in the proceedings. Heaving an audible sigh of frustration, I urged those near to me to head towards the forest. En route one of the ladies sidled up and asked why I was teaching in Africa and made her point that charity begins at home. I demonstrably retorted that my chosen art was not charity and that children the world over need education, so why not see the world at the same time. I hesitated but thought better of asking what the hell she was doing in Ethiopia. I escaped her simply by quickening my pace.

As I was catching up with the main party, I saw coming back towards us a sight most terrible. Two of the earlier breakaways had gone off and were now returning, still managing to pick yet more flowers while they each reeled under respective armfuls of Reed-mace, Iris, and a whole nosegay of wildflowers. I was furious and rounded upon them, shouting that it was far more socially minded to leave the flora in place for all to enjoy. They said they would report me to my headmistress for such rudeness and I informed them that I would be telling her well before they had their chance. It seemed that half the party had by now returned to the bus, probably because of a bit of light drizzle, which was falling. I suggested to the stalwarts that we investigate a nearby willow copse. As we walked, Mrs rotund-lady stopped and raised her binoculars. She pointed to a tree and said there was an Osprey sitting on the bole of a dead Eucalyptus tree.

"Ah yes, actually it's a young African Fish Eagle," I informed the group.

This awful woman went on to say that she had seen Ospreys in Scotland and stated most energetically that it was an Osprey.

"Very well, it's an Osprey," I said wearily as I swept my arm dismissively to the side. I then caught sight of her binoculars and asked if I could see them. I looked through them and thought at first that the lens caps must still be on. It was quite impossible to see, let alone identify anything through these archaic optics.

"They were my grandfather's you know," she piped up proudly.

"Indeed," I retorted as indignantly as I could muster.

The drizzle had turned to light rainfall and a few more people made their way back to the bus. There was now only Martin, myself and half a dozen others remaining. As we entered the copse a covey of partridges sprung up explosively (as they do) and an elderly gentleman, who already did not look a well man, was so startled he had to sit down on a log to be consoled by his wife. I truly believed he might die from shock but we were at least spared that event on this highly eventful day. The others now also returned to the bus, I presumed just to sit it out until the rain stopped. Even the water-bailiff was nowhere to be seen.

Martin turned to me and said, "Come on mate, let's get into that woodland out of the rain. This bunch of geriatrics don't give a toss about your words of wisdom – stuff the lot of 'em."

I didn't argue. As we approached the wood, we met a forestry worker who was pruning trees. We asked him where we might get a hot drink and he directed us along a path leading into the wood. He said there was a small shack which served as a café and bar for the foresters. We happened upon a rather dilapidated corrugated iron structure, which did indeed turn out to be the place we sought.

The door to the shack was ajar and as we entered, there before us stood a most beautiful, indeed quite etherial lady who was preparing coffee the traditional Ethiopian way (it would take a large chapter to explain this so I will spare you). In a grate a couple of logs were burning, such a welcome sight, and one which adequately warmed the small space. A hundred year old sofa, which had clearly lost much of its stuffing lay along the back wall and a low table lay before it. We had a couple of coffees each and then asked if she had beer. There was but it was not at all chilled and then she offered up a bottle of brandy. Martin and I were not spirit drinkers but, well, why not. We each supped a generous brandy, followed by another. We were in heaven. A few hailstones had penetrated the tree canopy and were pinging on the iron roof of the shack. Conversation became impossible but also unnecessary. As the hail subsided, Martin reminded me I was carrying the lunch. I reached in the pack and pulled out a load of sandwiches wrapped in a tea towel, something Aynellum had not done before. There was also a large bar of hazelnut chocolate. We established the barlady's name was Emebet and we presented her with a sandwich. They smelt wonderful and tasted even better. They were crab paste with mayonnaise and, with our sharing them with Emebet, they were soon all gone. We washed them down with another two brandies. Martin asked what time the bus was supposed to leave to get back to Addis. We had over an hour, so one final brandy would slip down easily. A couple of forest workers came in just as we were leaving and as I rose, I felt rather unsteady on my legs. Martin and I were giggling a lot, like a pair of naughty schoolboys. We handed Emebet the remainder of the chocolate and both of us promised we would return to see her in the near future. We did return a month later to take her a framed photo Martin took of Emebet and her daughter on our first visit.

It was still raining and quite heavily now. The forest floor was tough going as the soil was already water-logged and the place was a quagmire. Numerous rivulets ran across our path. The going was really slow, due largely to our intoxicated state. We simultaneously broke into a run on a drier patch to ensure we made the bus in time. Still we were giggling. I then hooked my foot under a tree root and took a tumble. My entire front was covered in wet mud and my face was slightly bloodied. Oh how Martin giggled. I must have looked like I had been on a commando course. With alternate walking, scraping clay off our boots and spells of running, we reached the edge of the wood. It was just ten minutes after the time the bus should have left but there it was standing 200m away.

We got to the doors and had a final scrape of our boots. Thirty faces stared back at us, some clearly angry, some sad and others simply blank.

"Sorry everybody, had to take shelter, managed to find some old shack – dead lucky really – certainly did come down didn't it?" I said, desperately trying to speak clearly.

"This old shack, made of gingerbread was it?" came a voice from the rear of the bus. It was the Ambassador.

"Anyway, only 10 minutes late – sorry again," I offered while carefully avoiding eye contact with anybody.

It was Dr Rory Dravers turn to speak. "Actually my dear friends, we've been sitting on this bus since two o'clock so you are in fact well over two hours late. Had you been with us, as I believe was the arrangement, we would now be back in Addis."

The Ambassador signalled the driver to set off. But before he could do so, Martin went to where the flower-picking ladies were sitting, grabbed the flowers up and tossed them demonstrably out of the door. The women said nothing. The only empty seats were immediately in front of where the Ambassador was sitting.

The bus made progress, although the moribund windscreen wipers struggled to do their job and it was very difficult to see out of the windscreen. That was the least of our problems. But at least the problems were over and all was quiet in the bus. That was not to last.

Sir Michael Samuels leant over the back of our seat and asked, "Got my pen?"

I felt urgently into the top pockets of the mud-caked canvas jacket I was wearing. Then the side pockets. And then I stood to fumble in my jeans pockets. I ran out of places to fumble. I dearly wished I had a cyanide suicide pill that spies reputedly carry. A massive surge of panic overtook me and for the first time in my life I was incapable of speech. My mouth would not work. Merely a sort of whimper was emitted. Finally, I explained that we had been running (I thought this might help) and that I had taken a tumble. I asked that the bus may be stopped so I might retrace my steps to find the pen. I explained I could probably find the place in about 20 minutes.

"What?" the Ambassador bellowed. "You keep us sitting here for well over two hours and now you want to delay these good people further." He turned to his wife and mumbled something.

I said I would of course replace the pen. "It was a Parker wasn't it your excellency?" I said with my voice sounding rather crackly.

He informed me that it was indeed a top-of-the-range Parker with a silver case and was a wedding anniversary present from his wife. His wife went on to say how the pen was engraved and that it had travelled much of Africa with her husband.

I stood up and shouted to the driver to stop. The Ambassador countered this and ordered me to be seated and to shut up, before he did something that would lose him his job. Some minutes passed as Martin stared out of the window and I stared down at my feet. Even Martin was now really fed up with me.

Time stood still. And then I became aware of Dr Dravers standing over us, with a menacing grin.

"My lunch Mr Denby, can I have it please?" he asked calmly.

Martin quickly responded to this and cast his stare away from the window and towards me. I heard him mumble, "My God, how on earth do you manage it?"

His brain was operating faster than mine but

mine was not that far behind. "Oh God Mr Dravers... Dr Dravers isn't it... I er... well we er... well it was more me... I forgot you had put it in our bag."

Martin by now had a hand over his eyes and was shaking his head in disbelief.

Dr Dravers spoke again, "Well I did not starve as you can see. But can I have it now please?"

After an age of silence and with a childlike whimper, I managed to convey the words, "We ate it."

Dr Dravers stroked his chin and then the back of his neck. Then he slowly raised his head until he was staring directly up at the ceiling and after maintaining this stance for some 10 seconds, bellowed, "They ate my lunch... they ate my bloody lunch."

Silence once more ensued. Still he stared at the ceiling and after some moments he bellowed, "You bastards, you total bloody bastards, you ate my lunch," he screamed.

Even the driver was looking round and appeared nervous. Slowly, Dr Dravers lowered his head and returned to his seat, saying not a word more. I looked at Martin, who immediately turned away, clearly disowning me.

As we neared the outskirts of Addis, I plucked up the courage to ask Martin if I should offer Dr Dravers our own sandwiches.

"If you did that my dear old boy," Martin relayed, "it would be your last act upon this earth. Stay put and shut up."

Dr Dravers came up to our seat once more and asked, "What chance of at least having my tea towel, which I wrapped round my sandwiches?"

I had to tell him that when I took my tumble in the woods, I had used it to bathe my wounds and had ditched the cloth there and then.

Next, addressing the whole bus, Dr Dravers gave his final oration on the day's proceedings. "Ladies and gentlemen, just imagine if you can just how much damage Mr Denby here could inflict during a three-day field trip with 30-odd students… doesn't bear thinking about."

This evoked some mirth among the passengers. I felt a bit hurt but could say nothing.

Neither Martin nor I ever went on a Wildlife Society trip again in the three years we worked there, and I was certainly never asked to lead one. And as for the write-up for the embassy publication… it never happened.

24. WARDEN'S EYE VIEW (1)...

I had just weeks before completing my boat building apprenticeship, which coincided pretty much with my twenty-first birthday. Having the proverbial 'key to the door' I was also on the threshold of permanently leaving home – flying the nest indeed. I was a member of the RSPB and on that freezing cold March morning my RSPB magazine arrived. I gave it an initial scan and then noticed the advertisements for summer wardens on its bird reserves. I possessed not a single O-level and certainly not a PhD in wildlife conservation. I had been involved in several birding activities in my home county of Essex. These included sub-editorship of the Essex Bird Report for a couple of years, regular monthly wildfowl counts along the Blackwater river and frequent sessions with the local conservation corps volunteers, which seemed to consist mostly of beating up and hacking to death noxious and alien Rhododendrons. My neighbour at the time worked for Bletchley Park spy outfit and kindly gave me a personal reference. I thought I did not have a snowball in hell's chance of success but I bunged in my application and (more or less) forgot about it. Three weeks later I received a phone call from The Lodge, the RSPB nerve centre in Bedfordshire. Told I was being offered a job, I was asked if I wanted to go to Balranald in the Hebrides or Fetlar in the Shetland Islands. I asked when they would need my decision.

"Now would be preferable," came the reply.

I plumped for Shetland – I knew it was more remote than the Hebrides and also, how many of us have seen a wild Snowy Owl?

Of the wardens, we were four in number, all with very different backgrounds and temperaments. We were all about the same age but I, for reasons unknown, was asked to be senior warden.

Digby had spent six weeks sailing to the UK from South Africa. He was a white South African who had had a bellyful of apartheid. He came to

Britain on spec and lodged with his godmother in Hampshire briefly. He had bought a copy of the Peterson Field Guide to the Birds of Britain and Europe in Pretoria and had osmotically absorbed it on his journey. His knowledge of British birds was exemplary even though he had actually seen hardly any.

Rob was a graduate of English and he wrote poetry. He read his stuff in a weekly slot on Scottish radio and had just published a short anthology of his work. He was not a birder at all but clearly was concerned about environmental issues.

Dave had the year before finished A-levels and was taking time out before going to Cambridge University to read Geography. He had an outrageous sense of humour and he and I got on famously and maintained contact for some years after this job.

Then there was myself. With no formal education and unsure of where life was taking me, I was however confident and quite adventurous. The only thing I was certain of was that I could not work in an office or indeed any aspect of business. I too had been blessed with a pretty bizarre sense of humour and wondered in fact how I would fit in to a small, possibly introspective island community flung far-off in the North Sea. As it happened, we wardens got on extremely well and there was never any animosity between us. Furthermore, we enjoyed almost total acceptance into the island community.

There was a fifth member of the team. Freda was a late middle-aged lady from Buckinghamshire, who busied herself with water paints and a palette whenever she could. Freda was our cook, appointed to feed this ragamuffin bunch of blokes and at first this concerned me. There was no need however. She did her job well and fitted in with our eccentricities, praising us for our respective unconventional ways. She did not open up much but reading between the lines she too had pursued quite a non-conformist and interesting life. She was not a birder but loved all things furred and feathered. She joined us a week after our arrival and looked a bit startled at the bowl of large spotted eggs standing on a shelf in the larder. Great black-backed Gulls were a real menace in the breeding season and would feed voraciously on wader chicks. We were obliged to help control these birds' populations and one way was simply to take the eggs. There were hundreds of nests and I am sure this method made little difference as the birds simply re-laid. Pricking the eggs is a more efficient way as the birds will then continue to sit. Gull control was hoped to give Whimbrel chicks and others a better chance of survival.

The entire Snowy Owl project was to run for five months and was supervised by the

RSPB representative, Bobby Tulloch. Bobby was a character indeed. We did not see him much but he came over once a month to bring us each a bottle of Jameson's and see how we and the Snowies were doing. Bobby was a baker in his early adult life but as a keen birder and wildlife photographer he was taken on by the society in 1964. He became internationally famous and his photos featured in numerous books and magazines. He gave public lectures, not just in Shetland, and wrote a couple of books on the Shetland archipelago. He had his own boat, not a modest affair and all in all had the perfect existence.

The society rented a two-up two-down bothy for the warden's use. There was no electricity, no generator and no frills whatsoever. Rob had brought along a radio and I a typewriter, both for general use. We did have a good clean fresh water supply, which came from a nearby spring. We had a chemical toilet, which was located in the adjacent barn. A pair of Blackbirds built a nest in the barn not five metres from the Elsan toilet. They became used to us and reared five young. I have a sad story about the chemical closet emptying rota. Towards the end of the incubation period, I made a bet with Digby that the fifth egg would not hatch. The loser would have to do the winner's toilet emptying for two weeks. I lost.

Our two luxuries were a very small gas-operated fridge and a telephone. In the kitchen was a Rayburn stove, which we kept going throughout the season, using coal provided by the society. Dave had returned late one night after a cavorting session and had cycled back in a torrential downpour. With no front mud-flap on the bicycle, his feet had been in a constant deluge. Stealing in quietly so as not to wake us, he put his trainers in the Rayburn oven and placed in some extra coal knobs. At breakfast time Freda, having a good sense of humour, served them up for breakfast, having placed them on a large plate. They were no longer white but a sort of bilious yellow and the soles were a tangled mush of re-hardened melted rubber. They were now three sizes too small. The smell was almost unbearable and was quite acrid making eyes water.

Every bothy on the island had a Rayburn and you could do anything on or in them - they were excellent for drying out wet clothing. Freda would bake bread, cakes and biscuits in the oven and there was always hot water whenever we needed it.

Fetlar, which is old Norse for 'fertile' by the way, is the fourth largest island of the Shetland archipelago, which comprises around a hundred islands. Only a few are inhabited but many of the uninhabited ones are used for sheep grazing in the summer. When we were there, Fetlar had 101 inhabitants, with less than 10 people below the age of 21. Fetlar's maximum population was quite a lot more than this in bygone days. In the 2011 census, Fetlar's resident population was 61, a dangerously low level. There were just nine surnames on Fetlar when we were there, some being those familiar sounding Scandinavian names like Anderson, Thomason and Petersen. Typically, there were quite a few elderly folk who lived alone and had been on the island since birth. Another interesting quirk was the long 'engagements' which now elderly couples had maintained. These close relationships had gone on for decades but the partners lived separately and never got round to marrying. Seemingly, all was very much above board. They may have had insular lives but many could spin a good yarn. Of special interest were the tales told by those men who had left Shetland in their twenties to work on the Great Newfoundland Banks on the cod fishery. Their return to the islands contributed to the ongoing ageing of the population generally, which in extreme cases led to island desertion.

Most able-bodied islanders went in for crofting, both men and women. This is the rearing of sheep mostly on common grazing land (scattald) which is controlled by the Crofting Commission. Crofters also grew vegetables in the fertile soils. In addition most of the crofters had a second job. There we had the island postman whose delivery round was once a week and took about an hour to complete in his brand new van yet he, Billy, was on a full postman's salary. Pretty cushy eh! Then there was the island plumber and the island taxi driver. There were only about half a dozen cars and four tractors on the island. One could often see one of the island's children aged 13 driving his dad's car on the two public roads – no one seemed bothered and there was no island police force. Any vehicles were brought ashore by lowering, by hand I stress, onto two planks astride the flit boat, a most precarious undertaking for sure. Our only means of transport was a single bicycle and we worked out a fair system regarding its usage.

Fetlar sits close to the 61st degree of latitude north. Being this far north means that during the summer months it hardly gets dark at night. On the longest day (June 22) the sun dips but briefly below the horizon. It is not like daytime but is an eerie kind of light impossible for me to explain. This change of day-length messed up visitors' circadian-rhythms and made it difficult to get to sleep and to stay asleep. I got used to it eventually and found I was living perfectly well on about five to six hours sleep a day. The Shetlanders called this period of non-darkness the 'simmer dim' (the summer dim). One must bear in mind of course that the exact opposite occurs during the other half of the year and on the shortest day (December 21) there are about five hours of daylight. During the winter time islanders tend to shut themselves away in their family groups. One of the former wardens I spoke to some years later spent a winter on Fetlar and said it was the most depressing and lonely time he'd ever experienced.

Fetlar's extreme dimensions are approximately 11km east to west and 7km north to south, its area being about 41 square kilometres. I estimated its coastline to be around 42km. At the end of the season the four of us plus about six other islanders elected to walk right round the island in a day, hugging the coastline as close as possible. We managed it but some had come with too little food for sustenance and we had to call in to a croft to refuel on a full-bodied potato soup. Like the rest of Shetland, Fetlar experiences powerful winds, the most powerful in Britain. Islanders, including us wardens, had to double peg washing on the line lest underwear end up in Norway. A demonstration of the power of the wind came on our third night on Fetlar.

Digby and I shared one of the upper bedrooms, he being situated immediately under the window. Around two in the morning a loud caffuffle broke out. I awoke and I sat up seeing Digby looking somewhat shaken. The wind had blown in the entire window and frame and it had landed intact across his sleeping body. Neither glass nor Digby was broken but it did lead us to check the other window fittings. The natural vegetation of Fetlar is mainly short coarse grass and sedge and areas of exposed rock. There are several small lakes and a few gurgling streams and springs on Fetlar. Some lakes had a pair of Red-throated Divers nesting on the margins while others had pairs of breeding Red-necked Phalaropes. The mournful call of the Red-throated Diver is one of the most evocative yet sad sounds I have ever heard. If I heard it today it would conjure up strong images of a desolate moody landscape and the half-light of the night in summer on Fetlar.

The large headland Lamb Hoga is moorland covered in heather as are other parts of the island. It was on this headland that Manx Shearwaters and Storm Petrels nested in their thousands. As with the divers, the shearwaters' calls are very evocative and difficult to describe - you just have to hear them and you'll know what I mean.

Peat digging was once common and old peat bogs were all over the place. Once we watched a Shetland Pony being rescued from a peat bog into which it had sunk up to its neck – it was a close thing. Shetland ponies can fetch very large prices so to lose one would have been quite a blow to a crofter as insurance payouts never fully covered true market values.

Fogs were common especially in the early mornings but these seldom lasted long. On one nightwatch I had to go down to the Snowy Owl nest site to move away a pony who was getting dangerously close to the nest. I led the pony away and turned to go back to the hut. I couldn't see a thing. The fog had dropped like a blanket. I had no clue in which direction to walk. Naturally, I feared the obvious – standing on the eggs, which were due to hatch. I also stood the chance of being attacked as indeed Rob was later in the season. I could not risk it, so I headed for a large rock outcrop and resigned myself to sitting it out. I had my jacket on and was in a recess and it would be just a few hours before the morning when the fog should clear. In the meantime, Rob had come to relieve me and found the door to the hut open, a half-eaten digestive biscuit and no me. He called down to the bothy but that did not work – our telephone system was temperamental, particularly in damp conditions due to the huge amount of exposed joints in the cable. The fog cleared by early morning and I walked into the hut to make my apologies to Rob about my Marie Celeste performance. I was ribbed over this by some islanders (and my trusty colleagues) for weeks afterwards.

Speaking of atmospheric phenomena reminds me of another experience I had on Fetlar. I was having evening tea with islanders, Kenny and Mimie, when their daughter rushed in shouting, "Merry dancers."

We all went outside to witness a display of the Aurora Borealis (Northern Lights). True, it was not one of those classic displays made up of shimmering sheets and rays of reds, yellows and blues but it was still most moving. This was mostly green and led one to imagine a group of people standing behind a curtain with green-light torches holding them up and making a shivering motion to cause the rays to sweep across the sky. I recall my hair tingling and crackling, which is not surprising when you know how this phenomenon is caused. Two years later, when doing O-levels in a tech college our geology lecturer organised a three-week expedition to Iceland which involved doing glacial surveys up in the north of the country. We so expected to witness a fine auroral display – this was not to be but I did see Iceland's two must-see birds, a single Gyr Falcon and a pair of Harlequin Ducks.

There were two large bays, the Wick of Gruting to the north and the Wick of Tresta to the south. Many afternoons would find me sitting on the fine sandy beach of the Wick of Tresta, ruminating, musing, philosophising (or what you will) on how beautiful our planet is and how lucky I was to have this enviable job.

It was there that I would write letters to friends, inadequately trying to get my emotions down on paper. This was all so new to me. I had changed so much in this short time and will be ever grateful to the organisation that sent me to Fetlar and to all those who contributed to this totally idyllic life I was having.

It was one such occasion when I was sitting on Tresta beach that Digby came screaming towards me, "Red-flanked Bluetail - Red-flanked Bluetail."

"OK," said I, "sit down, calm down and fill me in."

In his strong South African accent, he continued, "I'm telling you man, there's a Red-flanked Bluetail."

I was cautious. I was unaware of the status of this member of the thrush family in Britain but I knew it was surely a rarity. We sped across to where he had thrown down the bicycle and then, with me on the saddle and he standing and pedalling, we covered the three kilometres to the rivulet that flowed down through Houbie (pronounced Hooby). We walked up the watercourse, Digby clearly anxious that his bird was still around. Me too, of course. And there it was, sitting on the fence, a male Red-flanked Bluetail in fine plumage. Digby managed a couple of photographs, which turned out to be not that good but collectively they presented total proof of this bird. There was no internet then of course and the Field Guide did not make it clear if this bird had even been recorded in Britain before. We dashed to the phone box outside the shop to inform Bobby who lived on the island of Yell. He came over the next day and happily saw the bird. We also informed Rod the schoolteacher and he too, a keen birder and ringer also saw the bird. We asked Bobby to send in the record and it was accepted – the first record of RFB in Britain. This species inhabits the eastern parts of Europe and is most common across the vast expanses of coniferous forest, the Taiga, in Russia.

Most of the coast was sheer vertical cliffs with ledges on which numerous seabirds nested. These were busy, noisy places with Guillemots, Razorbills, Fulmars, Kittiwakes and Shags all vying for space and calling incessantly to their mates and young. Around the bases of these cliffs Black Guillemots, Long-tailed Ducks and Common Scoters swam in the sea. Eiders too floated in rafts as they collected food to take to their young on the Lamb Hoga headland.

Houbie was the main centre, just a cluster of croft houses, the community hall, a clinic (the nurse's house), a small shop and the primary school. It also had one of the two island red telephone boxes, the other in the middle of nowhere, which could come in handy if you were caught out in a storm. Houbie also had a landing pier with a flit-boat. All supplies came on to Fetlar via the MSV Earl of Zetland, which operated between all the inhabited islands and was indeed a lifeline. Too big to come right in to the Fetlar shore, the flit-boat would go out to meet the much larger supply vessel.

Houbie Tuesday was a highly social affair with about two-thirds of the population all meeting up on the pier to exchange crofting news and various bits of gossip, doubtless including the antics of the Snowy Owl wardens. On a few occasions Houbie Tuesday was not possible as the winds were far too excessive and dangerous to use the flit-boat. The island had an airstrip, which was used by a company called Loganair, which flew in visitors and various Shetland Islands Council dignitaries. On some days it was far too windy for the small Fokker Friendship single prop' aeroplanes to operate.

At the northern side of the island was a small pier and this had turned into a construction site. Preparations were being made for the introduction of roll-on/roll-off ferries, pioneered in Norway. These would ply between the islands and would be in service the following year, about half a dozen in total. They would take about four to five cars or a bus and around 50 people and bring enormous positive change to the islands. Another change looming was the Hydro. This was the scheme to bring electricity to these outer Shetland islands and was to be up and running during the following year. Until then the crofters were to continue with their generators.

Next to the proposed ferry pier site was the large but derelict Brough Lodge, the former home of the Nicholson family, the more recent lairds of the island. It was a depressing looking place, reminding me of when I tried to read the tales of Gormenghast by Mervyn Peake. Lady Nicholson was now in a home in Lerwick and the lodge was empty and in a state of advanced decay. Behind this sinister-looking pile was a veritable scree-slope of sherry bottles and cat food tins, this reputedly representing the great lady's lifestyle in her latter days. One young man on the island, who had gone once a week to the lodge to attend to Lady Nicholson's needs, told of how he had to don oilskins to protect him from the gang of semi-feral cats, which the great lady fed. He and several of the other islanders told me the place was haunted. Of course, I have no time for such nonsense but I have to say if I was going to make a Gothic horror-movie then Brough Lodge would be my chosen location.

The island enjoyed the services of a nurse, Ruby - Ruby from Houbie in fact. I had only once to succumb to her ministrations when I got cystitis, apparently a urinary disease more peculiar to women. Whatever my gender, it was bloody painful. Any serious illnesses were dealt with at the Gilbert Bain hospital in Lerwick, which is nationally famed for its high standards and was once the topic of a TV documentary. By the way, Lerwick is pronounced Lurwick and not to rhyme with Berwick and is the 'capital' of Shetland.

The island nurse was also needed when Rob was doing a nest check and the male Snowy Owl flew up from behind him and wrapped its wings around his upper body. It dug its claws into Rob's back, hissing loudly and surely scared the hell out of him. And this was the male, quite a bit smaller than his female. Rob had a few superficial cuts and was patched up but it could have been considerably worse. He was very badly shaken and it also taught us a good lesson in being careful in future. The eggs had all hatched at the time of his check.

Closing on matters medical, I must mention the nurse's husband, Peter. A nice enough chap to be sure, this funny little pear-shaped man had a story that he carried around with him and would relate it to anybody he met, even complete strangers such as tourists. His story was about how he met his wife, Ruby. Peter had attended a difficult lambing and needed to go home with the new arrival. He had to step over a barbed wire fence whilst carrying the lamb and had slipped and fallen awkwardly, his full weight bearing down on his crutch. It ripped his scrotum and he had to have immediate medical treatment. That is how he met Ruby, who became his wife. Ruby was aware of Peter's habit of telling this story to all and sundry and tried to discourage him but he insisted that it was important for people to know. So, there you have it.

One man of medicine worked with famous fellow medical pioneer, Joseph Lister, on the use of antiseptic carbolic acid in surgery. He had some connections to Fetlar at the time and the upshot of this is that a bunch of his descendants had a substantial property on the island and made annual pilgrimages so they could be particularly nasty to the islanders. During my time on Fetlar I had the misfortune to meet some of these vindictive people having had prior warning. They really did see themselves as superior human beings. They were the kind of people invented by authors and who only exist in books or films and not in the real world. To these characters the islanders were just quaint ignorant peasants who were convenient to keep their huge house and garden clean and serviced in their absence but never to be socialised with. And as for us wardens… we were verminous long-haired layabouts who should have a good dose of army life.

I was on duty on the hill when about six of this family came to see the Snowy Owls. I was aware of their presence not by the usual method of visitors phoning through from the lower hut but of someone uttering the words, "Oh Daddy, do make sure you get the nest in."

I looked out of the side slat of the hide and saw a leggy, mini-skirted teenaged girl standing there being photographed by her father. That explained why just one minute earlier the sitting bird had left the nest rather suddenly. I ripped into these ignorant, self-important souls and told them to get down to the lower hut. With a few surly looks and mumblings they actually did so but not before announcing who they were. I ignored this information. Yes, they did leave and what's more they continued past the lower hut and went back down the hill not bothering with the owls. I never encountered them again but I gathered in later years these people flourished in various careers and presumably bullied their way through their respective lives putting down lesser mortals who deigned to cross their paths.

The primary school had five students although the sole teacher/headmaster (Rod) still had to split these into three classes because of age differences. All children over 11 went off to a large secondary school in Lerwick where they boarded, coming home probably just at half-terms and major holidays like Christmas and Easter. One of the changes brought about by the introduction of the ferries was that the children could return to their homes every weekend.

The shop was well-stocked although notably expensive as everything had to be brought up to Shetland from Aberdeen on the MV St Clair and thence onto the Earl. The RSPB had an account with the shop and I recall getting a directive from the Lodge about keeping our cheese consumption down. Our late-night cheese-on-toast sessions were costing the society a small fortune. There was a hilltop coastal lookout and Rob volunteered to take his turns at doing nightwatches, looking out for the flares of distressed trawlermen. He was told that Russian trawlers would sometimes put up flares just to frustrate UK authorities.

Near to the wardens' bothy was the island manse, which housed the resident minister although I cannot recall ever having seen him. The manse had a high sturdy rock wall enclosing the only bushes and small trees on the island. In fact, it is only behind or enclosed by walls that trees can grow in Shetland, so terribly windy is the place. Consequently, this was a good place to look for migrant birds although most migration occurred before and after we were there. Of all the occasions us wardens had scoured the garden with binoculars, not once was anybody seen throughout the entire season. Yet we were assured that the minister was in residence. I am glad he wasn't looking after my soul.

Fetlar did have its own Post Office and when I was there this was run by Ina, who was 74 years old. I don't know how she kept her job with the then GPO but this she did. She was totally compos mentis but just a trifle slow. The society sent our monthly pay cheques to us in the form of Gyro cheques. These were quite revolutionary at the time and when we presented these to Ina for encashment she had no idea what to do. We had little idea ourselves, so weren't much help. She phoned through to Lerwick to get instructions and thereafter all was OK.

Dave sent a parcel to his parents and noticing Ina's poorly disguised inquisitiveness, handed it to her telling her that it contained a live Snowy Owl, asking her to take care. Ina simply stared for a moment and put the parcel in a sack. I thought this was a bit unfair of Dave, who probably assumed everybody was as weird as he was.

Of note, there was no pub on Fetlar, something which most islanders were very happy about. This is because sometimes macho testosterone-charged Norwegian trawlermen would come ashore in bad weather looking for alcohol... and women. On Fetlar they found none of the former and all of the latter were off-limits. Although, I was informed that one did try his hand at seducing an island man's wife. Sometimes Norwegian fishermen would come ashore on their rubber Zodiac dinghies already seven sheets to the wind. On finding no pub they could become aggressive and generally these true Vikings were not welcome. The island did not have a policeman and this meant that islanders were reluctant to have to deal with drunk fishermen without a police presence. Russian trawlers also used to take shelter in either of the two bays in bad weather. The trawlermen were not allowed to land on British soil (it was the time of the Cold War) but islanders would sometimes go out to them, albeit illegally. They would trade with the Russians taking out stuff like playing cards emblazoned with nude ladies, biro pens and ladies stockings. For such items, an islander could return with a fishing net or perhaps twenty gallons of diesel. Sometimes a few islanders would set out towards a trawler and be ushered away, highly indicative that the ship was there for purposes other than fishing. I once watched from a headland the crew of a Russian trawler doing exercises on deck, including women. It was an open secret that not all these Russian boats were engaged in fishing but probably more nefarious practices.

Speaking of fishermen, I learnt an interesting fact when on Fetlar. For the most part, fishermen do not swim. None of the adults I spoke to on Fetlar could swim. The year before one of the islanders was tipped overboard as they were lowering the nurse's new Mini onto the flitboat. He went under but his fellows managed to grab him and haul him out, spluttering and at the same time somewhat dazed. Islanders told me that their inability to swim was hardly noteworthy, just common sense. They maintained that if the sea was rough enough to tip a boat then it would be too rough to swim in. Additionally, the cold of the North Sea, even in high summer is sufficient to kill a person in three minutes. So, the logic goes, 'Get it over with.' I am not sure about this line of thinking. Furthermore, few of the islanders would wear life jackets when out fishing. They often went several kilometres offshore, distances too far to swim for an average person and again logic came to the fore. With sou'westers, leggings and wellies, fishermen would be so encumbered that they had no chance of swimming. Most of the island children were taught to swim at school but I know some of the parents were not too happy about this break with tradition. I gather this is not just in Shetland but an entire fisherman thing who have total respect for the sea and cannot regard it as a place to play.

Fishermen are very suspicious creatures and there are many strange beliefs that I heard of on Fetlar. For example, if they met a minister on their way down to their fishing boat they would turn back, as this was a portend of misfortune. Women were not allowed on boats. I am sure there were a few qualms involving the sightings and behaviour of birds but I do not remember them. I also learnt of various customs upheld in Shetland and these were mainly of a very positive nature. For example, if you went out and there was no one left in your croft house then you propped a garden fork against the front door. This saved your potential guest from traipsing up your track and having a wasted journey. Rarely did islanders lock their doors and we followed this habit – I don't think we even had a key to our bothy. This was at times to our advantage as islanders who had been out fishing could come to our bothy to leave us fresh fish, even though we were all out.

I never really thought much could happen

in the lady department but the island did have three young ladies about our age. Digby chummed up with Sheila within two weeks and I with Maris, shortly after. For me, this was a real 'Cider with Rosie' affair – all so idyllic and well... perfect. Digby had left a girlfriend behind in Pretoria and, knowing he would not be returning for some time did not expect her to await his return, stating philosophically that there were plenty more fish in the sea. He was certainly in the right place although I must stress that Sheila was not a fish. I had been pining over Maris for a few weeks and it was Dave who clinched it for me. He was late in relieving me from my watch and he met Maris as he was making his way to the track leading up to our huts. He persuaded Maris to go with him but did not let out too much information. On entering the forward observation hut, he apologised to me for lateness and at the same time invited Maris to sit down on the bench. I cast a glance at David, looking a little confused as to what was happening. She took a brief look at the sitting Snowy Owl and then asked if I was leaving. Indeed I was and she accompanied me down to our bothy where she came in for a while and I showed her the sort of stuff that us wardens were doing. And the rest is history so it is said. Dave had been very canny and clearly he had brought Maris as a peace offering.

There was a guesthouse on the island, which

did well out of the Snowy Owls, accommodating birding visitors. The proprietors were a dour couple from Edinburgh. They never settled into island ways and made all attempts not to integrate with the islanders. They did not rate us wardens highly either, unleashing their vitriol to their paying guests, assuming that their toxic words would not get back to us. Two young birders actually checked out of the guesthouse prematurely, saying they were not prepared to listen to their hosts' reactionary opinions. We let them stay with us for a few days when they helped out in some bird counts in exchange for a concrete floor at the back of our bothy.

Some visitors camped and on two occasions we let campers use this outhouse in bad weather. Our lack of a bathroom was solved independently with the four of us wardens. We each had an islander we would do odd gardening jobs or hay-stooking for in exchange for a good soak in a real bath. The islanders generally had a good knowledge and respect of their birds and had plenty of time for us wardens. It was clear that wardens from previous years had also enjoyed this wonderful hospitality as islanders would speak fondly of them and tell us the most endearing anecdotes, just a few bordering on the scandalous. We would sometimes return to our bothy to find a bowlful of freshly caught fish, mostly Piltock but also Saithe and Ling. The hospitality was overwhelming. It was sometimes difficult to pass an islander's croft without being summoned to the interior to enjoy a 'bit of tea'. One luxury was 'crappin'. While not having a very assuring name, Crappin is a kind of pâté made from shearwater meat and is a traditional fare in Shetland (and New Zealand) and highly rated by many. Any visit would result in sandwiches, bannocks, oatcakes or cake being provided along with countless cups of tea.

My parental islanders were Kenny (a jovial Popeye type character) and his wife Mimie. I spent quite a bit of time yarning with them, chatting about what life was like down south (in Shetland everywhere outside Shetland is branded 'down south') and I maintained contact with them for some years up to 1984 after leaving, making a further four visits to the islands.

Fetlar folk fully appreciated the RSPB work and they welcomed visitors. These were certainly good for the shop, the taxi driver (the taxi was a 12-seater VW Kombi), the local boatmen from other islands and visitors would also buy knitwear made on the island either knitted by hand or on machines. Most croft houses had a knitting machine and it was on Fetlar I saw my first sock machine where, once set up, you simply turned a handle like on a meat mincer as the sock emerged from the bottom. Shetland is famous for its fine knitwear with its unique patterning and of course Fair Isle is now an adjective applied to many Shetland made sweaters. Shetland knitwear is very beautiful to see and to wear but it is not very robust and its well-known soft texture is soon lost. It is the harsh windy conditions in Shetland that make the sheeps' wool so thick and soft.

Social events on Fetlar were mostly those held in the community hall, organised by a committee. Once or twice every week some islanders would play badminton and there I became quite hooked on the game, some two decades later teaching students how to play in the various African schools I taught in. Dances happened about once a month and these were further enlivened with hot and cold drinks and mountains of sandwiches and cake. Some of the men would sneak outside to swig from a small bottle as the donation of the hall to the islanders was conditional that no alcohol be imbibed on the premises. The dance caller would first sprinkle talcum powder all over the floor to give it a nice 'slide' as the dancers hurtled their way through various dances – the eight-some reel, the quadrille, the two-step and the gay Gordons. A few of the island men played fiddle and these too would perform, very professionally I must add. Almost all able people attended the dances and visitors were always very much welcomed, causing mirth as they bowled over on the slippery powdered floor. Oh such wonderful times. One evening one of the visitors, an archaeologist staying at the guesthouse was giving a talk in the hall on industrial archaeology. He had piles of slides of rock walls, telegraph poles, phone boxes, old barns, sock machines, boat winches, livestock weighing scales and so much more. The content was, I suppose, interesting to someone unfamiliar with Shetland but here was the most characterless boring man on earth, delivering stuff that all of the islanders knew – it was, after all, their own history. Most Shetlanders do not mince words and the next day many had cast their opinions of the talk. I sort of felt sorry for the speaker, for the first half hour, then as he droned on and on I started to feel somewhat irritated by this patronising old fart teaching his grandmothers to suck proverbial eggs. Back at the bothy we sat there trying to guess what this bloke did for a living. Diplomacy forbids that I tell you what we came up with.

An outdoor social event and one I very much enjoyed, was the annual sheep dog trials. Here, about fifteen dogs were put through their paces, each responding to the pips of whistles and monosyllabic verbal commands given to the dogs. Laura, one of the shopkeeper couple who were from Surrey and not crofters, entered their dog. It did not win but it did well and the islanders poured praise on her and her dog. Such events sometimes attracted the press, the *Shetland Times*. On one occasion, right at the end of the season, a reporter came over to interview us about the Snowy Owl success. The young had left the nest so it was safe to go to the nest itself. He was with us for an hour or so and went away happy. When we saw the following week's edition, we read his article. It was OK and accurate enough but I suspect he may have been better as a war correspondent. He gave a lurid description of the nest area using words like 'bloody mayhem' and 'widespread carnage'. Like us, Bobby was amused.

Incidentally, a name that sometimes came up in the *Shetland Times* was that of Councillor Blackadder. Little did we know that years later Rowan Atkinson would use such a name for his character in the TV series.

So much for all the social life we enjoyed on Fetlar, what of the job itself? Our first task was to clean up the bothy and check the roof tiles, which had taken a battering over the winter months. The next was to lay out the telephone cable from our bothy up to the forward hut from where we and the visitors watched the Snowy Owls. This was no mean feat and took four of us the best part of a day. The cable ran for nearly two kilometres and was laid straight onto the ground with no attempts to cover it. There were numerous joins along its length, each a potential for breakdown in communication. We had a phone link, primarily in case of getting unwelcome visitors in the form of egg collectors. We were the guardians of the rarest birds in Britain, just two Snowy Owls. The eggs of these birds would fetch a royal ransom in egg collecting circles so we did not make light of a possible attempt by collectors over the incubation period. We relaxed a lot once the eggs had hatched. I did once see a couple of people landing a boat some distance away from our observation hut. They landed, had a picnic and, happily went away. In the meantime I had called down for one of the others to come up as back up. I knew that egg collectors could be pretty desperate characters!

From the outset, we maintained a 24/7 watch with no days missed. During each of our six-hour shifts, we would note in the log just about every muscle twitch of the two birds. In the hut we had coffee making equipment and a constant supply of digestive biscuits. Woe betide he who left no biscuits for the relief warden! We had a substantial telescope, which I think must have come off a naval ship. It was mostly focussed on the nest being a heavy affair, while other observation when the birds were not sitting, we made with our binoculars. We had no form of heating in the hut but this was never a problem. A couple of times driving horizontal rain forced us to close the observation slats.

Also, during the first few days, in addition to calling round to various islanders to introduce ourselves, we erected the lower hut. This was about a hundred metres back from the forward observation hut and served as a repository of visitors. People would make the long trek up to the lower hut and then phone through to the forward hut. The duty warden would then give clearance for a small party (say three, maybe four) to head on up to the observation hut. The pathway between the two huts was clear to see, passing between large rocks and thus hiding them from the sitting Snowy Owls. Towards the end of the incubation period I started to get a bit nervous, fearing that collectors may make a concerted bid. Being senior warden, I decided I would spend some nights kipping in the lower hut and installed a camp bed and mattress, thus increasing manpower should a raid occur. This was in case any collectors carried out a night raid. I am no James Bond but my added presence might have swung the balance. A strange thing used to occur when I was staying in the lower hut. Ponies would stand outside and kick the hut walls. I shooed them away. They came back and kicked again. This went on until I gave up. They did this every time I slept in the hut but I never did fathom why they did this. I never saw them kicking when the hut was empty.

A typical watch nearly always had something of interest. As I implied earlier, we recorded just about everything that the two birds did. After a while one got to know what was going on in these birds' heads and some actions became predictable. As the birds came in they sometimes followed a sort of routine alighting on one rock, looking around, moving across to another and looking again before going to their sitting mate or their chicks to give food or to change shift. One thing I never predicted was when the female was being pestered by a persistent Hooded Crow, obviously trying to get at the eggs beneath her. This I observed for about 20 minutes and I could see the Owl was becoming tetchy. And then, all in a few seconds, she rose up, grabbed the crow around the neck and wrenched its head off with its feet. She then, after about five more minutes, picked up the headless bird and flew off with it. Call me anthropomorphic but I bet anything she had removed the crow to hide it from its mates. If she was going to eat it, why take the risk of leaving the nest to do so?

The owls were bringing in small birds like wheatears, meadow pipits and wader chicks (I hoped not those of Whimbrel or Dunlin). There were no lemmings in Shetland as they are restricted to more northern climes. Rabbits would have been a good substitute but there were very few of them due to myxomatosis, which was introduced to the island the year before. The energy value of small passerine birds is much less than that of lemmings so it was interesting to see how the owls would cope.

They coped by working flat out and three of the young reached flying stage. I shall not go into the detailed breeding biology of Snowy Owls. One of the wardens on the 1973 Snowy Owl project assembled the logs of all the years when these birds bred on Fetlar since 1967 and presented a fine paper (see Reading List).

In 1973 I called up to Shetland for a few weeks and helped out with the Snowy Owls, which were again breeding, in exchange for board and lodging. When up on Vord Hill (the breeding location) late in the season, I noticed in the distance a piece of white rag blowing on a distant barbed wire fence. That piece of rag was a recently fledged Snowy Owl trying out its wings. I removed my anorak, wrapped up the unfortunate aviator and took it back to the bothy where it was installed in the cook's room (she had already left) with a large wooden beam to perch on. One of its wing bones was clearly broken. A hole drilled through the wall enabled us to check up on the bird. We named him Baxter after a jar of pickles, which happened to be on the table. You are not, I know, going to believe this next bit, but here goes. Two evenings later a birding couple visiting Fetlar turned up at our bothy to ask what the chances were of seeing a Snowy Owl. We obliged them by taking them into the next room. And here is the punchline. The man was a vet! Using the kitchen table as an operating theatre, he did his best to attach a sort of splint to the broken carpel and suture the gaping wound. The couple then had to leave us. Baxter recovered well and he made his successful maiden flight just days prior to the wardens packing up their bags and heading south.

So, this was one type of wardening on a bird reserve involving close protection and monitoring of a particular species, very much like when the Ospreys started nesting in Loch Garten. In the next chapter, I shall give an account of the more usual type of wardening that takes place on a bird reserve. I refer to when I was an assistant warden on the Ouse Washes during the summer of 1977.

As a postscript, may I mention another owl anecdote? I managed, without trying, to see six species of owl in a three-day period. Leaving Fetlar with Cliff, I took one last look at a Snowy Owl. As we passed down through the islands, we called in to see Bobby Tulloch, the society representative, who was nursing a Long-eared Owl. Also, before reaching Lerwick, we encountered a Short-eared owl. As we approached Cliff's house on the Ouse Washes two nights later, we caught sight of a Barn Owl in the headlights and at breakfast two Little Owls were observed on the bird table. I then travelled down to Southampton (my university) where there was a Tawny Owl roosting in a tree in our hall of residence car park.

STUFF ABOUT BIRDS

25. WARDEN'S EYE VIEW (2)...

Monitoring the Snowy Owls on Fetlar was one form of wardening on bird reserves. I now move to a very different and the more usual manner in which reserve wardens go about their daily business. Bird reserves are really habitat reserves and of course all reserves have their own management needs. The point I wish to stress is that wardening on a bird reserve does not consist of simply looking at and recording birds – far from it. Reserve wardens must, over time, build up a comprehensive knowledge of their assigned 'patch'. You cannot conserve just various species of birds without understanding something of the ecology of their respective or shared habitats. You will need to be aware of and attend to where and how they live, how they cooperate or compete, the physical environment, the assemblages of other groups of organisms both animals and plants. You will have to consider both prey and predators and all other pressures and conflicts of interest being made on that particular ecosystem. All of these and more will need to be woven into the equation to achieve successful management.

It was April 1977 and I was involved in the planning of a second ornithological expedition to Ladakh in the NW Himalaya of India (see following chapter). I was phoning Cliff who I had first met when I went back to Fetlar in 1973 – he was senior warden on the Snowy Owl project that year. During our chat he asked if I was interested in a summer job, serving as his assistant on the RSPB (hereafter referred to simply as the society) bird reserve in the Cambridgeshire Fens. I turned over thoughts in my mind very quickly and confirmed my interest. I had a very unhealthy overdraft, which was becoming my albatross and here was a chance to go some way to reduce it. Instead of spending a significant load of money on another Ladakh trip, I would be earning and getting my board and lodging. I agreed to work with Cliff and then found a replacement ornithologist for the proposed expedition. I continued my involvement in the planning and fund-raising process.

I travelled to Cambridge from Southampton where I was at university and thence on a two-carriage train to Manea (pronounced may-nee) railway station. This lay about 5km from Cliff's society house in which I was to live. My actual employer was CAMBIENT - the Cambridgeshire and Isle of Ely Naturalists' Trust, which donated an assistant warden to the society each summer. Cliff collected me and without even time for a cup of tea I was whisked off to my first assignment.

The washes were still flooded bank to bank

and, coming at short notice, some of the graziers scarcely had time to get their livestock off onto higher ground. Cliff was helping with the rescuing of sheep, which were stranded up to their necks in the floodwaters. He took me off in the small flat wooden punt and we managed to haul three grateful sheep into the boat and take them to safety. The water level was in places over the tops of the barbed wire fences that criss-crossed the reserve so Cliff had to do some careful navigation. Looking out across the washes, I saw a half-submerged tractor, which had not been taken off in time before the water was let in and in this a pair of Swallows was currently nesting, flying to and fro, feeding their young. Having completed our ovine rescue mission, it was time for my welcoming brew.

The Ouse Washes lie between the two Bedford Rivers, which were cut in the mid-seventeenth century, firstly by the Fourth Earl of Bedford and then by Dutch engineer Vermuyden, who made a second parallel cut. The land in between serves as an overspill region for when the Bedford Rivers are in high spate and water is pumped onto them to avoid the flooding of a much wider area. High clay banks were constructed and the result was a linear basin sitting between the two parallel Bedford rivers (the Old and the New) about 1km apart and running a length of 32km. Separate fields (washes) were created by the digging of numerous channels all across the washland. In some places fences served a similar purpose. The washes were used to graze livestock, chiefly cattle and some sheep throughout the spring and summer months. It is the grazing regime established on the washes that serves to maintain just the right sward of grasses for nesting birds. This is achieved by subtle and skilfully controlled inlet and outlet sluices. With reed beds and occasional pools and the odd thicket of trees specifically planted in the early days, the unflooded refuge provides excellent habitat for a large number of breeding and migrant birds. The society acquired a substantial area of the washland and installed a resident warden and an assistant. Other organisations also took on some of the washes including the wildfowlers as a body. Reserve wardens need to be quite practical having mastery over tractors and hand tools as well as harbouring passions for all branches of natural history. They need also to have good public relations abilities. Such a huge expanse demanded an ambitious management programme to turn this into one of the society's most important wetland reserves. Indeed, the Ouse Washes rank very highly on the world stage with respect to wetland ecosystems.

Over subsequent years, hides were set up on the tops of the banks, a visitor information centre was built together with an accommodation building for volunteers. The warden's tasks were manifold and also involved a fair amount of diplomatic juggling as there was no lack of conflicting interests. The anglers, the winter wildfowlers, the birders and the graziers all had different ideas on how the place should be run, so the going was not always as smooth as it might have been. Anglers collectively would leave such messes and clearly resented our passing as we took the main boat along the river, carrying materials to complete management work or, on occasion, take special visitors on a river cruise. Sometimes graziers would block up or unblock drainage outlets when they fancied the current water levels were not to their liking.

The senior warden had an assistant, Les, who lived on the opposite side of the washes. For much of the time he took care of the affairs on his side but we did get to see him occasionally. We went round a couple of times to dine with Les and his Scottish wife, Anne. They were great fun and Les secured a society post in the Hebrides after his time on the Ouse Washes, much to Anne's delight to be once again in Caledonian parts.

And let me introduce Dave, a biology graduate acting as the society's own summer assistant to the warden. His principal task for the summer was to undertake a botanical survey of all the aquatic plant species living in the enormous total length of the lattice of channels on the reserve. For this, he was provided with a colleague, Mark. They both stayed in a large caravan in the reserve car park by the warden's house, which served both as their lodging and also their laboratory. Basically, their allotted task was to collect plants from every stretch of waterway using a throwing line and grapple and then identify the plants. Then they would quantify them and thus establish the frequency status of each species. They were guided by a somewhat elderly lady with a PhD in some aspect of botany and she came over periodically to see them. We had a regular throughput of visitors over the season including Joy, the head of CAMBIENT, various members of the society council including the president himself, wildlife photographers, groups of school children, volunteers, girlfriends and of course there were the day visitors. We wardens worked happily together and were kept busy. Dave and I enjoyed one day off per week but Cliff beavered on pretty much continually.

My days off were spent on trips to Cambridge, my favourite British city. I rarely had a particular programme, I just liked wandering around the place with its beautiful sandstone university buildings with their 'backs' and the river Cam flowing through the city. On one occasion I treated myself to a rowing trip. I did have two regular habits, however, and one was to dine at the Copper Kettle. The other was to call in to the CAMBIENT office to see Joy and have a chat about how things were going. Cliff always very generously lent me his car to make these delightful sojourns. I bought my own Morris Traveller towards the end of the season with some of my earnings on which I meticulously replaced some of the iconic woodwork adornment.

I turn now to some of the management chores we had to undertake. Dave and I would alternate in doing cattle counts, which involved walking along the tops of the banks, counting every bovine in every wash where they grazed. This was to ensure that none was lost by falling into the waterways as they stooped down to drink. In some areas there were special shallow sloping patches to prevent just this. There was clearly an art to counting cattle from a distance and if your count did not tally with that which you had on paper you had to enter the wash and check thoroughly. This was very frustrating and time-consuming and thus my least favoured assignment. Cattle which had fallen in were pulled out by attaching a rope around their necks and hauling them out with a tractor. Horses had to be roped around their front legs. In both cases the rescues looked pretty undignified and even dangerous to man and beast. Cattle counts gave us the opportunity to gather up some of the awful rubbish left either intentionally or unintentionally by the angling fraternity. Sandwich wrappings, newspapers, drink cans, bottles and fruit peelings were unsightly and fishing line and hooks were dangerous to wildlife. I once fished a broken fishing umbrella out of the river. Les did his cattle counts by trail bike.

Clearance of nettles around the hide approaches and mowing of the car park grass were carried out regularly. Other vegetation control included the spraying of Glyceria maxima (Sweet Reed Grass), a tall, tough, fast-growing reed-like plant, which would take over a site if allowed to do so. Crack Willow trees grew in several places and at times a dangerously imbalanced or overhanging branch may need to be brought down. One of my jobs was the creosoting of fence posts, which involved lighting a fire under a long metal trough filled with creosote. As fence posts were immersed they soaked up the heated thin black smelly oil right through to the interior, giving them a long life in often submerged conditions. It was a messy job and any clothes used had to be thrown away at the end of the season. It became part of a morning ritual where I spent the first hour after breakfast 'getting on to my creosote cycle'. I was not short of posts as Cliff and I had driven out in a hired van to collect four hundred from a supplier, already with their tapered ends cut.

The installation of new fencing and repair of the old was an ongoing task. For driving in the posts we had a marvellous piece of technology, which comprised a heavy metal cylinder with one end closed. On the side were two handles allowing the two opposite-standing operators to grasp as they alternately raised and forcibly pulled down the device. A fence post could be driven home with about half a dozen good downward thumps. Cliff had christened this piece of industrial archaeology a 'gadunker' employing the fine art of onomatopoeia. Three strands of barbed wire were strung between posts, being pulled super-taut with the aid of hooked crowbars.

A new hide demanded the erection of upright railway-sleepers on the back-slope of the bank. These had to be trimmed and this was done with a chainsaw. They were made of teak but it was like sawing through steel, as we laboriously took turns at a sleeper and had intervals for the chainsaw to cool down.

I have to say here that by far the most boring job I have ever done, anywhere, is spending three laborious hours sharpening a chainsaw blade with a rat-tail file. There are better therapies.

Apart from this large public hide Dave and I erected a small two-man hide for private use in a reed bed further down river. One of my allotted tasks was to build a stile. This, I accomplished, but not without having to have an anti-tetanus jab as I drove a substantial nail into my palm (tetanus is rampant in these sometimes anaerobic Fen soils). I recall as Cliff inspected my handiwork saying with my great wit, "Hey Cliff, d'ya like my stile?"

Another erection I was responsible for was the hanging of a long wooden gate. This was on the other side of the washes and I had to take the gate in the tractor and trailer.

As I lumbered past the warden's house half carrying and half dragging the proposed fixture, I called through to Cliff "……and here we see the warden, with his characteristic gate…"

Oh how unstoppable was my deluge of wit! At the same time as my gate erection, I had to check the Kestrel box and had brought along a ladder for that purpose. This was situated in a tall tree in a Crack Willow thicket. It was not in use (we knew that) but I gave it a clean out and checked it for need of repair. On one occasion, I had to take the tractor and trailer to collect a load of gravel, this being for the foundations of the volunteer accommodation unit, which we were about to start. On my return to the reserve with quite a load on the trailer, the nearside wheel of the trailer broke away with obvious consequences. I got a passing driver to make a call from the village phone box and Cliff came out with the necessary cavalry and equipment. I think he was rather worried about the society getting a bill from the council for fixing the rather long gash I had made along the tarmac surface. It took about ten minutes to find the escaped wheel, it having bounced off into the nearby beet field.

Speaking of tractors, I had to drive a Zetor four-wheel drive tractor from Norwich to the reserve. Being stuck at about 30kph I was constantly causing the back-up of a line of cars and trucks. I would pull aside whenever my embarrassment became too acute but this was not frequently enough for some who intelligently persisted in parping their horns and even trying some dangerous manoeuvres. This trip took me a considerable length of time and my constant intake of Fen dust was causing no small amount of discomfort.

On one occasion, Cliff called in a JCB chap, who was to clear some of the waterways of weed. He could keep the machine working without stopping as it moved along and at the same time alternately scooped up and then dumped its load. It was almost balletic to watch. On another occasion a JCB operator was called in to make a sizeable scrape, a feature which had proven so successful at Minsmere, another of the society's top reserves located in Suffolk and famous for its breeding Avocet population (and which is the symbol of the society), Bitterns and Marsh Harriers.

Pipe laying was one of our jobs and here we had to take great care not to part company with our fingers as the concrete pipes had to be totally abutted to each other and they were very heavy to boot. There were about eight hides dotted along the banks at differing intervals and these had to be maintained. It became clear that some anglers were sleeping in the hides and even worse, defaecating in them, giving us a most unpleasant task indeed. One of the warden's responsibilities was ascertaining and maintaining the correct 'grazing pressure' which determined the success of breeding birds. While the society did not own the cattle, they did want to maintain a record of how many beasts were on which washes. So much for the land management tasks. Before moving on to jobs that related to information and education. I will say something of a special activity, which the warden alone had to undertake.

Cliff, like the rest of us, was not really turned on by administrative tasks. However, every society warden had to produce management plans every five years and annual reports after each year. This was the bane of many a warden's life and eventually always caught up with them. I recall once when Cliff buried himself away in the 'office' to meet a deadline on an annual report. In 1977 there were no computers in the public domain. He was writing all the stuff out by hand and as each sheet was completed he popped out of the office to give it to me. I would then type it up on a typewriter I had inherited from my mum. This went on for a few days until the task was complete. I was only doing my job but Cliff was so grateful he presented me with a bottle of Famous Grouse. I was so glad for him that the pressure was now off.

School parties were welcome and one morning I had the pleasure of supervising a group of about 15 upper primary-aged youngsters with their teacher of course. This was the first time I had done this and did not recognise the potential pitfalls. We managed to squeeze all of us into the largest hide and I opened the slats. My heart sank. Right before us was a score of cows busily munching away. There was not a bird in sight. I struggled for ideas. Ely Cathedral reared up majestically in the far distance so I drew attention to that. This architectural wonder obviously had no appeal (perhaps these kids were from Ely?) and I could scarcely hide my embarrassment from the teacher. She was as supportive as she could be and kept up a breezy chat with the children and myself. And then the worst happened. A frisky cow walked up behind one of its chums and rose up onto its rear end, adopting a mating posture and even adding pelvic thrusts to make it even more convincing. I did not understand at the time why two cows should do this but have since learnt that this is quite normal behaviour among cattle. Even so, the pupils loved this and immediately the noise level of conversation peaked and the teacher looked at me with forlorn but sympathetic eyes. A Redshank kindly made an appearance but its presence had gone unnoticed. All in all the event was far from educational, not with respect to birdlife anyway.

For a few days we had the pleasure of the company of Mike, a professional wildlife photographer. He had set up a hide on one of the washes. It had long been proven that if two people walked into a hide but only one left, then the target birds would assume the hide now to be empty and thus not a threat. I had to do this with Mike enabling him to get on with his filming. While with us he also filmed a heronry at the far end of the reserve. For this he built a tall tubular metal tower, precariously roped to a tall tree adjacent to the heronry. My job was to take the tower down after Mike had done with it. This was not as straight-forward as I had expected. I was ever convinced the whole structure was going to topple as I climbed to the top. I did eventually achieve dismantling of the platform and tower with the help of another but it took a lot longer than it should have. It was from Mike that I learnt something most interesting about wildlife documentaries and films. They are scripted. I don't mean that the Black-Tailed Godwits chatted away to us but that the entire content of the finished piece is established in advance. I assumed that wildlife photographers just fired off loads of film and then went back to the film-lab to select the most interesting stuff. Not at all. Mike showed me his 'script' for the film he was then making. It had lines like 'raindrops falling on buttercups...

7 seconds', 'lapwing doing aerial display... 12 seconds' and 'Sedge Warbler feeding nestlings... 20 seconds.' And so it went on. Armed with a script the photographer then boldly goes to capture as much as he can keeping as close to the instructions as possible. Mike recounted several of his filming anecdotes and I came away having much admiration for his hardiness and patience. Sir David Attenborough takes years to complete any one of his superb wildlife series and he is supported by the world's leading film crews.

One opportunity to spread the word of conservation was the Manea Gala and at this we had a stand. Here we displayed photos of the work on the Ouse Washes and work of the society in general. We had suggested that Dave could stand on a podium and make bird calls. This was because he had a talent of knocking out tunes as he turned his inflated cheeks into a drum - his best was the William Tell overture. Not rising to this challenge we had to come up with other ideas. One of my contributions was to run a competition. Gala-goers were invited to guess the weight of a Grey Heron. It went down well and we had quite a few entries. People had to pay for entries and the proceeds were to go for the upkeep of a local sports field/facility. Cliff dug out some decoy ducks and people had to identify the species as they were suitably placed on an abutting pond. Another way we spread the word were with my articles for the CAMBIENT monthly magazine. These were to allow members to see where some of their money was going and what we had been up to in recent weeks.

In the reserve car park we had a blackboard with chalk requesting visitors to report any sightings of interest. We edited this every few days. Sometimes birders would call at the warden's house if they had something exceptional to report. One such occasion was when a transatlantic vagrant turned up. No, not an American chap in a grubby raincoat. This was a Wilson's Phalarope and obliged quite a few visitors as it fed some little distance from one of the hides. It stayed for about three days and remains the only American migrant I have ever seen. This was before the twitching frenzy took off in Britain and we were spared an onslaught. A rainy day activity was preparing bird identification boards for use in the hides.

My final topic here on information and education is the building of the visitor centre, which certainly warrants special coverage. This was by far the dominant activity of the season and involved Cliff, Dave and I in many weeks of enjoyment but not without some frustration. One of my earliest tasks on the reserve was to help complete the foundations. We had received the lorry-load of ready-mixed cement and tamped it out with a long thin wand of wood. This draws excess water upwards by capillary action and speeds up the hardening process. We gave it a few days to set hard and then set about the daunting challenge of assembling the hut sections of which there must have been a score or so. The manufacturers of the separate wooden panels had the holes already drilled so all we had to do was push the bolts through and fasten nuts to conjoin neighbouring panels. All was OK for the first couple of panels and then the trouble started. Some of the holes were slightly out of alignment demanding that extra push with a hammer to get the bolt all the way through. Then there came holes, which were way out of alignment and these had to be approached differently. Quite simply, we had to re-drill them. Fortunately, the good weather held and the outer shell was completed, including the roof although that would still need a layer of roofing felt. Belinda, a good-humoured nurse, lived just a hundred metres up from the visitor centre site and would sometimes ply us with comestibles. She was a good friend of us wardens and we had good times indeed. Once the outer shell was finished, we could order the lining boards. In the meantime, Cliff installed all of the electric cables, which had to be done before we lined the building. These completed and checked by a professional electrician they were connected to a main power output and all was well. We were electrified.

Next came the lining process and we had a huge stack of these lining boards in the building safely protected from any rain. These were rectangular boards of gypsum covered in hessian cloth. They were used to line all the walls and the ceiling being secured with long panel pins and needed no drilling. This was a slow job as many of the boards had to be cut to specific sizes and shapes as we worked our way around the building. Here is where I committed a huge blunder. After a session of lining the walls, we noticed that the electricity was not working. This was a mystery as it had been fine for the first couple of days. And then Cliff cracked it, at least the cause of the problem. We still had to locate it. He thought that the only explanation was that one of us had driven a panel pin through an electric cable and the whole system was shorting. He retraced where all the cables had been set so that narrowed it down a bit. It was looking disturbingly that I was the guilty party. Then, with tedious checking using an electrical screwdriver, he located the offending panel pin. Once that pin had been identified and removed it was clear that it was I indeed who had banged it through the underlying cable. So, now the electricity was restored along with at least some of my credibility.

By now Dave was allowed to concentrate on the botanical work. Being of a carpentry bent, I continued working on the interior of the visitor centre. I was to build a large counter behind which would sit some kind of education officer/receptionist/saleswoman when the visitors were pouring in. I managed to erect rather a robust structure and I was pretty proud of it. Only tectonic forces would move this item, built as a testament to human powers and appreciation of beauty.

A small storeroom followed and some shelving upon which various society goodies for sale could be stashed, was installed. A rack would display a range of pamphlets and brochures extolling the virtues of other society reserves and round and about there were to be photographic and information display boards and it is those we built next. These comprised each a pair of gypsum boards facing back to back and meeting at the outer end to form a V-shaped surface for the information/educational material. One morning during this period as I entered the centre, a Little Owl was sitting on my counter. It had obviously entered one of the open fanlight windows. I left the main door open but it would not go out, merely flying down to a corner on the floor. I painstakingly removed my fisherman's smock as I was wont to wear (its frontal pouch was convenient for carrying tools and I nicked the idea off Cliff) with the thought of catching the distressed bird. Having removed the garment, I approached the bird and it rose up, flew past my head and straight out of the door. I was relived as, although just a Little Owl, his little claws could inflict more than a little damage. With just a few more refinements we set about the outside of the visitor centre and a slabbed pathway was built from the bank down to the centre and an area of imported topsoil was planted with grass seed. I never got to see the actual displays until the following year when I visited Cliff. That visitor centre remains today although it has undergone a few modifications.

I mentioned earlier that we had volunteers visit the reserve. These came as organised groups under the umbrella of the Conservation Corps. A group of about a dozen, not always the same people, would come once a month and Cliff would assign them a single or several undertakings. One of us assistants would supervise them as they worked through the day, stopping once to have their packed lunches. The vols (as they were endearingly termed) were in some ways a double-edged sword. Their having to be supervised meant that one of us was taken up in overseeing them. Even so, they did aid us in getting things done and their enthusiasm and commitment was commendable.

By now it will be stunningly obvious that wardening entails a lot more than wandering around looking at birds. I would hazard a guess and say that if a typical society warden was to venture out to specifically birdwatch then it might be one day in a month. Of course we saw plenty of birds as we went about management business. One specific birdwatch was when Dave and I walked a long length of the reserve to undertake a Yellow Wagtail survey. This involved a lot of immersion in waterways or leaping across them if they were narrow enough. During our daily work we would see various Harriers, Ruffs, Black-tailed Godwits (a reserve speciality), other waders, Reed and Sedge Warblers, Barn Owls, Short-eared Owls and loads more. We had Little Owls sometimes on the garden bird table and in Belinda's garden we could sometimes witness three or four Hen Harriers gathering to evening roost. A pair of Spotted Flycatchers had built a nest in the workshop and for a while were tolerant of our comings and goings. However, the birds did end up deserting as, I suppose, it all got a bit too much for them. Les went through a stage of coming across to our side for the day and for this he used a trail bike. One morning he recounted how a Bittern had become entangled with the underbelly of the bike and how the bird escaped unhurt as he struggled to maintain control of the machine.

There was one job that Cliff had to perform and that was a personal service to me. It was to carefully remove butterflies from inside the house, especially my bedroom. Since the age of about eight I have had a strange phobia about lepidoptera (butterflies and moths). I cannot pick them up and if one is fluttering around indoors I am much troubled. Many people have very odd, irrational and inexplicable phobias and this is one. It is not a case of being frightened, no lepidoptera is going to attack or poison me. I think it is their fragility that offends my senses, I am not sure. In Africa we had plenty of large butterflies and moths including Mopane Moths, which are of the silk-moth family. These have wingspans of about 14cm and whenever one entered the house, Zandile had to put it out for me. One of the volunteers who came to our school in Swaziland shared this very same phobia, which I found quite a relief. Please don't get me wrong here, I would never do harm to a butterfly or moth. They are beautiful creatures and so essential for pollination and food for birds. I can now put them out myself, using a bowl and a piece of cardboard so by the time I am 150 I might even be picking them up. Strangely, I have no such aversions to spiders, bats or snakes.

Our domestic lives were well catered for, well-garnished with bonhomie and the occasional visits were most welcome. In the first half of the season before Dave moved to the botany caravan, he lived in a much smaller caravan about a kilometre down the road. He would, however, have meals with us. Those mealtimes were fun and we all got on so extremely well. Apart from Dave playing us Rossini's William Tell overture on his cheeks, he came up with the dictionary game. We would take turns to randomly open a dictionary and read out a seemingly new and strange word. The others had to guess the meaning. Words included were plaister (Scottish for plaster), pantophobia (fear of everything) and priapism (look it up, I can't tell you here). If you wonder why they all start with p I guess it's because p is more or less the middle of a dictionary and thus more likely to be selected. During one breakfast time a chap came to the door, entered, said, "Good morning," and dropped a dead male pheasant on the table. He explained that he had just killed the bird having hit it, accidentally of course, with his car. He asked if we wanted it. I am not sure who but one of us said that it would make a fine meal. The man was horrified. "What.... you're going to eat it?"

We asked him what he would wish us do with it. He said he thought we might like to have it stuffed and used in the visitor centre or perhaps we could do some research on it. What research he had in mind I have no idea - certainly not what killed the bird. Anyway, he left the fated pheasant and made a polite withdrawal. We thanked him and the bird was duly 'hung' in the warden's spacious larder. One very regular visitor we received, generally at meal times, was John the eel man. He was called this not because of his appearance but because he spent half the year catching and selling eels. His arrival was invariably announced by the kitchen door bursting open, followed immediately by a loud, "Y'aright!" delivered in his strong northern accent. He was a lovable rogue... well a likeable rogue anyway. He was quite short and gave a rather comic air as his waders were more than half his height. He always stopped for a brew and gave us the latest Fen gossip. On the occasion I tried to chop up one of his eels, I found it almost impossible, so slippery are these weird fish. Also in Cliff's larder lay a Yellow Wagtail found dead and immediately injected with formalin. This was clearly forgotten about until it was noticed some considerable time later. It was literally a heaving yellow bag of maggots despite its chemical intake. Still in the kitchen, there was a small cupboard, which was really an offshoot from the main room. This was known as the 'boot cupboard' as it was well-stocked with wellies, mostly those of earlier wardens and earlier days of the current warden. It also had various jacketry (a new word) such as old Barbour jackets, scarves and smocks and it had a collection of dead and moribund thick socks. It was Hell's Cavern and not a place for the faint-hearted. I recall once we had a bet one mealtime about something or other and the loser had to undergo a forfeit chosen by the others. This time it was my turn to undergo such a forfeit, which was two whole minutes of banishment into the boot cupboard with the door closed.

Now here is a good one. I always knew when we

were due to have a visitor from HQ or perhaps even the Duke of Edinburgh. It always happened early on the morning of the proposed visit. The large draining rack went missing. Cliff used to hide it if important visitors were coming. I never got to the bottom of his interesting ritual but ritual it was. It was as reliable a portend as a red sky at night. One evening after Cliff and I had made a long walk along the southern bank towards his house, he cooked up a huge field mushroom that he found earlier in the day. It really was a monster, the size of a dinner plate and this he sliced up and fried in oil. Meanwhile, a saucepan of rice was bubbling away on the stove. That was it, no greenery or anything else. He mixed the two together and the mixture became increasingly greyer as he did so. It called to mind some sort of builders' adhesive. A generous dollop was dished up for each of us. It looked disgusting. I took a mouthful, very gingerly and while the taste was not that bad, the texture was quite nasty. Sort of oily and lumpy at the same time, with just that hint of aniseed contained in many species of Agaricus mushrooms. A second mouthful found me glancing across to Cliff. He glanced at me likewise. There were no words. The plates were simply gathered up and placed safely to the side. Cliff then knocked up some bacon and eggs and all was well. That gastronomic event remains in both Cliff's memory and and my own. And finally before we leave the kitchen there is the Water Rail. I had been working out on the washes and returned to the house for lunch. Going to wash the sticky clay off my hands I was greeted by the sight of a Water Rail walking around in the kitchen sink. Muggins, Cliff's cat, had brought this bird in and yet there were no signs of physical damage nor aberrant behaviour. It was later released.

Other birds that came into our care included a Kestrel, which was poorly. We kept it in a shed outside and fed it cat food wrapped in fur and feathers. I recall Cliff tying a pellet of food to a string to encourage the bird to go for it. Birds of prey eat their food pretty much whole and fur and feathers all go down the same way. The bones and feathers are all cast up later in neatly packaged pellets and pellet formation is an integral part of such birds' digestive systems.

A broken winged Swift which was brought to me is mentioned elsewhere in this book. We had a Lapwing, which had a broken wing and a paddock was built for it to forage and dig for worms and whatever. Unfortunately, there were some who assumed that the RSPB was a specialised branch of the RSPCA and we would get phone calls from distressed people. A typical call might go along the lines that they had just run over a Greenfinch, its head looked crushed, it was bleeding at the mouth and its eyes were closed, but it was still breathing. In such hopeless cases we suggested dispatching the bird. Some were unable to do this and when we explained we were in fact not in the business of taking in injured birds they seemed quite put out. Of course these people meant well but far and away all accounts were of hopeless cases with only the one solution.

On one occasion, Cliff showed us slides of the washes in winter as neither Dave nor I had personally witnessed this. During this period the flooded washes are alive with thousands of ducks while Bewick's Swans and Grey Lag Geese grazed the fields just off the washes on adjacent farmland. Obviously management tasks took a bit of a back seat in the winter although there was plenty to keep the warden occupied.

Putting out grit for the wildfowl was an important job. Ducks, geese and swans need to take down sand and fine gravel to aid mechanical digestion in a special gastric intestinal organ called the gizzard.

Still inside the house I'll tell you of the 'Fen Blow'. No matter how much you dusted the house, it was not long before it was necessary again. The fen soil is very friable and as the wind blows across the flat exposed expanses it picks up fine particles of soil. It is highly penetrative and gets into all buildings, piling up on any flat surface. Over hundreds of years this has contributed to a lowering of the soil surface. Today, as you drive around the Fens you will see that half the telegraph poles are seriously leaning out of vertical, mostly outward away from the roadsides. You will also notice that the road you are on is a metre or so higher than the fields you are passing.

Social life outside the house was not lacking. Dave, Mark and I would frequently go down to the Ship Inn to down a few beers and discuss the day's events. Right outside the pub was a pontoon bridge, a floating structure made of plastic drums fastened together and with over-lying planking, the whole structure able to be swung open or closed to permit the passage of boats. This was convenient for visiting birders wishing to have access to the hides and also the pub.

Twice during my time on the Ouse Washes, Dave, Cliff and I went to a local 'western' evening. The Fen folk seemed to be very keen on country and western music (definitely not my favourite) and at these events many of the more committed people would dress up in cowboy finery. Some blokes even sported guns and spurs, indeed the whole shootin' match. These events were always in some farmer's barn and the tables and chairs were hay bales. Local C & W singers would knock out Johnny Cash, Dolly Parton, Glen Campbell songs of cowboy trouble and strife featuring prisons, jilted lovers and shoot-outs. Food was usually in the form of hamburgers and hot-dogs and there was certainly plenty of beer swilling and wild dancing with all the 'yee-hahs' you could wish for. Dave and I usually had different days off for obvious reasons but on one occasion he and I went out in his car to a site to see Golden Orioles nesting in the understorey of a White Poplar plantation, their favoured nesting habitat. We saw several birds although they kept pretty much to the canopy. I had acquired a girlfriend whose favours I had won when she came over with the conservation volunteers. She was a bright lady and was about to start at Cambridge University to read natural sciences. She, Eleanor and I travelled out some distance (it may have been Peterborough) one evening to see a play. It was about the First World War and the stage was set up as the aftermath of a skirmish with a couple of dead bodies lying before us as the soundtrack of gun and tank fire was played out. During the much longed for interval, Eleanor and I both agreed this was really depressing and we left the theatre and went off to find a bar.

While not actually social events, we would make weekly shopping trips to the nearest town of March. None of us were home drinkers but a bottle of whisky sometimes found its way onto the shopping list.

So, there we have it. A summary of a season working on a bird reserve. That season was to me one of the happiest and spiritually uplifting times in my life. If asked to sum it up in a word,

I would choose 'camaraderie'. All that I have written above comes straight from my memory, so much impact did that job make upon me.

In the next chapter I share with you the work on bird migration I was involved with over some years, living in the highest mountains of the world.

26. WITH THIS RING...

It is by now patently obvious that my main interest in the natural sciences is ornithology. Perhaps not so obvious is that within this subject my main focus, since university days in the mid to late '70s, has been the study of bird migration.

A university expedition to Ladakh, NW Himalaya, India in 1976 ignited my passion for this natural phenomenon, which totally defies belief once you delve into it. Three more expeditions to Ladakh followed and below is an account encapsulating all four, three of which I was involved with, both the planning/fundraising and in the field.

Ladakh (often spelt Ladak as it is pronounced such) is a region of northern India administered as a Union Territory. Covering an area of 59,100 square kilometres it is pretty much twice the size of Belgium. It lies on the eastern side of Jammu and Kashmir State in the NW Himalaya of India. It has been a bone of contention between India and Pakistan since partition (Indian independence) in 1947 and has been the source of various skirmishes between the two countries. Those differences still remain and a fragile peace reigns, at least for the moment. However, as I write, China to Ladakh's northern border is making menace and a skirmish resulted in 20 deaths just a few weeks ago. Thus it could well be described as being an extremely sensitive domain playing an important role in world politics. On all four of our expeditions, the Indian army showed a strong presence in Ladakh and was constantly on manoeuvres. Whilst part of India, Ladakh is culturally totally Tibetan, that country having been swallowed up by China in 1950. Tibet has never accepted this tragic takeover and still regards itself as an independent nation under unlawful occupation. If you were parachuted into Ladakh you would without doubt claim you had landed in Tibet. The language and script is much the same as Tibetan, the clothing, the Buddhist temples (gompas) sitting atop hills, their use of Yaks as both draught animals and providers of milk, the practise of polyandry and so much more.

The average altitude is about 3,000 metres and the terrain is, for the most part, dry stony desert with a fair smattering of snow-covered peaks, mostly unclimbed and unnamed, the highest being 6,153 metres. Local inhabitants are able to flourish by careful control of the glacial meltwater streams, which they direct to numerous hand-tilled fields by way of channels and the placement of small rocks. There they grow barley and generally manage two crops per year. The large range of vegetables that can be grown is amply demonstrated when you walk the main street in Leh, the 'capital' of Ladakh. The summers are baking hot and extremely dry while the winters bring much snowfall and way below zero temperatures. Around the end of October, the high passes from Kashmir into Ladakh freeze with roads being blocked by glacial ice and snow, causing Ladakh to be entirely closed off until around March or April the following year. The region had been closed to outsiders primarily for political reasons due to unrest to full blown war for over 30 years and in 1976 was just opening up. And so it was that we were on the way in.

Three climbers from my university (Southampton) whom I did not know, decided they would go to Ladakh that summer and climb a few peaks. I was in the student union bar one lunchtime in March 1976 when a student approached me and asked if I was Clive Denby. I acknowledged this and he followed up by asking if I wanted to go to Ladakh. "Probably," was my reply, "where is it?"

He gave me a quick run down and explained his reasons for wanting to go there. I asked where I fitted in to this plan and he said, "Science opens doors to money and I hear you are a bird man."

I was much impressed by his forthright approach. Having a lecture to go to, I arranged to meet him, Simon, up at the Crown and Sceptre, the nearby student pub, that evening. There, I was first introduced to two of his friends, Mike and Mark, and I learnt that all three were fellow climbers. We chatted, pored over a couple of maps and discussed my possible role as we supped our beers. I was to come up with a programme, which involved birds and Ladakh.

I managed to unearth some very old papers from the university library, written by early travellers to Ladakh, two of these being ornithologists, including one Colonel Meinertzhagen, who wrote a paper in 1927. This was to be my most recent reference to the resident birds of Ladakh. These accounts were quite brief and the diversity of birds did not seem that large. This is not a criticism – I am pleased that some of the earlier observers, often military men, undertook wildlife surveys and published their findings. I realized, however, that we would be in Ladakh for several months and that I would have the opportunity to build upon earlier work and would make my own study of the breeding birds of the region. The three students had all climbed together before but not stuff on a Himalayan scale. I suggested shortly after that we broaden our base and take along a botanist as well, which may also increase our chances of sponsorship.

Within a week we had met up with Janet, a third year medical student who was a keen botanist and eager to join us. She too created a programme of work. She would make a study of the plants of Ladakh, primarily the Indus Valley, including an investigation of the medicinal uses of plants if that were in fact the case. And a big plus point was having a medic on board, which gave us that much more credibility and would inspire confidence in our would-be sponsors. Her own department did indeed give a donation. With a lecturer friend and birder I knew back home in Colchester, Andrew, who would join us for five weeks, we had a strong team. The climbers, having written their own programme, we pooled all three and prepared a prospectus outlining the overall aims of the botanical, ornithological and mountaineering members.

Simon had managed to obtain Indian government permission for us to enter and carry out work in Ladakh so next was to send out a prospectus to any potential sponsors. With the aid of The Directory of Grant Making Trusts, which was housed in the library, we targeted about 20 trusts. We also had a splash in the local newspaper together with a radio interview. It was not too long before we started to get responses. Mostly, these were in the form of apologies and wishes of good luck but one day Simon walked into the union bar beaming and wafting a cheque for £100 from the Frederick Soddy Trust (no, we had not heard of it either much before then). With this the university was to become fully supportive and it too made us a monetary award. A Mr Eric Gordon, then the academic registrar of the university, advised us to secure Royal Geographical Society approval. He was an old hand at expeditions and had been on one studying blind white fish in Persian cave systems when studying at Cambridge University, some years previously. He was extremely supportive of our aims and offered to be our home agent. His secretary did any necessary typing for us and she too became quite involved, for which we were extremely grateful.

It was Mr Gordon who asked the Advanced Studies Committee to grant us an award of £100. Local and national bodies made various donations and, with our own proposed financial inputs, we knew that the expedition was unstoppable. A few lecturers were a bit miffed about the Advanced Studies donation as the fund was normally for their own research and not for a ragbag of undergraduates to 'have a good time' in the Himalaya. Various organisations and trusts topped up our coffers and national companies, notably Bachelors, supplied foodstuffs and their packet dried meat meals were a boon. We all had favourable credentials and with Mr Gordon fully captaining the ship, the whole outfit exuded an air of professionalism and confidence.

We all mugged up as much as we could on our various disciplines and Janet was chuffed to find that Ladakh did indeed use medicinal plants, a system called 'ampchi'. She also learnt that there was a military hospital in Leh where she could carry out her student elective, a piece of research, which all medical students have to undertake in places of their own choosing.

We purchased scientific equipment and the climbers purchased lightweight down-filled clothing, climbing ropes and accompanying hardware along with down sleeping-bags to combat sub-zero temperatures in the world's highest ranges. I needed just my binoculars. I had a pretty tired pair and treated myself to a new pair of Swift Audubons, my favoured optic by far. Over the years I have lost three pairs of Audubons. The first by having a badly secured bag on the back of my Vespa scooter (in my mid-teens) which contained my binoculars and another pair, which accidentally dropped over the side of an Irish ferry in 1983 after the well-worn lanyard broke, as I watched shearwaters. I replaced them with some less expensive glasses and in 1987 I bought a new pair of Audubons for Ethiopia, which were confiscated by Ethiopian customs as I entered the country. A replacement was smuggled into Ethiopia the following year and I still have them, miraculously!

In mid-June the five of us flew from London to New Delhi and thence travelled by overnight train to Jammu railhead. I recall eating just mangoes on that extremely long journey, becoming uncomfortably stickier and stickier, not wishing to brave the carriage toilet more than necessary. From there we moved by bus up to Srinagar, the main town of Kashmir, our heavy and laden packs put up onto the roof-rack along with scores of others and a tethered goat. There we stayed on a plush houseboat on the Dal Lake for two days while we picked up any last minute stuff we may need. While Kashmir and Ladakh are both in the same Indian state, the former is Muslim and tensions existed between it and Buddhist Ladakh. From Srinagar we again went by bus, up to Kargil, a whole day's journey. Spending the night in a rest-house we continued on the same bus to Leh (a distance of 130km) which took a long day due to the incredibly tortuous bends and the general condition of the road with ever-present sheer drops on one side. Drivers would overtake totally blind and simply rely on luck and possibly a short prayer. Having crossed a high pass called the Zoji La, which sits at over 3,500m above sea-level, we had left Kashmir and dropped down into Ladakh.

We set up a camp around 10km to the east of Leh in the settlement of Stok. From there the climbers would do their thing and Janet and I would independently go about our scientific business. Janet completed her botanical survey and also her medical elective and even found time to write a few well-penned poems, which she kept secret until the '76 Expedition Report was completed. I, together with Andrew, who had joined me, managed to amply swell the species lists of the earlier travellers and undertook a nine-week survey of the breeding birds. Andrew had to get back to the UK, leaving me for a short time as a one-man band.

Just before the end of my personal programme, I witnessed a fall of waders comprising about 10 species on the Indus River sandflats at Choglamsur, a bridging point across the Indus some way down from our camp. These were not breeding in Ladakh. They were palaearctic migrants, which breed in northern temperate climes. This told me something interesting. It told me that these migrants were here in the Indus Valley. But why?

That birds moved from their northern breeding grounds down to southern India and other parts of Asia was well established by the time of our expedition but it was assumed that these birds made a sort of pincer movement, passing around either end of the great mountain ranges that make up the Himalaya. However, if this were so then why would the birds be moving up or down the Indus Valley? It did not make sense.

The only alternative was that the birds were flying over hundreds of miles of high barren peaks and snowfields, breathing sub-zero temperature air, which was rarified (short of oxygen) and were dropping down as they came to the Indus Valley to replenish their fat reserves. This latter theory has pretty much been proven as a result of our four expeditions, although it may well be that different bird species use one or the other strategies.

Only with ringing stations set up at other Indus Valley sites in the Himalaya will sort this matter out further. My head was spinning that evening of the 'fall' as I mused on possibilities but I decided before turning in that we must mount as soon as we could a follow-up expedition, which concentrated on bird migration.

I was not a ringer but resolved to solve that problem by finding at least one. And so it came to pass that we organised a follow-up expedition in 1977, the '76 trip having met with considerable success, both scientific and with respect to the mountaineering. The climbers had 'knocked off' several peaks (some previously unclimbed), including Stok Kangri of 6,114 metres and Simon being an Archaeology graduate had done some detailed research into Ladakhi agriculture and the complex irrigation systems they used to grow their crops.

Due to financial stress, I did not take part in the '77 trip but was partly instrumental in its organisation. Another Simon was to be the other birder with myself, he holding a full bird-ringing licence (called an 'A' licence). This meant he could ring unsupervised using his own rings and that he could train others. Perfect!

I found a replacement for myself, Charlie, who was a biology student and a keen and experienced birder. Once again the same three climbers went along and did their own thing while Simon and Charlie did the bird work, this time involving lots of ringing. It was basically two separate expeditions.

The two birders were based at a village called Thikse (pronounced 'tiksay') and had the use of a forestry department hut courtesy of Tsering Narboo, the forest ranger based in Leh. It stood at an altitude of 3,300 metres, over three times the height of the summit of Mt Snowdon, UK. Use of the hut made an enormous contribution to the ringing work as Simon and Charlie had planned to operate from tents. Looking back, it is hard to see how the work could have been done nearly as well without having a fixed base. It was truly a ringing station. Simon trained Charlie to handle birds and to ring so between them they achieved a great deal and built substantially on my work of 1976. Tsering Narboo had more than a passing interest in and knowledge of birds and was incredibly supportive and remained so on future expeditions. Once ensconced in the hut, Simon and Charlie set up a few mist-nets in the plantation, which comprised willow and poplar along with Hippophae (Sea Buckthorn) bushes, which produced berries so important for birds later in the year. They then started the ringing programme, which ran for 63 days together with regular systematic observation, which yielded a burgeoning list of birds and they ringed over 960 individuals of 29 species.

Once again, a report was produced and our work was becoming known by, and accessible to a wider audience. The '77 trip was a huge success but even that was to be surpassed. It had not covered the northerly spring migration period around April/May and had not extended to the very end of the autumn migration period. It became obvious with myself and Simon having finished university, we could go for a longer trip. We found a third birder, John, who had just graduated in biology. Charlie was tied up with his PhD on over-wintering of aphids and was not going to join us. Having three birders was fine but again we broadened the research by finding two botanists, both fresh biology/botany graduates from the university. Clare and Anne were taken on board and once again a prospectus of work was drawn up. Sponsorship flowed in pretty well once we had been given the approval of the Royal Geographical Society, an essential requirement if any expedition is to get funding from elsewhere. In addition to university grants and those from trusts, we received a load of produce, theatre tickets from local bodies. These we raffled, having procured a licence from the local council. That raised £170. With air tickets purchased and examinations over, we were set to go, and left around mid-June.

So, we were embarking on the 1980 expedition and this time there was to be a variation.

We stopped off in Srinagar as before and there stocked up on various goodies we would need. These included a dozen three metre long bamboo poles for mist-net supports, which I never believed we would find. I struggled back from town with these over my shoulder and was thoroughly exhausted when I got back to the houseboat. Apparently, I collapsed there and was mumbling away piles of gibberish to the others (more than usual one informed me!). They diagnosed that I was delirious through sunstroke. Whatever it was, lots of water, sweet tea and a good night's sleep cured it.

We continued our journey by bus from Srinagar to Kargil and there, once again, overnighted but instead of moving onward to Leh the following day we headed south down the Suru Valley. There we would not do any ringing but take a look at the breeding birds. We travelled southwards down the valley by open truck about half of our proposed distance, over a hundred kilometres and camped for a couple of nights when it rained profusely. We then waited for another whole day for a truck heading south but few came and none could take all five of us. Finally, I decided I would walk, taking the pressure off numbers. John readily joined me so our departure may well give the other three a better chance of a ride. John and I walked for three days, spending two nights under canvas in a field that must have been a mosquito reserve. We were bitten to pieces but happily neither of us contracted malaria (they may not have been malaria carrying mosquitoes). We were not taking malaria prophylactics as Ladakh is supposedly free of the parasite, which causes the disease although the Suru Valley may have been a different story.

On that walk John and I were carrying substantial packs and it was quite tough-going but nonetheless rewarding. We did cook up a hot meal on each of the two evenings but during the day we would feed simply on tsampa, the barley flour, which serves as staple in Ladakh. Tsampa with river water makes a fairly good porridge made all the more palatable with sugar. We passed right by the snout of a huge glacier with a vertical front wall of about 10 metres thickness – it was just like something out of a geography textbook. We both had our first sightings of a Wall Creeper, such beautiful birds with their distinctive butterfly-like flight. John and I arrived at the settlement, which was to serve as our base for the next week. Coincidentally, the other three arrived by truck at precisely the same time as John and I, they having managed to get a lift. We had brought tents from Britain for both camping in the Suru Valley and also, possibly, at the Thikse site. We had no guarantee that the hut would again be available. We set up camp and the three birders birded and the botanists botanised.

I wandered off to a shallow pool where two

Black-winged Stilts waded on their beautiful red... stilts. A few other waders fed and then rose up as a large unidentified raptor flew high overhead. Unlike Janet in 1976, the two botanists were actually making collections of pressed plants and collecting certain pre-specified seeds. This they were doing for The Royal Botanic Gardens at Kew which was our most generous sponsor. I made a long walk out to the gompa (monastery) at Rungdom and laboured up the hill to introduce myself (I had yet to fully acclimatize to the altitude). On the wall a Tickell's Willow Warbler pecked around for insects. I was invited in and sat down in a wide circle of Buddhist monks. These were all, without exception, engaged in jovial chat and drinking 'chang', a sparkling and refreshing beer made from barley, the staple crop of Ladakh. Any society which has enough of its staple to go on to produce alcoholic drink is clearly faring well. This was my first taste of chang – absolutely wonderful and, reputedly, it does not leave one with a hangover. That later turned out to be true as we had loads of this stuff during this and the '81/2 expedition, which was to follow.

Down the Suru Valley was our first time using the Primus stoves and they were playing up - each had their own personality. They would frequently get bunged up and needed constant pricking. I think probably the problem lay not with the stoves but the quality of the kerosene.

We were constantly aware of the possibility of running out of kerosene (a large quantity would prove difficult to carry in our packs and make everything smell) and there at our camp we were indeed running a bit low. One evening, just over the way, an army truck pulled up and about five men stepped out. They erected a tent and got a fire going. They invited us over – they were in civvies and not, I suspect, on a military mission. They had brought along twigs and small branches and started liberally pouring loads of kerosene onto the pile, which they then lit. More kerosene was occasionally added most liberally as Simon and I exchanged glances of horror, as this precious liquid was chucked around with gay abandon. We explained our plight and Colonel Kumar gave us a few litres of fuel. He and his men sang us an Indian folksong and we tried to reciprocate by singing them Ilkley Moor Baa'tat… so much for British culture.

We awoke the next morning and they had gone with scarcely any sign they had ever been there – it must have been very early for we too were up at dawn. A few days later we prepared to head back north to Kargil. We had had a productive week, both botanically and bird-wise. We had a final birding session and saw a Pheasant-tailed Jacana padding over some water vegetation - as jacanas do, with the aid of their absurdly long lobed toes) some distance away, quite a sighting of a most attractive bird. We arranged a truck for the following morning and broke camp early. It took eight long tortuous hours to get to Kargil as all five of us alternately sat and stood in the back of a truck, which was also transporting a goat, held occasionally pinned to the truck side with the back of Simon's legs. The poor creature was constantly peeing (the goat, not Simon), which added to our luxury travel. Conversation was impossible as the ancient lorry rattled, banged and thumped its way along the narrow rock-strewn road. Any bird watching was totally out of the question. The dust was hard to bear and as the suspension was totally ruined, our internal organs were permanently re-arranged. It was a hell of a trip but we were very thankful. I suspected that even the goat needed some therapy. We spent a well-earned night in a Kargil rest-house and the next day set off for Leh.

Happily, once more we had use of the forestry hut and Tsering Narboo was there to assist us. The hut was perfectly placed. It was 15 minutes walk from the road to Leh, 100 metres from the Indus River and just 30 metres from our only neighbours, a Ladakhi husband and wife and their three children. The river flowed strong and wide from the south-east to the north-west. Either side of us loomed the Ladakh Range to the north and the Zanskar Range to the south, each having peaks in excess of 6,000 metres.

The children would often watch as we worked away on the verandah and occasionally they would bring us large bottles of chang, which the family had made themselves. We would in turn give them sugar, something they could not afford and which was welcomed. The parents were probably younger than they looked as the powerful sun's rays at this altitude gnarled the skin, making people look older. We thought that Ladakhi ladies had eye problems due to sitting in smoky huts but I believe that everyday exposure to the sun was also a contributor. Typically, a Ladakhi man would wear an ankle-length brown sack-cloth affair and a traditional Ladakhi hat that I am at pains to describe. If it helps it is much the same as a Tibetan hat. These were tall and chimney-like and had extensions, which hung down to protect the backs of the wearer's necks from acute sunburn and also ear-flaps, I presume for use in the frigid winters. The ladies wore a lot of turquoise on their hats and in beautiful chunky necklaces. Both sexes wore sort of sack-cloth shoes, which curled up at the toes. All adults and some older children would be seen with a spinning reel in one hand and a ball of raw wool in the other. Prayer wheels were also commonly held in the hand as they went about their daily affairs. The monks who all live in the hill-top gompas wear bright red clothing and characteristic hats unique to Buddhist monks in Ladakh. I do not wish to sound impolite here but Ladakhi people would rub butter into their skins and hair, which would turn rancid and give a characteristic 'bouquet', particularly in their houses. It served the purpose of keeping their skin moist and thus prevented cracking from drying out. One particular habit of Ladakhi people (and Tibetans) is the preparation of salt-tea. This is what it sounds like, tea with salt in it and not sugar. It is made by placing knobs of yak butter into a long wooden tube and next adding the tea, plenty of salt and hot water. The tea infuses, the salt dissolves, the butter melts and the preparer works a plunger up and down inside the tube. This makes a characteristic gurgling sound and thus gives the tea its onomatopoeic name of 'gul-gul chai'. It is topped off with a sprinkling of tsampa and the end product has a seductive pink colour. All of our team agreed that it was extremely refreshing and I could not get enough of it as I sipped it from small delicate cups in which it was served. The reason for the salt? It replaces that lost from the body by constant loss through sweating in the hot dry climate.

The two girls had gone off in a jeep with some botanical people and we would not be meeting up for a few weeks. Us three birders spent a day in Leh getting yet more supplies, largely fresh vegetables – as much as we could carry and kerosene for the stoves. We contacted Tsering Narboo again and he came down with us to the Thikse site. He assured us the hut was available once more but guessed it may be surrounded by floodwater. He was right but it was clearly going down. Even so, we returned to Leh and returned to the Thikse site two days later. We were able to stay but it would be a week before the nets could be set up. Oh what a relief – I dreaded having to operate from tents. Tsering Narboo had made arrangements for us to have access to the 10 volumes of Handbook of Indian Birds edited by the great guru of Indian ornithology Dr Salim Ali. This, published between 1968 to 1974 was a very handy reference. We were also able to refer to A Synopsis of the Birds of India and Pakistan, also by Dr Ali. The hut was made of dried mud and about the size of a medium bedroom. There was not a stick of furniture, no carpeting or even lino'. This was to be our home for five blissful months doing what we liked best. Annexed to the main room was a smaller one, which we used as a store. There was a porcelain urinal but it was not plumbed in. It did, however, come to be used as an excellent fruit bowl. There was a single light bulb in the main room, which gave a weak light in the evenings and had a habit of going off if it was windy. A couple of the windows were without glass although we did bung them up with cardboard. We had purchased a wood/coal burning stove in Leh complete with a metal chimney, which was arranged to take smoke out of one of the windows and that was a most welcome luxury in our lives. It was usually lit in the evenings, which were cold even in summer time. We could buy coal and wood from depots in Leh. The wood was bought in the form of huge single pieces. We had no decent axe and used to split a large log, maybe two metres long, first by forcing small flattened pebbles into cracks and banging them deeper with larger rocks until something gave, normally with a loud whip-like crack. This may have been done several times until our puny axe could reduce the timber to stove-manageable pieces. Our actions must have looked quite Palaeolithic. The stove worked very well and in our small room we were made readily comfortable. Sometimes, if the wind changed round we had to make adjustments to the cowling to prevent us being smoked to death. With sand blowing in through the door and windows together with the dust and fine ash particles generated by the stove, daily sweeping out of the hut became routine. We slept on the concrete floor in sleeping bags but we had karrimats, wafer thin but fairly effective even for me somewhat lacking in fleshy parts. Some of the food such as the tsampa flour and dried apricots had to be stored in cleaned bird bags and suspended from the ceiling. This was because a thriving population of mice was ever-present and busy foraging during the nights. We hardly ever saw them but we certainly could hear them. Happily, we were in a cockroach-free zone, nasty characters indeed.

A pressure cooker I brought from Britain

enabled us to cook efficiently at our altitude of 3,300 metres. Every evening we would take one of the packet meals (donated by Bachelors) and add quite an array of vegetables forming the most delicious, full-bodied and nutritious stews one could wish for. The curried meals were favourites. There was always plenty and we forever praised Bachelors for their kind donation – they had supported three of our expeditions and were to do the same for the fourth. For afters we would have fruit, often soaked dried apricots (chuli), which grew widely in Ladakh and were widely available in Leh. It was immediately after our much longed for evening meal that we completed the daily log and had various discussions about the day's events or about plans for the next day. The diversity of vegetables in Leh was most impressive and the ladies who squatted along the pavements who sold them kept the vegetables meticulously clean and neatly arranged, often piled in precarious pyramids. There would be half a dozen veg' ladies lined up next to each other with their fare and there were never signs of competing. We did try to spread our purchases out between a few of the ladies on any one shopping trip. Breakfasts followed a bit of a ritual. John became the japatti-man and prepared wicked japattis on which we had margarine and apricot jam, which we made ourselves. Tea flowed copiously throughout the day.

Our water supply was the Indus River, which flowed a stone's throw from the hut. This was simply scooped up in a bucket. Initially, we just used to drink from this but after a while we noticed some patterns of gastric disturbances. We were told that these were caused by suspended rock flour as the water was glacial. Thereafter, we would let the water stand overnight. Two centimetres of sediment could be seen the next morning settled on the bottom of the bucket. We each had our favourite washing sites, generally using the small streams that ran close to the hut and clothes too had to be washed - occasionally.

We went shopping once a week and just the one of us would go. The bus left from a stopping place about a kilometre from the hut at the base of Thikse gompa. I recall on one occasion when waiting (there was no timetable as such) watching a flock of Alpine Swifts. These large swifts are identified by their white throats and bellies and broad brown chest bands. As I watched them a male hobby, scarcely larger than the swifts, flew into the flock and grabbed one by a wing-tip, hanging on determinedly and taking the bird off, probably to a mate or young – it was a strange sight as the swift slowly beat its free wing. One could also watch a Hoopoe bringing in food to a pollarded willow where it had its nest. The clapped-out bus finally arrived and it would take over an hour to complete the 18km journey to Leh, billows of black smoke belching out from its exhaust due to lack of servicing and a clapped-out engine with shot piston rings. I rarely got a seat and even when I did I did the gentlemanly thing, generally regretting it after 20 minutes. The bus was always heaving with humanity and maybe a goat and a chicken or two.

The shopper would post our outgoing mail and collect any incoming mail from poste restante. We were advised to see that the stamps on our outgoing mail were franked before us as the stamps may be steamed off and sold again - this was ever the case in much of Africa as well I am sad to say. One perk for the shopper was to pop into a tea-house to luxuriate on lassi, an astonishingly ambrosial curd served in a tall glass. A shopping trip was basically a day's work as buses were not that frequent. One could return by jeep, which was infinitely quicker and saved the battles that ensued getting onto the bus but this was quite expensive. I did so on two occasions when fully loaded up with victuals and kerosene, having to stand on a small plate sticking out from the back of the vehicle. It would have made a health and safety nerd have proverbial kittens. Ferrying the stuff from the bus stop over the fields to the hut was also no mean task. Once I stupidly carried a heavy bag of coal to the hut and suffered for my folly for a fortnight, probably having crushed a nerve. For most of the season there was still standing water in the plantation so I built a series of very basic bridges over these rivulets with any bits of wood we could salvage, generally from old fruit boxes. These were appreciated by all as a net round (checking all six nets for birds) would demand crossing these streams every 15 minutes or so. The nets were opened straight after breakfast and kept open until about 1300hrs.

The afternoons were either spent carrying out observation, walking some 10 kilometres up to Choglamsur, or perhaps just to Shey lying halfway between Chog' and our hut. Shey marsh often produced some good birds even though it was only a few hectares in area. Sometimes one of us would use an afternoon to simply relax, read or maybe write letters.

One afternoon chore however was Simon's prerogative – sewing up torn mist-nets, a very slow and laborious process. The neighbours owned a yak, which had one deformed horn that hung slightly awry such that it would snick our nets when they were open. This yak would sometimes sit quite contented right outside our hut on the pebble-covered ground, probably chewing its cud. I had named him Yak Cousteau in honour of the great marine biologist (which I thought was rather amusing).

Ringing was our primary task, so I will outline here the process from capture to release of a bird. Having removed a trapped bird from a net, we placed it in its own canvas bird bag, which had a draw string (these we had made in Leh). We took it in turns to do net rounds and on each trip would generally come back with around half a dozen birds. These were processed on the concrete verandah fronting the hut. As one processed, another would act as scribe noting down the ring numbers and the biometric data including sex and age, if possible. After a bird was carefully removed from its bag it was popped into a weighing cone, using a finely calibrated spring balance. Then the bird would be ringed using special pliers ensuring of course that the correct size be fitted. The rings were supplied by the Bombay Natural History Society. Ringing was followed by taking a wing measurement using a special rule. Also the tarsus and the beak were measured as was the tail. Simon would be the one to check for moult as he was the expert in this. Finally, John would photograph the bird held in a hand and it would then be released, the entire processing taking about two minutes.

Occasionally, a bird would remain sitting on your hand and had to be given time and gently encouraged to leave. On one occasion the three of us were walking up to Choglamsur from the hut and an Ibisbill settled nearby. This odd-looking but most spectacular wader had been seen a couple of times by us but certainly not caught and ringed. Simon had a mist-net (I can't remember why) and he put this up without any shielding cover. Miraculously, we caught the bird but then learnt that we did not have the correct sized ring. I made a mercy-dash back to the hut (about half a kilometre) and returned a panting wreck (we were at 3,300m altitude!). He ringed it, one of the few waders we ever got to ring.

The other time we caught a bird in a net erected out in the open with no cover was when a Song Thrush I had seen some days earlier when on my own, flew past the hut and its call was picked up by Simon's excellent hearing. We caught and ringed the bird and I was so relieved as this turned out to be a new bird for India. To have been a sole observer was definitely not good and the record may well not have been accepted by the Indian birding fraternity.

Some of the observation afternoons were carried out by bicycle. We had bought two Hercules bicycles in Srinagar on the way through, which were most welcome. An additional aid to observation was a permanently mounted telescope on the verandah. This was useful for watching out for birds passing down along the Indus. There was a ten-day period when an Osprey sat on top of a distant telegraph pole right by the river and we would often see it working its way through a large fish.

Medically, things went very well and we had few problems. The most notable was when Simon was removing the only bat we captured (accidentally) during the season. It bit him. Bats are well-known for being reservoirs of rabies so he took the bat to the army hospital in Leh, hoping that if they identified it they may be able to administer a particular drug and that would be the end of it. This was not to be and Simon had to make four journeys to Leh over the following weeks to have jabs in the stomach. He was of course OK but it was quite inconvenient to have him out of service at any time.

Flatulence, hardly a disease of course, was far more than one was used to – something to do with differing air-pressures in the gut and the outer world, I gather. We did have eye-ointment with us and this was administered several times to our neighbours.

Ladakhi ladies spend a lot of time sitting in their smoke-ridden rooms and therefore suffer eye problems. Janet (our student/botanist) had identified this problem in 1976 and recommended any future expeditions come armed with eye-ointment.

During the course of all this busy ringing schedule, the girls came to join us for a while and also a couple of birding friends came out from the UK for a few weeks to assist. Clare and Anne ensured all their plant collections were in good order along with the seed collections. All in all the expedition had proceeded without much hitch and we had achieved all expectations and more. So, surely now with three trips in the bag that must be it. Not quite.

Chancing our respective arms, we put out cautious feelers for yet another expedition to Ladakh, once again with Simon, Clare and I with our names down. There was certainly plenty more to do but could we get the support? Our justification was that to go for a full year we could cover both the northward spring migration and the southward autumn migration. It would also incorporate a winter, which should prove interesting with temperatures down to minus 30°C. We knew from past experience we could muster up the personnel – there was no shortage of birders we knew between us who wanted to come out for short spells to help us. Even my own involvement was going to be fairly brief, just three months, covering the winter period. We decided to go for it and just for a change and lest the term 'Ladakh expedition' was becoming a bit hackneyed, we called it the University of Southampton Ornithological Project. As in the previous three trips we went through the process of applying for sponsorship. One huge boost was getting not only the approval of the Royal Geographical Society (essential for any expedition trying to raise money) but the RGS also made a monetary award of £250, the first time that financial aid had been conferred on a bunch of fresh graduates. Thereafter the money flowed in and with Mr Gordon once again the home agent, we had full university backing, despite the fact that all of us had graduated over a year ago. The Southampton University Convocation gave us £500, the British Ecological Society £500 and the prestigious Mount Everest Foundation £400 even though we were nothing to do with mountaineering. The largest single grant was from a bequest given via the Linnaen Society, the whopping sum of £700. And these were indeed whopping sums bearing in mind this was 1981. What would they be worth in today's money? Funding not only paid for air fares, travel within India, equipment, and our subsistence but also for the writing up and printing/distribution of our subsequent reports. We pretty much knew the ropes by now, how to get sponsorship, where to get the rings, how to undertake the ringing programme, how to maximise the benefit of those who would come out to help, how to obtain Indian government permission and how to analyse the data and present it in the form of reports and papers.

The '81/2 project started around early August. I was not able to get out until early November. For one thing I was busy getting the report for the 1980 expedition written up while at the same time doing a paid job. We all contributed of course to the report but I was pulling together a lot of the non-birdy organisational stuff (food, medical, fundraising). Once again it was to be our key man, Simon, working the programme. This time Clare accompanied Simon wearing a new hat - that of ornithologist. She had managed to gain a fair working knowledge of western palaearctic birds and this improved rapidly throughout the project. Charlie was to come and lend an experienced hand and a few others were lined up for various time slots. It was all pretty relaxed – people would come when they could.

For my own part, I flew out to Join Simon and Clare on November 7, 1981. Going this late I had to fly to Leh direct from Delhi, the roads into Ladakh being well and truly closed and snowed up. They would be closed until about early April. The road journey in to Ladakh was always epic, with hair-pin bends on rock-strewn roads winding their way precariously throughout the mountains. Most of the road was poorly surfaced, the gravel making progress very dangerous, especially when two vehicles had to pass each other on roads barely two trucks wide. The drivers would not hesitate to overtake blind and quite a few buses had gone over the side complete with passengers – so much for the value of human life in these parts. This time, flying in was also not without some excitement. Landing a Boeing 737 at Leh airport meant putting the aircraft down into a small basin between surrounding peaks. This demanded flying back and forth, bringing the plane lower and lower until it could be landed. I was informed it was one of the top 10 most dangerous airports in the world.

I arrived at the hut to hear of Simon and Clare's last three months and the autumn migration. I was able to hand them a copy of the 1980 report. Simon and Clare had much to share and it was mouth-watering stuff and I was sore that I had not been there. Anyway, I would at least spend the winter there. No ringing took place for rather obvious reasons and washing was pretty much abandoned during the winter. It did not matter, as firstly we were all in the same boat and secondly, bacterial action is much reduced in these frigid conditions. It was far too cold and therefore unsafe for birds for us to net them and also there was no lateral migration taking place. The previous few weeks had seen altitudinal migration occurring as birds breeding up in the hills moved down to the Indus Valley for the winter months. We kept a max-min thermometer on the verandah. During my winter stay the lowest temperature was -30°C and it never got above -20°C for several months. Water collection then involved smashing up ice, which had formed over the surface of the Indus River.

By the time I arrived, both Simon and Clare needed a well-earned break. I won't say rest unless walking many miles down a frozen river carrying a heavy pack and sleeping in caves at sub-zero temperatures constitutes a rest. Simon had gone 'down the ice' with a chap we met,

Dave, the year before. They were not entirely alone as local people went down the ice to trade with settlements far away. Clare did something a little more restful and went down to Plains India for a few weeks. This meant that for about a month I was left alone at the site.

I managed to get out most days to carry out observation and there was plenty going on. Even on days when I would have preferred to stay in the hut, I went out about mid-morning for a few hours, normally walking up to Choglamsur and back. It was nowhere as busy as at other times of year but I generally managed a score or so of species on each trip. Cracking open the tree logs with pebbles kept me busy but I did have some coal to use in the stove. Staying out for much of the day extended the life of the fuel supply. I could have done with a radio in the evenings, particularly for music but I stayed happy.

I longed for a guitar, but carting one around India was a non-starter. I had an Icelandic sleeping bag but that became insufficient even in the hut and I bought an ex-army sleeping bag in Leh using one inside the other. I did not have to shop as frequently of course but I enjoyed it when I did go into Leh.

I shall not list my winter birds save to mention the flock of about twenty Tibetan Sandgrouse I observed from our verandah flying some way off and making calls, which sounded like a gaggle of geese.

STUFF ABOUT BIRDS

At Shey marsh a Bittern sat in the same spot every day for weeks, its body temperature doubtless keeping an area unfrozen so it could still catch fish. I thought it might be worthwhile taking black and white photographs during the winter, feeling this may produce some dramatic shots of both people and snow-covered peaks. I was right and pleased with my efforts. I had these made into slides and at the end of any subsequent public talks my black and white winter shots always went down well and evoked comment.

I left our hut in mid-February to go off to an RSPB job but four others were to come out separately to help Simon and Clare cover the spring migration period including Charlie who was on the 1977 trip. Everyone always fitted in well and there were never any significant issues arising between personnel.

Here is not the place to start reeling off lists of birds – you can follow up the reference given in the appended Reading List at the back of the book, a paper which was prepared by Simon and Charlie in 2014 covering all four expeditions along with lists, tables, photos and a map. However, below is a summary of the bird action on the '81/2 Project, which lasted for just three weeks shy of a full year.

A total of one hundred and ninety species was recorded, mostly long-distance migrants, the majority of which were moving either north or south between the northern Palearctic and lowland India. Just under twenty species were Palearctic – African migrants. Thirty-four species were hitherto not seen before in Ladakh and eight of the nine birds new for India were seen on the project. The 'new' birds were all passerines: Black-browed Reed Warbler; Sedge warbler; Great reed Warbler; Common Redstart; Eurasian Linnet; Song Thrush; Lesser Grey Shrike and Yellowhammer all of which were caught and ringed with the exception of the last. A Garden Warbler caught and ringed in 1980 was also a first for India. Four bird species constituted second records for India. The number of birds ringed was over 5,500 of fifty-five species. We had more than a thousand re-traps of our own birds. By far the most numerous ringed species was Guldenstadt's Redstart (2010) followed by Mountain Chiffchaff (475), House Sparrow (334) and Common Rosefinch (212). Brown Accentor, Hume's Lesser Whitethroat and Red-spotted Bluethroat all numbered well over a hundred each. A further twenty-two species each numbered less than ten birds and twenty species each had just the one representative. Of the species which were just observed, twenty-nine were raptors including four different Harrier species, Short-toed Eagle and Merlin. Other non-passerines featured Little Egret, two crake species, Demoiselle Crane and both Long and Short-eared Owls.

When we come to consider all four expeditions collectively we can boast two hundred and thirty-one species, seventy-one of which had not been recorded in Ladakh before. A total of 7,623 individual birds of sixty-nine species were caught and ringed, most of which were passerines or near-passerines. We were all scientists in various disciplines but that does not detract from our collective sense of wonder of feathered, hollow-boned creatures, some weighing as little as 8.3 grammes (eg Mountain Chiffchaff) making their way over these forbidding mountain ranges as they moved to more favourable conditions. The wastage rate is surely enormous but provided that nature can balance the books then all these inveterate travellers will sustain their populations for many millions of years to come.

Simon and Clare furled the mist-nets for the last time on July 10, 1982 and we were surely done with Ladakh by now. We have each since taken jobs in conservation and teaching and have kept in touch, meeting up about once a year to re-cap on old times together up in them-there hills doing what many can only dream of. We were all lucky, very lucky but having said that, you can to a large extent make your own luck. We left it to others who so wished to further our work which, allow me to say, was the most comprehensive trans-Himalayan bird-ringing study ever undertaken in Ladakh and indeed probably the entire Himalaya. It all happened thanks to climber Simon who had told me in all honesty in a bar that 'science opens doors to money'.

27. GETTING COLD FEET
- MAY BE, MAY BE NOT...

If you asked any child or indeed many adults to define a penguin you would probably get something like 'A black and white flightless bird, which feeds on fish and lives in icy places'. This is fair enough but as a birder this is in no way good enough and needs looking at. Firstly, 'penguin' is a broad term covering a whole family of birds. Within the family are six genera and these together contain 18 species. The black and white bit is basically true although 10 species of penguins do display some bright colouration (yellow and orange) especially about the head and neck region. Flightless is certainly correct but you can be pretty sure their ancestors did once fly. Penguins have not lost their wings but they are much reduced... but far from useless. See penguins underwater and you may well think they are flying, so adept are their old wings now converted to flippers (of course I am talking on an evolutionary timescale of millions of years). Feeding on fish is for the most part correct but one species hardly utilizes this food source. Now, here is the best bit and a way to win bets. Two thirds (yes, two thirds) of penguin species never set their feet on ice as they do not inhabit or venture onto the great landmass of

Antarctica. These live in the continents of Africa, Australia and South America while New Zealand also has representatives. One penguin species lives bang on the equator in the Galapagos Islands. So, only six species of penguin ever get cold feet!

Let's consider some features characteristic of the family. Birds spending a lot of their time on the sea are usually black and white. This is all about camouflage. From below the white underparts make the birds difficult to see and thus protects them to some extent from predators like sharks and leopard seals. Predators from above will not readily see penguins as their black upperparts blend in with the dark sea surface. The auks of the northern hemisphere have adopted the same principle although they are not closely related to penguins.

Penguin sexes are generally alike but males may stand taller and be heavier than females. Both sexes take part in incubation and rearing of the single young. All species are monogamous, sticking to the one partner unless one dies. In all species the wings have, over evolutionary time, been modified to form flippers for swimming. Some use them to work their way through dense vegetation such as Little Penguins. In all species the feet have large strong claws and the feet are webbed. Birds have hollow bones for obvious reasons but penguins are the exception. Their bones are solid to permit the birds to stay under water for protracted periods – hollow bones would make them too buoyant. All can dive to considerable depths (Emperors up to more than 500m) and can reach speeds of around 15km/hr, their bullet-shaped bodies affording efficient streamlining. A common habit is that of 'porpoising', where a bird charging rapidly through the water suddenly leaps up and out of the water, gliding for a few metres enabling it time to grasp a fresh lungful of air. This action may also help a bird escape being caught by a predator. Penguins, like all birds, moult annually and when doing so they are unable to enter the sea. Bills of penguin species are quite varied ranging from short and squat to long and fairly thin. All young birds are fed by the parents regurgitating food. Adults contact their young by being able to identify their calls. Adults also communicate with each other by both calls and body language. When left alone while the parents are out at sea feeding, the chicks huddle together to keep warm. Chicks can survive for long periods without food because of their generous fat (blubber) reserves. Adults, which live in extremely cold conditions on the Antarctic ice sheet including King and Emperor Penguins, also huddle, those birds on the outside slowly getting to move inwards, a true sign of altruism in my opinion. Penguin huddles may number many thousands of individuals. The huge colonies (sometimes numbering millions of birds) comprising both adult and young birds of the one species are called 'rookeries' which are very busy, noisy and smelly places. Ice-dwelling penguins move by waddling but also sliding on their bellies (tobogganing) is important. Courtship displays by the males involve standing erect with necks outstretched and flippers held wide apart, braying rather like donkeys. Any interested females may copy the male's actions. Fights may break out between either sexes when birds try to steal nesting material from their neighbours.

Killers of penguins are chiefly Leopard Seals, Sea Lions, some shark species and Killer Whales, the latter known to tip up ice-flows on which penguins are resting. Skuas and gulls will readily feed on penguin eggs as will introduced animals like cats, dogs, foxes and ferrets.

Eight species live on or around the margins and islands of Antarctica: Emperor, King, Adelie, Gentoo, Royal, Rockhopper, Chinstrap (Bearded) and Macaroni Penguins. Three inhabit South America: the Magellanic, the Peruvian and the Galapagos Penguins. Yellow-Eyed, Fjordland and Snares Penguins are found in New Zealand and a further two occur in Australia, the Little and the Erect-crested. Jackass Penguins live on the western coasts of South Africa and Namibia.

We'll now take a deeper look and delve into the lives of three very differing species: the Emperor, the Little and the Fjordland penguins.

As its name suggests, the Emperor Penguin is the largest of the family, standing at about 1.3m tall. Antarctic penguins will lose a lot of weight over the breeding season and an Emperor will range between just over 20 – 45kg making it the heaviest non-ratite bird on earth. Being so large enables it to cope with the coldest conditions ever to beset a penguin, breeding in the Antarctic winter months. The temperature may plummet to -40° C and add to this the chill inflicted by winds of over 140km/h. The dense feathers and up to three centimetres of subcutaneous fat each serve to keep the birds warm. In addition, the feathers can be made to stand erect thus trapping air close to the body. Keeping the feathers compressed ensures that good waterproofing is maintained when diving.

The sexes are alike in size and plumage being the standard black and white but they have yellowish upper breasts and necks. Just after breeding, the adult plumage turns brownish immediately prior to the annual moult. Emperors have a life expectancy of around twenty years but there are suggestions that this may be more than doubled. Emperor and King Penguins are together known as the 'Great' penguins.

Emperors, like their smaller cousins, feed on fish, crustaceans, krill and cephalopods such as squid. A feeding foray may take the bird down to 500m and an underwater stay of about twenty minutes. They have a special kind of haemoglobin in the red-blood cells, which helps them make greater use of a lungful of air. As with other penguins, a bird can return to its mate or young on land with a full crop and then regurgitate its catch. A single crop-load may weigh four kilograms.

They breed on stable pack-ice often some way offshore and can do so after their first three years. The female lays a single egg, which is initially incubated by the male while she goes off to sea for up to a couple of months. The male has to sit it out as he burns up some of his valuable fat reserves. When she returns with a crop full of food, having travelled up to 1,000km at sea, it is the turn of the male to go off feeding and have a break from standing on the ice. There are nearly fifty breeding colonies of Emperors in Antarctica. Some individuals have been seen as far north as South Georgia and even New Zealand.

In 2009 a census counted over half a million birds. Natural predators are Southern Giant Petrels, which take up to one third of chicks. Leopard Seals and Killer Whales will frequently take adults. Natural predation is all written into the balanced equation but Emperors, along with nine other species of penguin, are today classified as endangered species. All ten species are undergoing falling food stocks with industrial harvesting and climate change working together. Tourism is also of concern but it is not yet understood how the increasing presence of humans affects the birds.

Let's move to the other end of the penguin scale and discuss Little Penguins. These are clearly the smallest, standing at about 33cm high. Also called Fairy Penguins, these are found on the coast of South Australia, and also New Zealand where they are known as Blue Penguins because of their slate-blue upper plumage instead of the more usual black. There is no yellow or orange in the plumage but they do have pink feet. They weigh a mere 1.5kg, just three per cent the weight of an Emperor. This is because of their lifestyle, which does not demand a thick layer of blubber under the skin. They spend most of their days at sea feeding on much the same as their huge cousins but will also dine on crab larvae, jellyfish and sea-horses, the latter being just another kind of fish. They tend to feed quite close to the shore and do not often dive to great depths, hence further obviating the need for blubber. They can remain under water for only about one or two minutes but they have no need for protracted dives.

Little Penguins breed mostly on islands dotted along the South Australian coastline including Tasmania and also around the entire coastline of New Zealand. The more successful colonies are those breeding on islands free of feral cats and foxes. During the southern hemisphere winter the males come to shore to repair or to build afresh their burrows, digging with their feet. Some birds will use the old burrows of other animals. All burrows are generally close to the sea. Mated birds breed either colonially or in isolated pairs. Some pairs will alternately share a burrow with prions or maybe Short-tailed Shearwaters. Those not preferring burrows may use caves, rock crevices or even nest under man-made structures. The Littles are the only penguins to lay more than one clutch per year and may even have three broods. Both sexes share in care of the eggs and young. One, two or three eggs are laid and incubated for five weeks. The chicks will fledge about seven weeks after hatching. Various reptiles will feed on the eggs and chicks while adults will be taken by Australian Sea-Lions, sharks and Barracuda. Bird predators include White-bellied Sea Eagles, Kelp Gulls and Brown Skuas. As if that weren't enough, Little Penguins have to contend with introduced mammals and, near human habitations, fires and being struck by vehicles. Oil-slicks at sea and plastic pollution can be added to the list of hazards. Birds can even die of over-heating due to climate change. Notwithstanding this basket of life hazards, a Little Penguin can expect to live on average for about six-and-a-half years although this may soar to twenty-five for birds in captivity.

Finally, in this chapter we come to those penguins who I am sure will surprise many of you. Fjordland Penguins, which stand about twice the height of Little Penguins, live along the south-west coast of South Island, New Zealand. Since early human occupation they were once found all the way up to the north of New Zealand but proved palatable fare for the Polynesians. They average about five kilograms and they, just like many other penguin species, never place their feet on ice. When not feeding in the sea, these birds are in the dense temperate forests along the coastline. The adults have bluish-grey uppers and the usual white below but they, like Emperors, enjoy a splash of colour, bearing yellow crests on the sides of their heads. They have red bills and pink feet.

They nest in scattered colonies among tree roots and rocks, laying two eggs each of differing sizes. Surveys in 1990 estimated two-and-a-half thousand pairs of birds but once again the threat of introduced mammals rises to the fore and these birds are, consequently, classified as endangered. Their diet comprises eighty-five per cent Arrow Squid with a mere two per cent fish. Krill is also taken.

Fjordland Penguins have been little-studied but what is certain is that they are on the slippery slope towards extinction. Yellow-Eyed Penguins are also inhabitants of New Zealand forests, their numbers being well down to around one-and-a-half thousand pairs, once again due to mammal introductions.

I shall mention briefly here some of the other penguin species, Jackass Penguins are the only birds of the family to live in Africa, being found along the western coasts of Namibia and South Africa. They are so-called because of their characteristic donkey-like braying call. They are also called African or Black-footed Penguins. About the same size as Fjordland Penguins these birds have dwindled from millions of several centuries ago to just fifty thousand pairs today due to hunting and loss of habitat. They would make their burrows in guano deposits but these have been fully exploited by humans for use as fertilizer. One conservation effort is that of providing the birds with artificial burrows.

Some penguin species do make some attempt at nest-building such as the Gentoo Penguins, which may pull together a few pebbles, little more than a token nest. Neighbouring birds may try to steal another's pebbles leading to fights.

So, yes, fights can break out even amongst penguins, these cute and cuddly birds, which feature so widely on T-shirts, duvet covers, wallpaper, coffee mugs, cushion covers, Christmas jumpers and wherever else. Because of the way penguins waddle around with 'arms' hanging downwards, we impose upon them human attributes – anthropomorphism gone rampant.

The prize for living the furthest north goes to the Galapagos Penguin, nesting on those islands lying some way off the Ecuadorian coast and straddling the equator. This island archipelago is today fully protected as a World Heritage Site and is part of the nation of Ecuador, whose name incidentally means equator in Spanish.

Just to add an afterthought here, I shall refer to a recent text written for children with the aim of teaching tolerance of homosexuality. The basic theme of this book is to use a pair of male gay penguins who steal an egg (how else could they have got it?) from a pair of straight penguins and raised the hatched chick as their own. I believe that if you really do find it necessary to teach people of such a young age about sexual orientations then at least have the courage to deal with it head on and make reference to humans and not penguins. Did the author feel that using penguins for his masterly treatise would 'soften the blow' for children being enlightened thus? Parent or not, we do not know precisely what goes on in the mind of a young child. How many children now harbour the belief that homosexuality is a penguin issue?

28. ALL AT SEA...

Selected from the Rime of the Ancient Mariner by Samuel Taylor Coleridge.

> *At length did cross an Albatross,*
> *through the fog it came;*
> *as if it had been a Christian soul,*
> *we hailed it in God's name.*
>
> *God save thee, ancient Mariner!*
> *From the fiends, that plague thee thus!*
> *Why looks't thou so – with my cross-bow*
> *I shot the albatross.*
>
> *Ah! Well a-day! What evil looks*
> *had I from old and young!*
> *Instead of the cross, the Albatross*
> *about my neck was hung.*

Well at least I spared you the other 151 verses of Samuel Taylor Coleridge's rather lengthy poem of 1834, which relates the tale of an unwise sailor who kills one of these birds, long upheld by sailors as the protectors of seafarers' souls. Of course, albatrosses have little to fear from crossbows these days. Instead they have a whole new basket of problems. By far the biggest single threat to nearly all albatross species is the practise of long-line fishing. The lines are baited and the albatrosses are attracted to them as a source of food. It seems that little is being done to reduce this problem despite a range of suggestions, including the weighting of lines so they rapidly sink, the retention of offal on the fishing boats to prevent initial attraction of albatrosses, setting the lines at night and using brightly coloured bird scarers. Trawl-netting by South African fishermen also presents problems for some albatross species. In addition to long-lines and trawls, introduced mammals like cats and rats wreak havoc in some breeding colonies. Three-quarters of the albatross species are globally threatened.

Let's consider this family of sea birds in a bit more detail. They belong to the order Procellariiformes, which contains four families: albatrosses, petrels and shearwaters, storm petrels and diving petrels. All of the birds in this order are 'tube-noses', the birds having two special horny tube-like structures at the base of the upper mandible, believed to have a role in the elimination of excess salts accumulated as they forage over the oceans. Another characteristic of the order is the production of a viscous stomach oil. This serves several functions: it can be food for chicks when conditions demand and it can act as a fuel for the adult birds. A further function is its use as a deterrent to potential predators.

When working in Shetland in 1971, I was walking below a cliff upon which many birds were nesting, including quite a few Fulmars. I received a huge splodge of this disgustingly smelly and sticky oil and I reeked for days of this distinctly fishy odour. I ended up throwing away my jersey as it was impossible to get rid of the stuff. Apparently, rock climbers ascend cliff faces in fear of Fulmars for this very reason and I gather it is becoming policy not to climb where Fulmars are nesting. Albatrosses are of the family Diomedeidae, which itself contains twenty-two species. Examples include Wandering, Grey-headed, Black-browed, Yellow-nosed, Black-footed, Laysan and Sooty albatrosses - nearly all being birds of the southern hemisphere, nesting on the plentiful array of islands either those way out in the oceans or the sub-Antarctic islands. Albatrosses may feed over relatively shallow shelf seas or they may be pelagic, feeding out in the vast open oceans well away from the continental shelves. Some birds venture into the North Pacific realm. They are extremely long-lived and can take up to ten years to reach sexual maturity. This still affords many birds a further fifty years of reproductive life. Their foraging areas may cover thousands of square kilometres of ocean. A single egg being the norm and several species breeding only every second year, albatrosses have the slowest reproductive capacity of all birds.

All species of albatross spend the non-breeding season well out in the oceans and it seems that different species use different areas of ocean. It even seems that juvenile birds have innate information about such areas and can find their own way after becoming fully fledged. Whereas terrestrial birds have distinctive landmarks to follow, enabling them to navigate their two-way migrations, pelagic species such as albatrosses would appear to have to cope with a featureless ocean-scape. However, there is considerable evidence that birds can identify patches of ocean by reference to observed currents, wind directions, and other sea-surface features, even possibly including odours. It is well-known that salmon species can taste or smell the water chemistry, thus aiding in their migrations. That this ability should extend to our long-winged wayfaring friends should therefore not be so unbelievable.

The largest species is the Wandering Albatross, having a three metre wingspan and weighing between eight to twelve kilograms. Wanderers are one of the four species nesting on South Georgia where birds gather in areas of tussock grass known as 'greens' to do their courtship displays. They need quite a bit of space to use their long wings in such spectacles. It may take two or three years to establish a bond but once achieved it should last for life. Wanderers can cover 110,000km in ten to twenty days. They lay their single eggs in December and these hatch in April. The young fledge at the end of the year, having been fed on fish, squid and carrion. The parents will then take a year off.

The Black-browed Albatross is the most widespread and numerous of the family, nesting on twelve islands or archipelagos including South Georgia, Falklands and the South Sandwich islands. They forage over the shallow shelf seas, unlike some of their cousins like the Grey-headed, which are pelagic. The 2005 census came up with six hundred thousand pairs, two-thirds of these breeding in the Falklands. Its black eye-stripe is an identification feature as is the broad black edging to the undersides of the white wings. They are of medium size with wingspans of about 2.4m and averaging 3.5kg. They can live up to seventy years.

Albert (so appropriately named) was an individual who summered in Scottish gannetries over some years and in the Faroe Islands one bird made its home with Gannets for more than thirty years. Any birds of this family seen in British waters are likely to be Black-browed or Wandering Albatrosses.

Largely restricted to the NW Hawaiian Islands is the Laysan Albatross, one of the smaller of the family. They have a wingspan of just two metres. A bird ringed in 1956 was seen in 2016 rearing a chick making the bird at least sixty-six years old. Female-female pairs are not uncommon and these will successfully raise their single chick once the male of course has done his bit. Laysans feed mostly on cephalopods (squids, octopuses and cuttle-fish). On Midway Atoll, one of their breeding sites, lead poisoning from the paint on now derelict buildings is a serious problem and kills many birds annually.

The smallest albatross is the Yellow-nosed weighing around 2.5kg and having a wingspan of a little under two metres. Many islands where albatrosses breed have now become reserves due to the marked decline in populations during the last half century.

29. 'TWAS A COLD DARK NIGHT...

*The Owl and the Pussy-cat went to sea
in a beautiful pea-green boat.
They took some honey and plenty of money
wrapped up in a five pound note.*

I think Mr Lear was exercising poetic licence when he wrote this memorable nonsense poem. Owls can be found almost anywhere including coniferous and deciduous forests, marshlands, grasslands, desert, farmland, riversides, lake shores and even urban areas - but not the sea. Owls occur in every continent except of course Antarctica and they thrive way up in the north well beyond the Arctic Circle. All owls are in the order Strigiformes. Of the 172 species of owl, 14 are types of Barn Owl (family Tytonidae) and the rest are placed in a separate family Strigidae, the 'true' owls.

The true owls are themselves split into scops and screech owls, eagle owls, wood owls, eared owls, fishing owls and owlets, this latter not referring to young owls. While generally believed that owls are nocturnal, this is indeed the case in most but quite a few species are diurnal while others are crepuscular (dusk and dawn hunters). Short-eared Owls and Burrowing Owls are diurnal while Pygmy Owls are crepuscular. There exists a very wide range of size from the diminutive Elf Owl, which is sparrow-sized and weighing around 40 grammes. Contrast this with the four kilogram Eurasian Eagle Owl. I recall when in Ethiopia entering a bat cave and a Spotted Eagle Owl whooshed past my head – I was rather shaken by this, my first sighting of any Eagle Owl. Presuming this bird was using the bat cave as a regular roost, there's no guessing what it had for breakfast.

Owls are characterised by their distinctly upright stance, forward-facing eyes and somewhat cryptic plumage, this being a mix of browns, greys, black and white feathering. The plumages are the same in both sexes. Most owl species have distinctive facial discs wherein the feather arrangement serves as a shallow bowl directing sound to each of the outer ears. Other features of most owls include relatively large heads and short tails, in some species the ends of the primaries extending beyond the tail tips when the birds are at rest. One of the backward pointing feet is reversible enabling the bird to maintain a grip on its prey. Many owls have feathered legs, more so in birds of higher, colder latitudes. In other species the legs and feet remain bare, as in the fishing owls whose feet feathers would not do to be repeatedly wetted as they catch fish from the surfaces of rivers and lakes. Most feed on small mammals such as mice, rats and lemmings but lizards, other birds and various invertebrates may well feature in the diet. Those that feed on fish do so exclusively apart from the occasional frog.

Owls are not prone to eating carrion. The smaller prey items are swallowed whole, the bones/fur/feathers being brought up later in the form of pellets. The catching of prey is aided by the ability to turn the head through 270 degrees as they get an accurate fix on, say, a mouse a few metres away feeding in pitch darkness. With their ears being placed asymmetrically on either side of the head, the owls achieve super-stereoscopic hearing. Ultra-fine 'tuning' by minor adjustments of the head position allows the bird to pin-point its prey. This flexibility in the neck is permitted due to some owls having fourteen cervical vertebrae instead of the more usual seven possessed by most vertebrates (including giraffes by the way). No species demonstrates this prey-locating accuracy as well as the Great Grey Owl, a high-latitude species, which can hear the rustling of a mouse buried under half a metre of snow.

Owls are generally non-migratory although a few may undertake short-distance seasonal movements north-south such as the Northern Saw-Whet Owl. Some owls will disperse widely after a good breeding season, Snowy Owls being a prime example. The white eggs of owls are more or less circular laid on minimal nest-lining material. Owls may take to nesting boxes and today, many green farmers are providing such, appreciating the pest-control value of these birds. And are they wise? I would guess that they are as wise as any other bird and we should not be taken in by outward appearances. It is probably this idea of the wisdom of owls that led to the collective name for owls, a 'parliament' and which unjustly confers upon our politicians false mantles of omniscience.

Not much predates on owls, apart from other owls. However, smaller birds such as various Passerines but also crows will 'mob' an owl, collectively sweeping down upon it and sometimes actually making contact. My science teacher, when I was in lower secondary, brought in a stuffed Tawny Owl and stood it outside. It remained untouched for a couple of days and was then seriously attacked by a group of Pied Wagtails and Blackbirds, some even ripping out feathers. It is well worth trying this if you have a stuffed owl to spare.

Owls are steeped in tradition and have not, for centuries, enjoyed a good press. Their nocturnal habit, their sometimes ghostly appearance, especially Barn Owls, their eerie cries and bright staring eyes all contribute to their undeserved reputation of being associated with witchcraft and demons.

When teaching in Swaziland and Botswana, I became all too aware of the widespread hatred of owls. In southern Africa a type of medicine called 'muthi' is practised. This may well involve the use of owl parts and can be used to put spells on your undesirable neighbours. Even the most highly educated people I met in Botswana, including fellow science teachers, lived in fear of muthi and all the superstition that enshrouded it. Native Americans, for the most part associate owls with death. In modern Japan the owls get a break and are considered good fortune. Pliny wrote that owls' eggs were a good hangover cure! JK Rowling featured owls in her Harry Potter books, the birds as messengers, bringing forth both good and bad news.

Let us consider several species of owl, starting with the largest, the Eurasian Eagle Owl. These birds have wing-spans of nearly two metres.

They nest on cliff ledges, in rock crevices and sometimes old nests of other birds. I was aware of a pair nesting in a disused Hamerkop nest in Ethiopia. They average two eggs and incubation is by the female only. Both adults will feed their young for around five months. Siblicide (eating their brothers and sisters) occurs with the chicks of this and other owl species. There are twelve sub-species of Eurasian Eagle Owls, which seem to obey Bergman's Rule (see Glossary). An estimated ten to forty pairs now nest in the UK. It is thought that they can live for twenty years in the wild and a captive bird has been known to reach 68 years of age! Eagle Owls are apex predators, having nothing which feeds on them. The more common causes of death are by electrocution from power lines, collisions with traffic and by being shot. More terminal than death of any owl is extinction of a species. The Laughing Owl, a New Zealand endemic, was a ground-nesting true owl and was laughing no more by 1914, having had its eggs and young taken by introduced cats, rats and goats.

Elf Owls, the smallest of all owls, have a wingspan of just 25cm. They occur in the southwest USA, the Californian peninsula and Mexico. Most distinctive are the yellow eyes and the white eyebrows. They breed in holes in Saguaro cacti made by woodpeckers. They are crepuscular and feed mostly on insects, often drawn to outdoor lighting to feed on the moths, which are attracted. They themselves are predated on by hawks and other owl species. Elf Owls can feign death when captured or held in the hand.

Pel's Fishing Owls are birds to behold. They are bright ginger-brown and one of the larger owl species, the female averaging two kilograms. Quartering along rivers and over lakes at night, they catch fish in their non-feathered talons, taking all manner of fish species and also frogs. They may lay two eggs but normally only one chick reaches the flying stage. Pel's Fishing Owls can be seen over much of Africa. I was lucky enough to see these birds although I never saw one actually catching a fish.

Barn Owls are one of the most cosmopolitan birds on Earth and occur in all continents except Antarctica. There are thirty-five sub-species of Barn Owl. While not strictly diurnal they do often hunt by day, feeding on small mammals, lizards, amphibians and insects. Pellet analysis has also revealed that bats may be taken although how such aerial acrobats are caught doth boggle the mind. I assume the bats are taken whilst roosting but this raises the question of how such a manoeuvre may be accomplished in pitch dark. Barn Owls may be killed by Eagle Owls and, sadly, by ignorant people. I found two maintenance men throwing stones up at a Barn Owl's nest in school grounds in Botswana. I asked the head to address this but I had cause to believe that nothing would be done, so deep does this aversion to owls run in Africa, only to be surpassed by the fear of snakes.

I would have mentioned at this point Snowy Owls, which breed way up above the Arctic Circle but I have given a whole chapter to these birds covering the time I was working for the RSPB in Shetland where a pair was breeding.

30. AUTOMATIC PILOT...?

The swifts belong to the order Apodiformes, which includes over a hundred species of true swifts (family Apodidae), just three species of tree swifts and a staggering 334 species of hummingbird (yes they are very closely related). The Eurasian or Common Swift (Apus apus), which breeds throughout Britain and Europe, belongs to the largest genus Apus together with the swiftlets, an equally large genus. Sub-species are plentiful among swifts with the White-bellied Swiftlet of S and SE Asia having twenty. Swifts occur in every continent except Antarctica, the majority of species in Asia followed by Africa and South America. Both Europe and North America each have fewer than half a dozen species. In addition to the Eurasian Swift, we have in Europe (but not Britain) the Alpine, Pallid and White-rumped swifts. In North America the Chimney Swifts are the most common. Swifts breeding in temperate regions will migrate to the tropics in winter. Some species can survive sudden cold spells by lapsing into a semi-torpid state. Collectively, swifts are the fastest flyers with a White-throated Needletail clocking up nearly 170kph. The sizes of swifts range from the Pygmy Swiftlet (5.5 grammes) to the Purple Needletail at over 180 grammes, thirty-three times the weight. Swifts tend to lay fewer eggs than Passerine species and have longer incubation periods.

Swifts and swallows together demonstrate convergent evolution, wherein two species have similar features due to having similar lifestyles and not because they are genetically closely related. Unlike the swallows, swifts are not even Passerines, being separated by quite a few orders. Swifts follow immediately the order of nightjars, their closest relatives outside their own order. Swifts do not perch on telephone wires and do not settle on the ground like Hirundines (swallows and martins) and if you see flocks of birds circling way up high they will be swifts, not swallows.

Our familiar Common Swift (Eurasian Swift) of the UK and Europe, while appearing black is in fact sooty-brown. It has a pale whitish throat, long scythe-like wings and a slightly forked tail with no streamers. As in all swifts, the sexes are alike in plumage and in size. Their piercing screams are also very distinctive. They have a wingspan of approximately 35cm and weigh around 40 to 50 grammes. Their legs and feet are much reduced, hence the name of the order. Despite the extreme relative wing-length, they still conform to having ten of each the primaries and secondaries on each wing (I checked this when I held an injured bird in my hand). These birds fly up from their wintering grounds and arrive in Europe in early May, late for our summer migrants. They remain for just three months, time enough to rear their single brood of young. Only Cuckoos match such short stays – being brood parasites they have no need to hang around caring for eggs or young, leaving that to pipits, wagtails and Dunnocks mostly.

Common Swifts take four years to become sexually mature, after which they will lay their first clutch of eggs. They can expect to live a further five or six years although one ringed individual reached 21 years. They have few predators but a Hobby will sometimes take a swift (see chapter 27). They nest high up in substantial houses, church towers and, even better, cathedrals. They need to be high up so they can 'fall' into the air when going off to feed. By all means put up special swift breeding boxes but not if you live in a bungalow, which is too low to prevent them tumbling to the ground. They are highly gregarious birds and nest colonially. I was once called to view and write about a colony of Little Swifts nesting in the capital of Swaziland under an overhang of a very tall building bang in the heart of the city. Wishing to estimate the number of nesting birds, I was obliged to lie on the pavement and stare up looking through my binoculars while passers-by presumed I had absented myself from some institution. I estimated around four hundred pairs nesting in the colossal structure.

Pairing for life, the males and females of a pair will meet up at their established nest hole and a new nest will be built or an old one repaired, using vegetable material glued with saliva. Monogamy is the norm among swifts. There just two to three eggs will be laid at two to three day intervals and these can withstand lengthy periods of chilling when parent birds are delayed in their foraging. Delays simply slow down egg development for a few days and will not damage the integrity of the developing embryo. Unusually, incubation starts from the first egg so young in the nest will be of different ages and stages of development. This is a survival strategy and ensures that at least one bird will be successfully reared, it having received the lion's share of the food provided by the parents. Feeding of young may be impaired by bad weather necessitating the adults to go off further afield in search of the particular aerial insects on which they feed. UK breeding birds have been encountered feeding in Germany as they have been obliged to go far in their foraging. In the nest the young can close down their metabolic rates reducing them to semi-torpid states. This might retard chick development by a couple of weeks but will not harm the bird in the long-term. The young are fed on balls of insects including ants, aphids, wasps, bees and aerial spiders. Larger insects may include dragon-flies. The adults have much the same diet and water is scooped up in flight by the adult birds or they may even catch drops of rain. After two or three weeks the young will start to exercise their wings and are able to fly after about six weeks. A few days after leaving the nest they will commence their long-distance flights down to sub-Saharan Africa, taking them all over including right down to the Cape at the tip of South Africa. The chicks will already have good fat reserves and do not have to wait to stockpile body fat as fuel for the journey. Young birds do not have to accompany their parents and will navigate their own way to their wintering quarters.

It was believed, until as recently as the late nineteenth century that swifts (and more so swallows) hibernated in mud at the bottom of ponds. Even the highly respected Gilbert White (of Selborne) got labourers in the mid-eighteenth century to dig down to see if they could find dormant birds.

Before their maiden breeding season, Common Swifts spend their first three years almost entirely on the wing, feeding and sleeping in flight and hardly ever coming to land. They can never alight on the ground as their wings are far too long and their feet too short to permit take-off. So, how on earth do these birds seem to defy the laws of science? That swifts are indeed capable of sustaining non-stop flight for many months has long been suspected. In an attempt to clarify this, in 2013 Swedish ornithologists tagged twenty birds with dataloggers, which were able to record many of the birds' movements and positions. The results confirmed that many of the birds had settled for just two hours in eight months! A similar study was made by Swiss scientists on Alpine Swifts, again confirming the mind-blowing ability of swifts to sustain absurdly prolonged flight. One possible explanation is that the birds use a technique used by dolphins whereby they are able to shutdown half of their brain at a time, enabling them to be constantly active. Another thing swifts cannot do is preen while flying, so they are, not surprisingly, infested with feather parasites. When I examined one in the hand (mentioned in chapter 26) I was aware of quite large flat-flies crawling all over the body.

Another remarkable swift fact is that some, notably swiftlets, use echo-location to navigate locally within cave systems. The Three-toed Swiftlet even uses this outside of the caves in which it nests.

You will almost certainly have heard of bird's nest soup. This is prepared from the nests, which are made totally of the saliva of the Edible Swiftlet – so it is not the bird which is eaten but its nest. The only benefit of boiling these nests down to soup is that they contain plenty of iron, calcium, potassium and magnesium. Over-harvesting of these rather flavourless and supposedly aphrodisiac nests has led to a decline of the species. I find it absolutely sickening that any animal should be threatened with extinction just to satisfy some ignorant bloke's sexual urges, as is also the case with rhinos of course.

As I write, the RSPB is operating a project wherein it receives records of breeding Common Swifts in order to ascertain reasons for the sharp decline in numbers and possible remedies. Loss of suitable nest sites due to modernisation of old tall buildings is largely responsible but also climatic change is affecting insect populations in the birds' wintering quarters. Globally, about eighteen species of swift are classified as 'near-threatened' in the Red Data Book.

So, we met Samuel Coleridge in chapter 29. Here now, a lesser-known poet will close this chapter. This was penned eight years back by Ruth Marden whom I got chatting to on a train journey in England in 2019. I so appreciated her company and conversation fuelled by our common interest in birds, that I gave her my email address on parting. We have since maintained contact and below are a few of her well-chosen words about our globe-trotting masters of the air.

SWIFTS, SALISBURY 2012

Perhaps they were cheated this summer
of whatever it is they came for

in their extravagant style,
without pause, from Africa.
They slipped in, didn't command
the sky, in their usual way.
When it rained, they stayed hidden.
Did they huddle, fasting
or had they called off the whole show,
turned round, sped home?
In rare snatches of sun
they'd appear again
as if to confirm that the world's
still on course.
At last near the end of July
they put on a display
in full force –
more than we'd dreamt were here –
then returned us to silence. A blank
saps the remains of our summer.
But this evening – yes! Again
that faint familiar piping
and far, far up, a detachment, purposeful,
makes off in a close formation.

Ruth Marden

THIS IS ALL FOR YOU MY CHILD...

What follows is not specifically about birds. It is about the general collective problems be they local, national or global, which in turn are having knock-on effects on the environment as a whole and its myriad inhabitants. Any opinions expressed are my own but factual correctness has been ensured.

Whenever I taught I always laid emphasis on the fact that there is hope for our spaceship Earth and all of its passengers. What kind of teacher would fill his students' heads with feelings of gloom and despondency for the future? I was very privileged. I taught in international schools, which made my job a sheer pleasure. Numerous children in parts of Africa and other developing countries never go to school, especially girls as they have to remain at home looking after younger siblings, helping on the land, fetching water. Many parents simply cannot afford to send their children to school. I taught in seven African countries and only one, Botswana, provided free education and that even included board and lodging as most schools there are rural and remote. In nearly all countries it is a legal requirement that all children attend school, both primary and secondary but that does not always work out, unfortunately. Children may end up working in factories and other places of work - so called child-labour.

When I was passing through Kashmir on the way to Ladakh, I visited a carpet emporium in the main centre, Srinagar. It was indeed impressive, the beauty, intricate patterning and colour of Kashmiri carpets being world famous and reflected in their exorbitant prices. However, the owner of the factory was in no way abashed to tell me that the carpets were woven by young children as they had small and dextrous fingers. He even seemed quite proud of the fact. Those children lucky enough to be in school may suffer being in huge classes. In Ethiopia I taught in the main international school in Addis Ababa but once I asked to spend a morning in a state school. Please believe this... all of the classes were in the region of 60 to 70 pupils but some, such as English or Maths had over 120! How oh how do you teach 120 children at the same time. You do not of course – you simply talk 'at' the amassed throng. Most students were without pen and paper and I doubt those sitting at the back could hear properly. My classes wherever I was teaching in Africa were never more than 24 students but all were, I must say, international schools where this is pretty much the norm.

I discovered over the years that increasingly

fewer children today have hobbies or special interests. I learnt this when I was teaching in three schools, two in Swaziland and one in the UK and after I had returned to the UK. I carried out surveys and asked students about how they spent their spare time. The answers were very predictable. Computer games and texting came out as number one, while watching TV and videos was the next. With a few exceptions such as football or playing some form of musical instrument, that was pretty much it. In Ethiopia we did have one exceptional student, an Australian lad who loved to paint birds - dead ones. Any dead bird was brought to him and I would put it in my laboratory fridge for him (his mother would not oblige) having injected the corpse with formalin. He did a beautiful painting of a male Black Headed Oriole, which he presented to me when he graduated - I was most chuffed and it now hangs on my wall.

I need no reminding of how important it is to protect our children but I do honestly believe that in the UK at least, we do tend to be over-zealous to the point of total absurdity. I am no fan of political correctness or health and safety when it goes over the top. When I was 13 and above I would go off camping for weekends with Stewy, my next-door neighbour friend and when I was 15 (and Stewy was 16) we hitch-hiked down to Istanbul, with our parents' full support. My dad was always up for adventure and one day when we had to vacate a rented house he went out and bought a defunct double-decker bus from the council and parked it in his brother's field. I was 11 at the time and we lived in it for 14 months. Stewy and I built a treehouse in the local woods and got up to all manner of stuff including bird-watching of course. It was this freedom and my connection with nature that enabled my early passion for wildlife to blossom and my adventurous spirit to develop. It is no coincidence my first teaching job was in a war-torn African military dictatorship, namely Ethiopia. Those were the best three years of my life until I went off to Swaziland (another dictatorship) some years later.

At university today, UK students receive government loans so they spend the first few years of work in crippling debt. I maintain that education is any government's most important investment. Children and adolescents are the future. As if these student loan debts are not damaging enough what legacies shall us old'uns leave our youth?

Let's look at the UK first. Do we have problems? Just a few! We have a seriously ageing population, placing enormous pressure on the health and pensions service. Despite the fact that human life expectancy is increasing, not all elderly people reap the benefits if they are physically or mentally impaired as dementia seems to be taking a firm foothold. We have so many cars and trucks that we even have traffic jams on our motorways, notably the M25 ring road. We have a big litter problem with fly-tipping being carried out all over the show. Britain even 'exports' waste, notably plastic, for processing by other countries. We have a disturbing lack of police, doctors and nurses and teachers are leaving the profession in droves. I don't really blame them as I gather that teaching in the UK is riddled with piles of tedious and unnecessary paperwork, something I was always spared in Africa. We have hardly any land left for landfill sites. We have an extremely high suicide rate and I gather that this is the commonest cause of death in our under 45 year-old men. British people have to join long waiting lists for medical treatment such as surgery and also for housing. Reputedly applicants for employment send off scores or even hundreds of letters and CVs. We are forever destroying natural wildlife habitats to make way for housing, industry, roads (especially by-passes) and railways. The HS2 project is a good example - this white elephant is ripping up a wide range of habitats including several SSSIs (Sites of Special Scientific Interest). SSSIs are just that…until needed for some form of development, public or private.

Our standards of education have fallen markedly since I was at school due to governments dumbing down the syllabuses so as to compensate for falling grades due to austerity moves. GCSEs are less demanding than their precursors, O-levels.

Moving to a more global view, what do we have in store? In 2019, Sir David Attenborough aired a fine series of programmes on the life of our oceans. There he highlighted the dire problem of waste plastic, millions of tonnes of which enter our oceans every year. This had the effect of leaving me feeling so down for a couple of days and I hated the whole human race, including myself.

Most of the world's weather systems are generated over the oceans and much of our oxygen is produced from the photosynthetic action of phytoplankton (plant plankton). The TV series was a wake-up call and it made a huge impact certainly in this country and I am sure everywhere else. I think it may well have led many to consider environmental degradation generally. Just occasionally, between C19 reports we get snippets of information on other global problems such as Tropical Rain Forest felling in the tropics. Despite the fact that we know that TRF also supplies much of the world's oxygen (through photosynthesis) its destruction continues at alarming and largely unchecked rates. It is a free for all. The forest is being sliced up into smaller and smaller fragments in the mad rush to reaps its riches. This is reducing extensive areas of rainforest to islands of forest too small to be able to support viable populations of various species. Logging, both legal and illegal is ripping out hardwoods such as Ebony, Oak, Teak and Mahogany. Mineral prospectors clear huge expanses as do ranchers who then graze cattle.

Devastating wildfires have destroyed vast expanses. Many animal and plant species are being lost even before they have been discovered. How do western countries who have already decimated their own forests tell countries like Brazil to stop deforestation? It is worth noting here that many of the companies pillaging the Amazon are not, in fact, Brazillian. Poaching of animals in and out of the world's game parks is rampant and much of Africa's remaining megafauna is being killed. Rhino horn and elephant tusks are prime targets, which still find unscrupulous markets. The Northern White Rhino is virtually extinct with a the death of a 31 year-old female leaving just the one male and three females. We can't even take care of our close cousins Chimpanzees, Orang Utans and Gorillas.

The melting of Arctic ice means a shorter period of time each year for the Polar Bears to rear their young. Female polar Bears hibernate, so I presume they may be finding it increasingly difficult to find suitable ice caves. Turtle eggs on remote beaches around the world are overharvested, cheetahs are suffering from a weakened gene pool leading to genetically inferior offspring and the too few Blue Whales have trouble finding each other in the vast oceans. The Red Data Book is ever expanding and every year there are extinctions of animals and plants although most of these don't make the news as there are so many of them and unless you are a specialist you will remain unaware of them.

Supertankers with their cargoes of oil ply the ocean waves and spillages are not uncommon, either by the flushing out of tanks at sea or the crashing of ships onto coastal rocks. On my various stays in Shetland, finding oiled seabirds was a daily occurrence. I had to put several birds down as they gaped helplessly, taking their last breaths – a tragic sight indeed. I also found a few birds with legs entwined in old fish-netting.

Although electric cars are making inroads, that electricity still has to be generated somehow and fossil fuels still constitute 84 per cent of world energy production, at the time of writing. Lakes and rivers globally receive sewage and industrial pollution.

Working on the Ouse Washes bird reserve, the head warden and I would find fishing line and hooks along the river banks, along with litter left by thoughtless fishermen.

Norway and Japan refuse to stop killing whales despite world pressure – Japan says it is for scientific research and Norway claims that it is traditional. Overfishing has left some fisheries permanently damaged such as the cod fishery off the Newfoundland Banks, which was overfished during the 1970s.

Discarded computer and auxiliary equipment contain heavy metals, which are particularly nasty when allowed to get into the environment.

Tourism is threatening wilderness areas, even Antarctica, which plays host to those wealthy enough to go on cruises around the continent.

Air conditioners and fridges pump out Chlorofluorocarbons (CFCs), which destroy ozone in the upper atmosphere. Ozone, a form of oxygen, protects life on Earth from ultra-violet radiation. Bathrooms, kitchens and garden sheds all over the world are home to myriad chemicals such as cleaning agents, fertilizers, weed-killers and a whole host of nasty toxins we can throw at our environment to make life that little bit more bearable or our lettuces that much larger.

Alien species are introduced either intentionally or by accident as humans travel around the globe. Rhododendrons may look nice but in those places they have been introduced to (from the Himalaya) they have caused environmental problems such as soil acidification and have proven to be pernicious weeds.

Plants may be spread around the world by means of seeds sticking to travellers' walking boots or the wheels of aircraft. Kenya exports cut flowers to various countries in Europe, including Britain and The Netherlands and 'rogue' plants and seeds may find their way into foreign parts. Slugs and harmful insects such as beetles may also move around in flower, vegetable and fruit cargoes. Farmers grow monocultures, which totally lack biodiversity and are sterile environments devoid of other plants and nearly all animal life.

The introduction of the Grey Squirrel from North America has driven our native Red Squirrel numbers way down, leaving it extremely localised. Ring-necked Parakeets are now flapping around Britain and parts of Europe taking nest sites away from Tawny Owls (holes in trees). I recall when living in Brussels sometimes hearing a flock of about thirty of these aliens as it congregated at nightfall to roost right outside my window.

Politicians and business people are often corrupt, especially in developing countries where accountability is less strict and slackly enforced. Let me quote the story of when I was in Kenya. A government minister built a house in Nairobi Game Park without anyone noticing! Happily, he was finally caught out and never got to live in it. It was used thereafter as a roost by a group of Marabou Storks for whom I had a much greater respect. Humanity's huge dependence on computer technology means that nations may be subject to cyber-crime such as being held ransom or suffering prolonged shutdowns served to frustrate by disgruntled groups and governments.

We are currently (as I write) undergoing a return to the Cold War with much of the world turning against China or Russia or both. Fake news has become very fashionable and although I don't really understand why it is generated it is certainly out there doing lots of damage.

Racism is alive and kicking in the USA and never really went away in South Africa. Zandile, my Swazi partner and I stopped going down to South Africa as it was so painful for her when we went into pubs and restaurants together and were either completely ignored or treated badly. And here in the UK we still quite frequently hear the statement, "I'm not racialist but...... "

Drugs and alcohol have wrecked certain societies and this problem seems to be filtering down to even the very young. Sadly, some teenagers seem to think stabbing someone who has a different postcode is fair practise.

Countless people all over the world are exploited, overworked, underpaid, unemployed and even trafficked into modern slavery and prostitution.

Nuclear war is still a black cloud hanging over us although this has been rather overshadowed now by climate change (and of course viral attack). AIDS continues to take it toll despite significant medical advances, leading to numerous orphans who will almost certainly get a raw deal in later life.

Raped women may be legally forced to give birth to their rapist's baby and still today, even in developed countries women earn considerably less than their male counterparts and have fewer opportunities.

Circuses continue to humiliate animals such as bears, big cats and elephants and some zoos keep captive animals in the most dire of conditions.

Poverty and ignorance are the two greatest enemies of mankind and his fellow creatures and will prevail unless serious measures are taken to change our economic and social systems along with our misguided attitudes of our role in the natural order of things and to accept our stewardship of all life on Earth.

The most powerful man on the planet (deposed just a few weeks ago at the time of writing and reinstated in 2025) is distinguishably ignorant of many things including science and continues to blunder his way from crisis to crisis, seemingly oblivious of the damage and under the impression that everyone else is wrong. His taking the USA out of the Paris Climate Accord has serious implications and serves to indicate this man's utter contempt for environmental affairs. His total denial of climate change and branding it as a 'hoax' is staggering.

Oppressive regimes exist worldwide and we can see both China and Russia today clamping down on civil liberties. Dictators either military or monarchical keep tight reins on their countries such as Ethiopia and Swaziland respectively, both of which I have lived and worked in. [It's OK so long as you keep your nose out of politics!]

So, inheriting this cornucopia of problems our children and more so our grandchildren will have plenty of challenges to keep them occupied as they slowly pay off their burdensome student loans. They won't solve this basket (neh, this truck-load) of problems entirely of course but they may make some inroads into improving the state of the planet.

How on earth did Homo sapiens, the 'wise ape' manage to create this plethora of problems for himself along with all of his co-inhabitants of this beautiful planet?

I firmly believe that one fundamental cause is religion (aaargh, shock horror!). Many many wars have been fought and are still being fought because people choose to worship different gods. The Christian soldiers who marched onward 'as to war' (according to the stirring song) have a lot to answer for. Millions of people who were just getting on with their lives were slaughtered during the Crusades of the eleventh to thirteenth centuries. The opening lines of the book of Genesis include the following words of wisdom:

> *Let us make humankind in our image, according to our likeness; and let them have*
>
> *dominion over the fish of the sea, and over the birds of the air, and over the cattle,*
>
> *and over all the wild animals of the Earth, and over every creeping thing that creeps*
>
> *upon the Earth.*

Somewhere else in this opening book of the 'greatest book ever written' we are encouraged to go forth and multiply – it didn't consider a world with eight billion of us and still counting. Books have been banned for less damaging sentiments as these. Still many of us believe that we are the only species that matters and everything is here just for us. Forty per cent of people in the USA take the bible more or less literally while this figure is a slightly more reassuring twenty-five per cent in the UK. In the States there is a strong lobby against the teaching of evolution in schools and this may add that creation must be taught either as well or instead. I feel that such beliefs release Christians from responsibilities for taking good care the planet.

When teaching in Ethiopia, we had a reverend from Norfolk, who was head of English. I used to challenge him on his fundamentalist beliefs and the subject of extinction came up.

"I can assure you, Mr Denby, God won't allow the extinction of any of his creations," was his enlightened reply.

He was clearly an educated bloke but had he not heard of the dinosaurs, sabre-toothed tigers, mammoths, the Dodo or indeed our early hominid forbears? Was he truly unaware that so many creatures' existence hang in the balance. I asked him how God managed to create light a few days before he thought about making the sun as the book of Genesis so informs us. Predictably, he informed me that God acts in mysterious ways and it is not ours to challenge. What chance have we when gullible people's minds are polluted with such garbage? He wanted to introduce religious assemblies at the school. No international schools have religious functions for very obvious reasons. Our headmistress, herself a practising but private Christian, pointed this out to him so he used to allow his beliefs to permeate his English lessons... until some parents complained. The very reverend reverend was told to lay off, then continued to do his stuff. He was subsequently found out to have forcibly seduced one of the maintenance worker's teenage sons and then... he was fired there and then. Not one of us saw him off at the airport as was normal custom for leaving teachers. He doubtless continues his nefarious practises in the fair county of Norfolk.

Have we learnt anything from the C19 pandemic? I do believe that we have, at least for the moment but whether it lasts and leads to change is another matter. Many of us have been shown just how vulnerable we are despite all our wondrous technology. Even so, it has clearly demonstrated that we seem unable to cooperate effectively when it comes to combatting a common foe. It has long been asserted by many scholars that microbial infections could well be the greatest risk to all humanity. That may yet be proven correct. Our far too relaxed attitude to and mis-use of antibiotics means that a lot of bacteria species have developed immunity to our armoury of drugs. The malarial parasite, Plasmodium, is now totally resistant to quinine in many parts of the tropical world.

Of much concern should be what is going to happen to all of the PPE (Personal Protection Equipment) being used during the C19 pandemic. Already, after just nine months many masks and plastic aprons are being found in our oceans and washed up on our beaches. The number of gloves, aprons, face-masks being used just once and then discarded does not bear thinking about. May God, or someone please help our oceans. I was told that I was wicked to even consider what happens to all the rubbished PPE while humans are dying in their droves. This attack stems from the deeply held belief that humans are really all that matters and above all else together with total ignorance of the world systems that sustain life.

It is a strange irony that never before have we been able to literally hold almost the sum total of human knowledge in our hands in the form of smartphones. Who would have believed this in days gone by? Despite this, it seems that an unhealthy majority of smartphone users employ this super-technology to play pretty pointless war games and send trivial texts to people they may see every day. It is like a disease and I fully expect humans will evolve a special third arm exclusively for smartphone use.

We can enjoy wonderful wildlife documentaries where the standards of photography just get better and better. Over the last few years I have sometimes found it difficult to watch these as just before the end you can predict the twist, the warning of the threats to this or that animal or ecosystem – on one occasion I intentionally did not watch a programme on rainforest destruction as I knew it would adversely affect me.

We are also living in a period of the greatest biodiversity the Earth has known. Paradoxically, it is also an age where the amount of potential extinctions of plants and animals across the planet have never been more.

As a final note, let me tell of the time I was asked to judge a competition set up by the English department of a school in Swaziland. Students had to pick any animal they wished and then write about it explaining the problems and solutions related to the animal's conservation. When I came to look through the forty or so entries, I almost immediately noticed the distinct absence of birds. There was not one and 90 per cent of the animals were iconic mammals such as Polar Bears, Giant Pandas, Giant Ant-eaters, lions and elephants (there was a frog and one snake, I recall). I was hard-pushed to judge the students' work but I managed to keep most people happy. This did make me realize however, just how easy it is to fall into the trap of making more fuss of cuddly mammals than of seemingly lesser creatures. Of course, Giant Pandas, Polar Bears, and cute Meerkats are important but not as much as those lower in the food-chains or food-pyramids. How many of us appreciate that it is the base of the pyramid that keeps everything above going. The base is of course land plants and the phytoplankton living in the upper levels of our oceans. I have read that the dry weight of all the Earth's phytoplankton would be greater than that of all our grasslands and forests put together. Terrestrial and aquatic plants provide our only source of oxygen. If we continue to damage world ecosystems we do so at our peril. Without these oxygen liberators there is no us...and not even a few left to read the history books.

APPENDIX (I)

GLOSSARY OF TERMS

Definitions are in the context **as used throughout the book** and may not cover the broader range of meanings of any particular one. For example, I have defined albumen as the white of an egg. Outside of this book, the term may be used with respect to a substance found in some plant seeds as well. Some of the following may have been partly explained in the text but for convenience, definitions of a wide range of terms are presented together here. The definitions are my own and not taken from any specific source.

Adaptation

The acquisition of new structures or the modification of old structures or changes in behaviour by any organism, which enables it to be better suited to a new or changing environment.

Aerial display

A nuptial display carried out by some male birds whilst flying in order to impress females. The display may show off brightly coloured plumage and special structures.

Ageing population

Of humans, the increasing percentage of elderly people within the overall population such that there is a high percentage of unproductive people who may well be dependent on medical services.

Air mass

A body of air, either cold or warm, which moves as an independent mass and brings specific weather conditions. Two air masses meet at a 'front'.

Albumen

The white substance of a bird's egg providing both cushioning and various proteins for the developing embryo.

Algae

A group of non-flowering plants, living either on land or in the sea.

Alien species

Any species which intentionally or accidentally enters an ecosystem in which it did not evolve and thus may upset the ecological equilibrium.

Altitudinal migrant

Any bird which moves down to lower levels to find food and shelter at the start of winter.

Angels

Unidentified blips seen on WW2 radar screens, which later proved to be flocks of migrating birds.

Antarctic

A large continent covered almost entirely by a freshwater ice-sheet or ice-cap lying in the south polar region. It has no permanent human inhabitants. It is administered by ten different countries.

Anthropomorphism

In writing or in speech, incorrectly conferring human characteristics onto animals.

Antibiotics

Chemical compounds prepared and administered to kill bacteria. They do not work on viruses.

Anting

A process carried out by some bird species whereby ants are allowed to crawl over their exposed body and wings for the purpose of ridding the birds of parasites.

Apex predator

A top predator in any food chain or pyramid and having nothing preying on it.

Arboreal

Living either temporarily or permanently in trees.

Arctic

That region above the Arctic Circle (66 degrees north) which has variable amounts of floating sea-ice throughout the year. There is no underlying continent.

Assemblage

The total collection of organisms living in a particular ecosystem.

Auks

The family of sea-birds, which includes Razorbills, guillemots and puffins.

Aurora borealis

A natural phenomenon caused by electro-magnetic particles entering the Earth's upper atmosphere in the northern hemisphere's high latitudes, giving rise to colourful luminescent displays in the night skies. Aurora australis is the same occurring in the southern hemisphere.

Avifauna

Bird-life, either locally, regionally, nationally or globally.

Bacteria

The kingdom of single-celled organisms, which may be pathogenic or provide services to higher organisms.

Barbs

Extensions of keratin on either side of the central shaft of a bird's feather, forming collectively the vanes.

Barbules

Micro-extensions of the barbs on a bird's feather, which fit neatly into corresponding sites thus maintaining the integrity of the vanes on the tail and flight feathers of a bird.

Beaks

The 'noses' of birds, which contain the nasal cavity (nostril). They are very varied between species according to the birds' feeding habits and other essential activities such as nest-building, nuptial displays and preening. Also referred to as bills.

Bergman's rule

A dictum in biology, which states that there exists a tendency for individuals of a species to become larger at higher latitudes, as a means to heat preservation.

BES

British Ecological Society.

Billion

One thousand million or 1,000,000,000.

Binomial

The two-word scientific name of an organism.

Bins

The familiar word used by birders for binoculars.

Biodiversity

The variety of different species of organisms inhabiting a habitat, biome or the entire planet.

Biogeography

The distribution of organisms over any given area.

Biomass

The collective dry weight of a given number of organisms.

Biome

An extensive latitudinal band of a particular vegetation type, which will have its own assemblage of organisms.

Biometric data

Various measurements taken from birds in the hand during the ringing process such as wing length, bill length, weight and sex.

Birder

A familiar term for one who watches, studies and maybe maintains records of birds.

Bird observatory

A special site with building(s) used entirely for the process of catching and ringing migrant birds. They are seasonally operated.

Bird ringing

The placement of a uniquely numbered aluminium (or coloured plastic) which is placed on the leg of a bird for monitoring purposes.

Bird strike

The accidental collision of a bird or group of birds with an aircraft, which may cause the aircraft to crash especially if birds are taken into the jet engines.

Bleaching

The whitening (and death) of coral caused by the acidification of sea-water due to human activities.

Blind spot

The region at the back of the eye where the optic nerve leaves to go to the brain. This site has no light receptors.

Blubber

The layer of sub-cutaneous fat deposited by animals, which inhabit cold places such as seals, whales and penguins.

BMS

British Medical Society.

Botanist

One who studies plants.

Botulism

An acute form of food-poisoning caused by bacteria affecting birds (especially gulls at landfill sites).

Bristles

Specialised feathers lacking vanes at the base of the mandibles of some insect-catching birds serving as a net, as with swifts and nightjars.

Broad Spectrum

As in pesticides, those which kill a wide range of pest organisms rather than a single target organism.

British list

The list of the total number of birds that have occurred in a wild state in Britain.

Brood parasitism

The laying of a bird's egg in the nest of another species of bird in order that the hatched chick of the true parent will be cared for by the foster parent at the expense of its own eggs or young.

BTO

British Trust for Ornithology.

Bush

The word used informally for the open Savannah/scrubland of Africa (and other regions).

Bush-meat

The meat of wild animals, which are taken from the wild to sell and use as food.

Calamus

The lower end of the central shaft of a bird's feather which has no vane.

Call

The sound of either a male or female bird made to its mate or young to alert of danger.

Call-over

In a bird observatory, the end of the day group recording of all the birds seen that day.

Carbohydrate

Any simple soluble sugar such as glucose or more complex compounds such as starch and cellulose.

Carboniferous

A period in geological history of the Upper Palaeozoic noted for the formation of coal.

Carnivore

Any animal which consumes the flesh of another animal. Some plants are carnivorous.

Carrion

Dead rotting flesh.

Cave painting

Any pictorial representation of animals, hunting

scenes or other human activity today found on the walls of caves throughout various countries. These were painted/drawn by our hominid ancestors and highly prized as evidence of environmental conditions in times past.

Cellulose

A complex long chain carbohydrate used in the cell walls of plants.

Census

The systematic counting of any particular species of animal or plant.

CFCs

Chlorofluorocarbons which can damage the ozone layer of the upper atmosphere. Common sources are refrigerators and air-conditioning units.

Chordata

Animals with backbones or primitive semblances of such.

Class

A group (taxon) of organisms such as Birds which is made up of a number of orders.

Classification

The orderly grouping of organisms based on their evolutionary relationships.

Climate change

Disturbances and rapid changes to global weather patterns caused by the burning of fossil fuels. Carbon dioxide and other gases enter upper atmosphere and cause the entrapment of heat around the Earth especially in its oceans which generate the world's weather systems.

Clutch

The total number of eggs which a bird lays in the one breeding session. Also called a brood.

Colony

A group of birds of the same species which all nest together within a confined area.

Competition

That state which exists when different species both have the same ecological requirements such as food and nest sites. Animals of the same species will compete for mates.

Cones

The cell structures in the retinas of animals which are used in day vision and for the appreciation of colour.

Coniferous

Of trees, cone-bearing such as pine, yew and spruce.

Continent

A landmass covering a very extensive area such as Asia or South America. There are seven continents.

Contour feather

The non-vaned feathers of a bird which lie above the down feathers.

Convection current

A circular movement of any liquid (or 'plastic' material) resulting from the upward travel of heat from a source such as the core of the Earth.

Convergent evolution

The resulting similarity between different species of organism arising due to adopting similar behaviour or characteristics which suit any given type of environment. A good example is swallows and swifts which are two unrelated families.

Coral

A hard calcareous (chalky) substance secreted by some marine organisms, often forming large reefs.

Core

The moon-sized sphere of nickel and iron in the centre of the Earth.

Creation

The belief held by some that a God somehow produced all existing organisms at the same time.

Creching

The gathering together of eggs or young into the one nest of some ground-nesting birds including Ostriches.

Crepuscular

More active at dawn or dusk particularly with respect to feeding such as nightjars.

Crop

The pouch in a bird's oesophagus used for storage and later digestion of food.

Crystallisation

The formation of crystals which are aggregations of atoms or molecules which have a regular internal structure.

DDT

Dichlorodifluorodichloroethylene, a chemical used to kill external parasites of animals and agricultural pests.

Deciduous

Of trees, the systematic loss of all of the leaves at the onset of winter.

Decomposer

Any organism such as a fly, a fungus or a bacterium which feeds on dead organic material and thus returns nutrients to the soil.

Deforestation

The widespread clearance of trees to make way for farming and developments.

Desert

A dry barren region which has an annual rainfall of less than 250mm a year. Deserts may be covered is sand, gravels, bare rock or combinations of these.

Devonian

A geological period of the Palaeozoic.

Dimorphic

The situation in birds where the size or plumage of either sex of a given species are different.

Dinosaur

A member of the diverse group of reptiles which ruled the Earth during the Jurassic and Cretaceous periods. They became extinct around 65 million years ago.

Diurnal

Feeding and active during the daylight hours. It is the opposite of nocturnal.

Dodo

An extinct member of the pigeon family which lived on the Indian Ocean island of Mauritius.

Down feathers

The feathers of a nestling bird or those retained by the parents below the contour feathers providing body insulation.

Dust-bathing

The practise of some birds where the crouching bird flicks dust over its body and wings to help it rid itself of parasites. Ostriches are a good example.

Echo-location

The system used by bats and some bird species whereby emitted pulses bounce back to the senders' ears and provide information about what lies ahead.

Ecology

The study of the relationships between organisms and their environments or between organisms and other organisms.

Egg tooth

The horny extension of a chick's bill which assists it in cracking open its shell upon hatching. It disappears shortly after use.

Endemic

Living in just the one region or country.

Entomologist

One who studies insects.

Environment

The total of the physical conditions surrounding animals and plants such as topography, altitude, climate, liquid water and other resources.

Enzyme

A chemical found within organisms which either speeds up or slows down the speed of a chemical reaction.

Eocene

A geological time zone of the Tertiary period.

Equator

The line of latitude of value zero degrees which separates the northern and southern hemispheres.

Ethology

The study of animal behaviour.

Evolution

The process whereby an organism undergoes slow and successive changes over time due to environmental pressures such that it may subsequently become a new species which can only breed with its own kind.

Exotic

From foreign parts (a term often mis-used to mean hot, tropical and idyllic).

Extinct

No longer having any representatives of that particular species living on Earth. Dead individuals cannot be referred to as extinct.

Facial disc

A shallow near-circular dish-shaped depression on the faces of some owl species which serves as a parabolic reflector to concentrate sound waves emitted by prey.

Fall

The sudden appearance of a number of migrant birds, often of the same species at a particular site.

Family

The taxon (group) of organisms made up of one or more genera such as the crow family.

Feather

An ultra-lightweight structure unique to the class of birds used to enable flight and maintaining body heat. Feathers contain pigments for plumage and camouflage.

Feral

The condition of any animal arising from domesticated stock to a wild state such as cats.

Field-guide

A specialised book furnished with numerous paintings or photographs of bird species and text used as an aid to identification.

Field of view

The width of the area to the front of the eyes

which affords clear vision, normally quantified as an angle.

Flight

The wing action of birds, insects and bats which sustains the creatures in an airborne state.

Fly-by-wire

An aeronautical term meaning to fly an aircraft by means of looking down at familiar landmarks by which to navigate. Some birds use this technique during migration using rivers, mountain ranges, valleys.

Fly-tipping

An illegal (and highly immoral) human habit of dumping waste material in non-designated places in the environment. It is a huge problem in the UK.

Follicle

A pit in the skin from which hair, fur or feathers grow.

Food chain

A succession of organisms starting from a plant (producer) followed by what organism (consumer) feeds upon it, and then which consumer feeds upon that and so on to the top (apex) consumer.

Formic acid

A chemical contained within the bodies of ants.

Frugivore

An organism which feeds exclusively on fruits such as fruit-bats and oil-birds.

Fungi

A kingdom of organisms lacking chlorophyll which feed on living or dead organic material. They are important decomposers and serve as food for many animals including man.

Game park

A specially designated area set aside for wildlife. Many have been established throughout Africa such as the Serengeti and Kruger National Parks.

Gas flare

At an oil-drilling site, the flame produced by the burning off of unwanted gas from tall towers. This may attract and disorientate and even kill migrating birds.

Gene pool

The sum total of genes existing within a species, the greater the number being more advantageous.

Genus

The taxon (group) comprising a single or many species such as Homo in humans.

Geology

The study of the rocks and minerals and processes such as vulcanism, earthquakes and plate tectonics.

Geothermal power

The power generated from naturally heated water rising up through the crust of the Earth, widely used in Iceland and New Zealand and of increasing importance globally.

Gizzard

A special structure in the intestinal tract of an animal for the containment of sand or small pebbles, these aiding in mechanical digestion found in duck species, Ostriches and many other birds.

Global warming

The not so gradual warming up of the world's oceans and, to a lesser extent, the world's landmasses due to human activities. It gives rise to extremes of weather and weather perturbations, hence the alternative name of climate change.

Glossopteris

A primitive plant known to have been widespread in Gondwanaland but now found separately in those continents, which broke away from the great single landmass.

Gondwanaland

A former single landmass comprising Africa, South America, India, Australia and Antarctica located in the southern hemisphere.

Granivore

Any organism which feeds exclusively on seeds and grain such as many finches.

Graze

To feed directly from the ground as with cattle, most antelopes and also flamingoes.

Green farming

The increasing practise of farmers to manage their farms in an environmentally friendly way such as using non-persistent and less toxic pesticides and placing nesting boxes on their land.

Guano

The accumulated mass of bird faeces which was formerly gathered up commercially in some northern S. American countries and sold as a fertilizer. Cormorants were the more usual providers.

Habitat

The location where an organism lives such as a Beech forest, a pond, an area of marsh, a shoreline.

Heavy metal

Any metal such as lead, mercury and cadmium

Heligoland

A location on the north German coast which serves as a refuge for moulting wildfowl. It is also the name of a large special funnel-shaped fenced and roofed trap used for catching migrant birds at bird observatories.

Hemisphere

One of the two halves of the Earth either side of the equator - either the northern and southern hemispheres. The terms eastern and western hemisphere may also be used for those halves either side of the Greenwich meridian.

Herbivore

An animal that feeds exclusively on plant material, such as rabbits, elephants and antelopes.

Hibernation

The process whereby an animal escapes the hardship of winter by entering a deep state of sleep during which the metabolic rate shuts down to a minimum. Hedgehogs, most bats and one species of bird carry out hibernation.

Hominid

Any member of the Order of primates in the family Hominidae, including humans.

Hovering

A special kind of flight where a bird can remain stationary in the air as an aid to hunting. This is a distinctive feature of some birds of prey such as Kestrels and Black-winged Kites. Also, hummingbirds are very adept at hovering as they feed on the nectar of flowers.

HS2

A highly controversial high-speed rail network proposed to link London to Manchester and Leeds, using trains capable of 360km/h. Its construction will demand much habitat destruction.

Incubation

The process carried out by birds involving sitting on eggs, keeping them warm as they develop chicks which eventually hatch.

Industrial revolution

A period in history, starting around 1760 in Britain during which numerous inventions changed the way in which humans went about their business. It brought about much environmental change, generally non-beneficial.

Insectivore

An organism which feeds exclusively on insects and/or spiders.

Introductions

Species of organisms taken by man either

intentionally or accidentally from their places of origin to other places where they frequently exert a lot of ecological damage by competing aggressively with native species for food or breeding sites.

Invertebrate

Any organism lacking a backbone such as an octopus or a house-fly.

IUCN

International Union for the Conservation of Nature.

Jurassic

A period in geological history set in the Mezozoic. It is the time when dinosaurs ruled the Earth and when many limestone deposits were forming – these today yielding numerous fossils. Birds evolved during the Jurassic period about 180 million years ago.

Keratin

The substance of which the feathers of birds (and also our fingernails) is made of.

Kew gardens

The familiar name given to the Royal Botanic Gardens at Kew based in London and which houses numerous plants and seeds from all over the world.

Kingdom

The major taxon (group) used in the classification of organisms such as animal kingdom. There are five major kingdoms.

Landfill

The collective term used for all types of human rubbish taken to special terrestrial sites for storage and possibly treatment.

Larder

A feature created when some shrike species impale their caught prey (lizards) onto thorns such that they may be eaten at a later stage.

Larva

The grub stage of many invertebrate organisms such as dragon flies, from which the adult form will emerge. Plural larvae.

Latitude

Any line on a map lying to the north or south of and parallel to the equator progressing up to either of the poles, measured in degrees and minutes. Britain lies roughly between latitudes 50 and 60 degrees north.

Laurasia

The once single landmass which in the geological past comprised North America and Eurasia, excluding India.

Lek

The practise of some male birds to display

themselves in a special arena to prospective females. Some grouse and also Ruffs employ this technique of seduction.

Lemming

A guinea-pig sized rodent occurring, often in huge numbers in the Arctic regions of the northern hemisphere.

Life expectancy

Having survived infant-hood, the age to which an individual of any given species is expected to live.

Lift

The phenomenon of the process which allows a bird to remain aloft during flight which is dependent on the cross-sectional shape of the wing (upon which we design aircraft wings).

Limestone

Rock formed from the calcareous shells of micro-organisms, often richly laden with fossils. Much was deposited during the Jurassic period.

Loch Ness Monster

An aquatic creature supposedly resembling a plesiosaur which inhabits the depths of Loch Ness in Scotland, UK. Despite numerous attempts to prove its existence, not one reliable photograph has been forthcoming.

Logger

One who either legally or illegally removes timber from forests for commercial gain.

Luddite

A person who is reluctant to accept new ideas and devices, preferring to hang on to the 'old ways' such as preferring a typewriter to a computer.

Lumpers

Those who, in classification of organisms tend to favour the combining of subspecies into the one species, such as Carrion and Hooded Crows.

Macaque

A medium-sized Old World monkey.

Magnetite

A magnetic iron-compound found in some migratory birds' skulls.

Mandible

Either of the two parts of a bird's beak, the upper and the lower mandibles.

Mantle

That region in the Earth's interior lying between the core and the crust.

Marsupial

Any member of the mammal class which bears an abdominal pouch for the early protection and continued development of its young, such as kangaroos and wombats.

Mechanical digestion

The breakdown of food in the gut by means of the movement the gut itself or of stones and fine gravel taken in by the bird.

Megafauna

The larger mammals of any continent such as elephants, hippos and lions of Africa.

Metabolism

The chemical reactions occurring within the bodies of organisms which result in the production of energy.

Meteorite

Any rock object entering the Earth's atmosphere having originated and travelled from outer space.

Metric

The system of numbering used in weights and measures which operates on increasing factors of ten, also called the decimal system.

Microbe

Any single-celled organism which may or may not cause disease such as bacteria and protozoans.

Micro-plastics

Microscopic particles of plastic resulting from

the breakdown of larger plastic items discarded into the environment by man.

Midden

In archaeology, a domestic rubbish pit.

Migration

The intentional movement of organisms away from unfavourable climatic conditions to those offering better feeding and breeding opportunities.

Milk teeth

The teeth which appear first in humans, numbering twenty-eight in total. These are shed throughout childhood and replaced individually by the 'adult' teeth which will number thirty-two.

Million

One thousand thousand written as 1,000,000.

Mist net

A very fine net used for catching birds during migration studies or other special projects.

Mnemonic

A memory aid used by those wishing to recall lists of things such as colours of the rainbow or the planets. 'Rowntrees of York gives best in value' is one I use to recite the former, in order (red, orange. yellow, green, blue, indigo and violet).

Mobbing

The action of smaller birds which collectively harass a larger bird, normally a predator in attempts to drive it away. Physical contact may or may not be made.

Mollusc

A member of a group of invertebrates including slugs and snails.

Monoculture

In agriculture, the growing of a single crop in one field such that biodiversity is totally lost.

Monogamous

Having just the one breeding partner, at least for the season.

Monograph

A separate treatise on any given organism such as David Lack's 'The Life of the Robin'.

Moult

In birds, the systematic loss and replacement of feathers, normally after each breeding season.

Mustelids

The family of mammals which includes stoats, weasels, pine martens and badgers.

Myxomatosis

A man-made disease prepared and released to kill wild rabbits.

Nancy's café

At Cley village in Norfolk, UK an end of terrace café which provided the exclusive service of being a telephone nerve-centre for information on UK sightings of rare birds.

Natural vegetation

That dominant vegetation type existing in any given region or country which would remain intact without human activities altering it. In most of Britain this is Oak woodland.

Nectar

A sweet sugar-laden substance at the base of some flower-heads used to attract and reward its pollinators.

Neolithic

Of the New Stone Age.

New world

Collectively the continents of North and South America including Canada and Greenland.

Niche

A micro-habitat such as a rock crevice or a hole in a tree.

Nominate race

That member of a group of sub-species which was the one originally described and named such as Blue-headed Wagtail in the Yellow Wagtail species.

North Pole

The single point lying at latitude 90 degrees north and from which any direction away must be south.

North polar region

The region north of the Arctic Circle which is 66 degrees north.

Nuptial

In birds that relating to courtship as in nuptial plumage or nuptial displays.

Oil pollution

Generally at sea, the intentional or accidental discharge of oil from ships.

Old world

Collectively the continents of Europe, Asia, Africa and Australasia.

Order

The taxon (group) of organisms which collectively belong to a class. The order Passeriformes belongs to the Class of birds.

Organism

Any living thing ranging from a bacterium to a Blue Whale or a sphagnum moss to a giant redwood tree.

Organochlorines

Chemicals used in pesticides, many of which are now banned.

Ornithologist

One who studies or at least watches birds.

Over-harvesting

Taking more out of a resource than allowing it to replenish itself, such as over-fishing.

Ozone

A layer of gas in the upper atmosphere which is a form of oxygen containing three oxygen atoms and not two. It shields life forms from UV radiation.

Ocean

Those vast expanses of water which together cover seventy-five per cent of the Earth's surface. The five oceans are the Atlantic, Indian, Pacific, Arctic and Southern.

Omnivore

Any organism which feeds on both animal and plant material such as hedgehogs, foxes and humans.

On the origin of species

The shortened title of the classic work by Charles Darwin (pub. 1859) in which he describes the improvement and adaptation of organisms over time by the process of natural selection (see Reading list).

Pair-bonding

Any action which serves to re-enforce the bond between a male and female of the species. For example, albatrosses may engage in bill-clapping or offer one another nesting material.

Palaearctic

Collectively, Eurasia, the Middle East and North Africa. It is one of the six zoogeographic zones.

Parasite

Any organism which feeds on or gains advantage from another living organism such as mites, ticks and tapeworms.

Paris Climate Accord

An agreement drawn up in 2015 between most of the world's nations to reduce carbon emissions into the atmosphere and thus help slow-down or even prevent drastic climate change.

Passerines

The largest order of birds comprising the perching or song-birds.

Pelagic

Feeding way out in the open oceans as with many albatrosses.

Pellet

A cigar-shaped structure comprising bones, fur

and/or feathers which is egested by birds of prey which swallow their food whole.

Permafrost

A layer in the upper level of soil in Arctic regions which contains water that is permanently frozen. Much of this is currently melting due to global warming, releasing methane in the process which is also a greenhouse gas leading to further warming.

Persistent

Of pesticides, those which remain in the environment for a long time and are not readily broken down.

PhD

A post-graduate degree undertaken for about three years to study a very narrow topic in great depth. Completion of such allows the person to adopt the title of Doctor.

pH scale

The logarithmic scale of acidity/alkalinity of a substance which ranges from 1 to 14, water having a neutral pH of 7. Below 7 is acidic and above 7 is alkaline. A pH of 5 would be ten times more acidic than 6. A pH of 4 would be 100 x more acidic than pH 6 (i.e 10 x 10).

Phylum

The next taxon (group) down from Kingdom

such as Chordata, animals with backbones.

Pioneer

A species of plant which is the first to move into a newly formed environment.

Pirating

Used by skuas and some gulls, the action of forcing other birds to give up their own catches while still in the air. It is a form of parasitism.

Plankton

The single celled plants or animals which float in the upper ocean levels, known as phytoplankton and zooplankton respectively.

Plate

In geology, the name given to a chunk of the Earth's crust which moves slowly in relation to adjacent plates, leading ultimately to the drifting of continents.

Plate boundary

That line between any two plates.

Plate tectonics

The study of the movement of plates and subsequent Continental Drift.

Plasmodium

That single-celled organism which causes Malaria and is carried by some mosquitoes.

Poaching

The illegal hunting of animals, either within or outside of protected areas.

Porpoising

The practise of porpoises, some small whales and penguins which, during fast swimming leap out of the water and take in a lungful of air as they descend.

Preen gland

The gland at the upper base of a bird's tail which secretes preen oils used to maintain the condition of feathers including the waterproofing of feathers essential in water-birds.

Preening

The act of distributing preen oils over the feathers of a bird which serves to repair attachments of the barbules and ridges of feathers and to create waterproofing in the case of aquatic species.

Primaries

The outer wing feathers of a bird's wing, usually ten in number and used exclusively for flight.

Primate

Any animal of the order of Primates which includes humans, gorillas, chimpanzees, orang utans, monkeys, tarsiers, lemurs and bush-babies.

Protein

Any nitrogenous organic compound made up of amino acids which form the basis of living tissue in all organisms.

Psittacosis

A respiratory disease affecting humans which is spread by members of the parrot family.

Pterodactyl

An extinct flying pterosaur which had a long neck, body and tail and a toothed jaw.

Rachis

The central shaft of a flight or tail feather of a bird.

Rain Forest

A tropical forest comprising numerous species of deciduous trees such as The Amazon, Congo and SE Asian rain-forests. The world's greatest biodiversity occurs in rain forest.

Raptor

Any bird of prey.

Rarities committee

Any committee of ornithologists which receives and either accepts or rejects submitted reports of unusual bird-sightings. These may be at county or national level.

Ratite

Any one of five species of flightless birds such as Ostrich, Emu and Rhea. They each lack a sternum to which flight muscles would otherwise be attached.

Rectrices

The tail feathers of a bird, normally twelve in number.

Red data book

A book maintained by the BOU which includes those species threatened with extinction. It contains an alarming number of species which is ever-increasing.

Refraction

The apparent bending of an object immersed in water due to light passing through two different mediums.

Regurgitate

The bringing up of food by a parent bird from its crop in order to feed young.

Reintroduction

The release of animals or plants into regions where they once flourished but have since become rare or extinct, such as Great Bustards on Salisbury Plain in England.

Remiges

Flight feathers.

Re-trap

In bird-ringing, the capture of the same bird more than once.

Rift valley

A huge linear fissure in the Earth's crust formed either at plate boundaries or along extensive fault-lines.

Rodent

The order of mammals which includes mice, rats and porcupines.

Rods

Those cells of the retina which are responsible for black and white vision.

Rotifer

Microscopic, aquatic single-celled animals with cilia which rotate as in a wheel.

RSPB

Royal Society for the Protection of Birds.

Sahara

The largest desert in the world covering north and parts of Central Africa.

Savannah

The vast open expanses of grassland throughout sub-Saharan Africa.

Saw-bill

Any member of the group of ducks containing mergansers, Goosanders and Smew.

Scandinavia

The collective name for the northern countries of Europe: Norway, Sweden and Denmark. Some authorities argue that Finland and Iceland should be included.

Scavenging

Feeding on dead organic material as practised by vultures and Marabou Storks.

Science and Maths Fair

An annual competition held in many countries wherein people (often school-children) prepare and enter scientific or mathematical projects.

Scientific community

All those scientists existing all over the world, practising their different disciplines and who may form collective opinions on various issues.

Scientific name

The Latin name of any organism. It is formally written in italics and underlined, often in parentheses.

Scrub

Open grassland with occasional bushes and low trees, characteristic of much of Africa.

Sea-level rise

The rise of sea-level due to either thermal expansion (caused by ocean-warming) or by melting of ice, particularly that of the polar regions. It threatens many low-lying countries and coastal settlements.

Secondaries

The flight feathers lying next to the primaries, usually ten in number.

Semi-circular canals

Special structures in the inner ears which are responsible for maintaining balance.

Sensory organs

Any organs which receive signals providing information about the environment such as eyes, ears and noses.

Sexually mature

In adult birds, old enough to produce their own young.

Siblicide

The killing and usually eating of one's brothers and sisters, as in some bird of prey chicks when food is scarce.

Song

The vocal out-pourings of male birds in order to establish territorial boundaries and attract mates.

Space-ship Earth

A term used to denote that the Earth is just like a space-craft, fully equipped with all its passenger's needs. The term serves to accentuate the fragility of our planet.

Species

The smallest taxonomic group of any organisms (excepting sub-species).

SSSI

Site of Special Scientific Interest.

Stereoscopic

Three – dimensional.

Sternum

The breastbone or, in a bird, the keel.

Strata

Layer of sedimentary rock.

Sub-cutaneous

Lying just under the skin of an animal.

Sub-Saharan Africa

All of Africa lying south of the Sahara.

Sub-species

A group within a species that has branched off due to geographical isolation. Sub-species are able to interbreed but are often in differing regions and do not generally do so.

Sunning

The action of a bird, lying prostrate allowing its plumage to be bathed by the sun, thought to rid the bird of parasites.

Super-tanker

An extremely large ship specifically for the purpose of transporting oil across the world.

Symbiosis

The relationship between two organisms of different species wherein both parties gain benefit, such as lichens which comprise a fungus and an alga, each mutually dependent.

Taxidermist

A specialist who preserves animals by stuffing and mounting them, often for exhibition in museums.

Taxon

In classification, a group such as Order or Family.

Taxonomist

One who engages in taxonomy, the classification of organisms.

Territory

That area claimed for itself by an organism in which all the resources such as food, potential mates and shelter are provided.

Thermal

A spiralling upwelling mass of warm air upon which birds may rise to great heights to locate prey from above, such as eagles and buzzards. Birds may also rise up to enable them to glide downwards for long distances as an aid to migratory flight.

Thermal expansion

The expansion of sea water due to even slight rises in temperature caused by global warming.

Tobogganing

The practise of penguins sliding on snow and ice on their bellies, this being a lot faster than walking.

Top predator

In a food chain or feeding pyramid, the last predator in the succession such as a Polar Bear, a Bonelli's Eagle or a human.

Torpidity

A shallow kind of hibernation, where all bodily activities slow down to a minimum. This is done on a daily basis in such creatures and hummingbirds.

Trade-off

A compromise in nature where the development of one benefit is curtailed to allow also for another benefit. A peacock will develop its back feathers to form a beautiful 'tail' but it loses this immediately it has completed its function to enable it once again ease of passage through Asian forests.

Tree-fern

A taxon of ferns which have trunks like trees which hold the fronds above ground level.

Trinity House

The organisation responsible for Britain's lighthouses.

Trinomial

The three-word Latin name of a bird in which the third name identifies any sub-species that may exist for that species.

Tropics

That region of the world lying between the Tropic of Cancer and the Tropic of Capricorn, each lying at 66 degrees north and south of the equator respectively.

Tube-noses

Birds which have strange tubular structures on the upper mandibles, thought to have some role in salt control. Albatrosses, Fulmars, petrels and shearwaters have such structures.

Tundra

High latitude regions with low temperatures and short-growing seasons. Vegetation is typically grasses, sedges, rushes, lichens and mosses.

Turkish Van

A breed of domestic cat from Turkey which has a penchant for swimming and is regarded as unusually intelligent for its species.

Uniformitarianism

The principle in Geology that the 'present is the key to the past'.

Up-ending

The feeding strategy of some duck species whereby they sit on the water surface and then swing the entire body through 90 degrees, thus immersing their heads enabling them to feed.

UV radiation

Ultra-violet radiation emitted by the sun and which is harmful to life if not filtered out by the ozone layer surrounding the Earth.

Vane

Those areas on either side of a flight or tail feather made up of numerous parallel barbs.

Vestigial

The non-functional part of a structure of an organism which, through evolutionary time has outlived its purpose. The wings of an Ostrich are vestigial, at least for the purpose of flight.

Viable

Of a population, workable, containing enough

individuals to perpetuate the species of various organisms, all of which have a minimum threshold level below which the population is not likely to recover. White Rhinos are probably below the threshold level and may well become extinct.

Vitamin D

A chemical essential for the healthy formation of teeth and bones, being a controller of calcium utilisation in the body. Lack of this vitamin causes rickets in children.

Wader

A member of a large group of long-legged, long-billed birds which characteristically feed on sea-shores and lake margins such a sandpipers, redshanks and Sanderlings.

Wildfire

A forest fire which has become totally out of control. These are occurring with increasing area and frequency as the world undergoes warming causing forest trees to become tinder-dry.

Wildfowler

A person who derives pleasure from shooting ducks and other birds during 'open seasons'.

Wildlife and Countryside Act 1981

An Act passed by parliament which affords

heavyweight protection of UK wildlife, especially birds.

Wintering grounds

Those areas where a bird may migrate to after the breeding season. Many palearctic wading birds will move southward for the winter.

World Heritage Site

A site which has universal appeal and/or huge ecological importance and is thus conserved for posterity. The Great Barrier Reef, the Okovango Delta and the Florida Everglades are all classified as such.

Yolk

The yellow part of a bird's egg which serves as the food supply for the developing embryo. It is often mistakenly believed to be that part which forms the chick. Neither the yolk nor the white develops into a bird.

Zoogeographic region

One of six zones on Earth characterised by their own climates and assemblages of animals and plants.

APPENDIX (II)

RECOMMENDED READING LIST

BOOKS

All dates are of those when the book was first published. Many of the books have been reprinted since the dates given.

Attenborough, D. *The Life of Birds* BBC 1998.

Carson, R. *Silent Spring* Houghton Mifflin 1962.

Cawardine, M. *Last Chance to See – in the footsteps of Douglas Adams* Collins 2009.

Cramp S. et al *The Seabirds of Britain and Ireland* Harper Collins 1975.

Darwin C. *On the origin of species* John Murray 1859. Numerous reprints by various publishers.

Denby, C. A. *Of Giraffes and Toothbrushes* Happy fish productions (Swaziland) 2007.

Delany, S. N. *Bird Migration Across the Himalayas* Edited by Prins, Herbert H.T. and Namgail, T. Cambridge University Press 2017 Chapters 4 and 5.

Delany, S. N. et al, *An Atlas of wader Populations in Africa and Western Eurasia* Wetlands International 2009.

Fothergill, Alastair *Life in the freezer – a natural history of the Antarctic* BCA 1993.

Gould, S. J. *Wonderful Life* Hutchinson Radius 1989.

Hartman T. *The Last Hours of Ancient Sunlight* Mobius 2001.

Hillstead, A. F. C. *The Young Birdwatchers* Faber and Faber 1959.

Hosking, E. *An Eye for a Bird* Hutchinson 1970.

Howard, R. & Moore, A. *A Complete Checklist of the Birds of the World* Academic press 1980.

Huxley R. (Ed) *The Great Naturalists* Thames and Hudson 2007.

Lack, D. *Ecological Isolation in Birds* Oxford University Press 1971.

Lack, D. *Swifts in a Tower* Methuen 1956.

Leakey, R. and Lewis, R. *The Sixth Extinction* Weidenfeld & Nicolson 1995.

Lockley, R. M. *The Island* Andre Deutsch Ltd 1969.

Lovelock, J. *Gaia a new look at Life on Earth* Oxford Landmark Science 2016.

Mead, C. *Bird Migration* Country Life 1983.

Petersen, R., Mountfort, G. and Hollom P. A. D. *A Field Guide to the Birds of Britain and Europe* Collins 1954.

Ponting, C. *A Green History of the World* Sinclair – Stevenson Ltd 1991.

Sinclair I. *A Field Guide to the Birds of Southern Africa* Struik publishing 1992.

Tulloch, B. *Shetland* Macmillan London Ltd 1988.

Weisman, A. *World Without Us* Virgin Books 2007.

Williams, J. G. and Arlott, N. *A Field Guide to the Birds of East Africa* Collins 1980.

PAPERS AND REPORTS

Delany, S. N. and Williams, C. T. et al *The University of Southampton Ladakh Expeditions 1976, 1977, 1980 and 1981/2.*

Robinson, M. *Snowy Owls in Shetland* British Birds 79 pp 228 – 242 May 1986.

APPENDIX (III)

BIRDS NAMED THROUGHOUT THE TEXT

Adelie Penguin, African Fish Eagle, African Hoopoe, Alpine Accentor, Alpine Swift, American Robin, Andean Condor, Ant-bird, Arctic Skua, Arctic Tern, Ashy-headed Wagtail, Avocet.

Barn Owl, Barn Swallow, Bearded Tit, Bearded Vulture, Bee Hummingbird, Bewick's swan, Bittern, Blackbird, Black-browed Albatross, Black-browed Reed Warbler, Black-capped Sibia, Black Guillemot, Black-headed Bunting, Black-headed Gull, Black-headed Oriole, Black-headed Wagtail, Black-footed Albatross, Black-tailed Godwit, Blue headed Wagtail, Blue Tit, Brown Accentor, Bufflehead, Burrowing Owl.

Californian Condor, Carolina Wood Duck, Cassowary, Chatham Island Robin, Chaffinch, Chiffchaff, Chimney Swift, Chough, Cirl Bunting, Common Buzzard, Common Redstart, Common Rosefinch, Common Scoter, Common Snipe, Common Starling, Common swift, Cormorant, Corncrake, Count Raggis' Bird of Paradise, Crested Lark, Cuckoo, Curlew Sandpiper.

Dartford Warbler, Demoiselle Crane, Dodo, Dunnock.

Edible swiftlet, Egyptian Plover, Eider Duck, Emperor Penguin, Elf Owl, Emu, Erect-crested Penguin, Eurasian Eagle Owl, Eurasian Linnet, Eurasian Robin, European Nightjar.

Familiar Chat, Ferruginous Duck, Fieldfare, Finchlark, Fjordland Penguin, Flightless Rail, Fulmar.

Gadwall, Galapagos Flightless Cormorant, Galapagos Penguin, Gannet, Garden Warbler, Gentoo Penguin, Giant Petrel, Golden Eagle, Goldeneye, Golden Oriole, Goldfinch, Goosander, Gorgeous Bush-Shrike, Goshawk, Graceful Tern, Great black-backed Gull, Great Crested Grebe, Greater Flamingo, Great Grey Owl, Great reed warbler, Great Skua, Great Spotted Woodpecker, Great Tit, Greenfinch, Green heron, Green Woodpecker, Grey-headed Albatross, Grey-headed Wagtail, Grey Heron, Greylag Goose, Griffon Vulture, Guillemot, Guldenstadt's redstart, Guttulated Forest gleaner, Gyr Falcon.

Hamerkop, Harlequin Duck, Harrier-hawk, Hawfinch, Hedge Sparrow, Hen Harrier, Hobby, Hooded Crow, Hoopoe, House Martin, House Sparrow, Hume's Lesser Whitethroat.

Ibis-Bill.

Jackass Penguin, Jack Snipe, Jay.

Kakapo, Kentish Plover, Kestrel, Kingfisher, King Penguin, Kitlitz Plover, King of Saxony Bird of Paradise, Kittiwake.

Lady Amherst's Pheasant, Lady Ross's Turaco, Lapwing, Lark Bunting, Laughing Owl ,Laysan Albatross, Leach's Petrel, Lesser Flamingo, Lesser Grey Shrike, Little Egret, Little Owl, Little Penguin, Little Stint, Little Swift, Little Tern, Long-eared Owl, Long-tailed Tit, Long-tailed duck, Long-toed Stint.

Macaroni Penguin, Magellanic Penguin, Magnificent Frigate Bird, Magpie, Mallard, Manx Shearwater, Many-coloured Bush Shrike, Marabou Stork, MistleThrush, Marsh Harrier, Merlin, Montagu's Harrier, Moorhen, Mountain Chiffchaff, Mute Swan.

New Zealand Wren, Nightingale, North American Brown Pelican, Northern Saw-whet Owl, Nuthatch.

Oil Bird, Osprey, Ostrich, Oystercatcher

Pallid Swift, Paradise Wydah, Passenger Pigeon, Peacock, Pel's Fishing Owl, Penduline Tit, Pennant-winged Nightjar, Peregrine Falcon, Peruvian Penguin, Pheasant, Pheasant-tailed Jacana, Pied Kingfisher, Pied Wagtail, Pintail, Pochard, Poor Will, Puffin, Prince Rupoli's Turaco, Ptarmigan, Purple Needletail, Purple Sandpiper, Pygmy Kingfisher, Pygmy Owl.

Raven, Razorbill, Red-breasted merganser,

Red- flanked Bluetail, Red-necked Phalarope, Red-rumped swallow, Redshank, Red-spotted Bluethroat, Red-throated Diver, Red-winged Starling, Reed Warbler, Resplendent Quetzel, Rhea, Ringed Plover, Ring-necked Parakeet, Robin Accentor, Rockhopper Penguin, Rook, Royal Penguin, Ruff.

Sabine's Gull, Sand Martin, Sardinian Warbler, Scarlet Macaw, Scaup, Schalow's Wheatear, Secretary Bird, Sedge Warbler, Shag, Sheld Duck, Short-eared Owl, Short-toad Eagle, Short-toed Lark, Short-toed Treecreeper, Shoveler, Smew, Snare's Penguin, Snow Goose, Snowy Owl, Sociable Weaver, Song Thrush, Sooty Albatross, Spanish Wagtail, Sparrowhawk, Splendid Starling, Spotted Eagle Owl, Spotted Flycatcher, St Kilda Wren, Stone Curlew, Storm Petrel, Subalpine Warbler, Superb Starling.

Tawny Owl, Teal, Thrush Nightingale, Tibetan Sandgrouse, Tickell's Willow Warbler, Treecreeper, Tufted Duck, Turnstone.

Variable Sunbird, Velvet Scoter, Verraux's Eagle Owl.

Wall Creeper, Wandering Albatross, Water Rail, Wheatear, Whinchat, White-backed Vulture, White-bellied Swiftlet, White-bellied Turaco, White-Eye, White-rumped Swift, White-throated Needletail, White Wagtail, Wigeon, Willow Warbler, Wilson's Phalarope,

Woodpecker Finch, Wood Pigeon, Wren.

Yellow-billed Duck, Yellow-eyed Penguin, Yellowhammer, Yellow-nosed Albatross, Yellow Wagtail.

ALSO AVAILABLE

A Year in My Garden: The Artist
and the Gardener
by Sue Goodchild
The Path Less Trodden by Don McNeil
The Path Less Trodden (Again) by Don McNeil
The Canticles of Spring by Frank McMahon
Averse to Poetry by Garry Davidson
Writing from Life by Jo Foster
Stronghold of Happiness by Devina Symes
We Cry to Thee by Stephen Constance

tsaunderspubs.weebly.com

Printed in Dunstable, United Kingdom